S0-AIZ-354

WHO WAS
**DORIS
HEDGES?**

WHO WAS DORIS HEDGES?

The Search for Canada's First Literary Agent

ROBERT LECKER

PAPL
DISCARDED

McGill-Queen's University Press
Montreal & Kingston · London · Chicago

© McGill-Queen's University Press 2020

ISBN 978-0-2280-0369-4 (cloth)
ISBN 978-0-2280-0477-6 (ePDF)
ISBN 978-0-2280-0478-3 (ePUB)

Legal deposit fourth quarter 2020
Bibliothèque nationale du Québec

Printed in Canada on acid-free paper that is 100% ancient forest free (100% post-consumer recycled), processed chlorine free

This book has been published with the help of a grant from the Canadian Federation for the Humanities and Social Sciences, through the Awards to Scholarly Publications Program, using funds provided by the Social Sciences and Humanities Research Council of Canada.

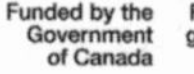

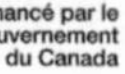

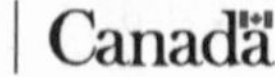

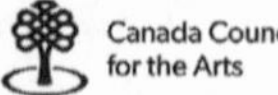

We acknowledge the support of the Canada Council for the Arts.

Nous remercions le Conseil des arts du Canada de son soutien.

Library and Archives Canada Cataloguing in Publication

Title: Who was Doris Hedges? : the search for Canada's first literary agent / Robert Lecker.
Names: Lecker, Robert, 1951- author.
Description: Includes bibliographical references and index.
Identifiers: Canadiana (print) 20200287311 | Canadiana (ebook) 20200287400 | ISBN 9780228003694 (hardcover) | ISBN 9780228004776 (PDF) | ISBN 9780228004783 (EPUB)
Subjects: LCSH: Hedges, Doris, 1896-1972. | LCSH: Authors, Canadian—Biography. | LCSH: Literary agents—Canada—Biography. | LCSH: Canadian literature—20th century—History and criticism. | CSH: Canadian literature (English)—Women authors. | LCGFT: Biographies.
Classification: LCC PS8515.E28 Z735 2020 | DDC C813/.54—dc23

This book was typeset by studio oneonone in 10.8/14.2 Minion

CONTENTS

FIGURES AND TABLES

FIGURES

TABLES

ACKNOWLEDGMENTS

The Social Sciences and Humanities Research Council of Canada provided funding that was crucial to the completion of this book. I am deeply grateful for this support. It enabled me to work with several research assistants whose dedication was invaluable. My sincere thanks to Matthew Rettino, who provided enough tantalizing information to get me hooked on the search for Doris Hedges. I am also thankful to Sara Farah, who assisted me in the early phases of the project, and to Sophie Weiler and Emily Szpiro, who contributed a great deal to the book in its later development. A special note of gratitude must go to Sabrina Aguzzi, who, seriously infected with the Doris bug, brought me information and insight over four years; her organizational skills and her investment in the project meant everything to me. I also want to thank Joel Deshaye and Mary Williams for their insightful comments on an early draft. Lonnie Weatherby, the Liaison Librarian of the McLennan Library at McGill University, generously provided his expertise and assistance over several years. I am indebted to the helpful staff at the McCord Museum and the Canadian Centre for Architecture. Finally, I would like to thank Mark Abley, my editor at McGill-Queen's University Press. Mark appreciated the project immediately, offered speedy and supportive help, and took the special initiative of locating original photographs related to the project.

WHO WAS
DORIS HEDGES?

INTRODUCTION

Who was Doris Hedges? I first encountered her name while researching the history of literary agents in Canada. I was supposed to be exploring the now widely recognized observation that as soon as literary agents entered the British and North American publishing scenes at the end of the nineteenth century, literature itself began to change. I would build on John O. Jordan and Robert L. Patten's argument that "any new paradigm of publishing history" must consider how "mediating agencies altered the nature, pace, and result of publishing."[1] Of these mediating agencies, literary agencies play a crucial role in the process of literary production. The same holds for Canadian literary production. That could certainly be a subject for study. But the more I found out about Doris Hedges, the more my original project got sidetracked. Instead, it turned into a long search for more information about this ambitious woman who had more or less vanished from Canadian literary history.

Although some individuals advertised themselves as Canadian literary agents in the 1930s,[2] the first professional agencies in Canada – by which I mean agencies operating as viable business entities with bricks and mortar offices – did not emerge until after the Second World War. However, a common misconception is that professional literary agents and agencies were not active in Canada until the founding of Matie Molinaro's Canadian Speakers' and Writers' Service in Toronto in the early 1950s.[3] While the history and correspondence concerning Molinaro's activities are reasonably well documented, with extensive archival holdings at York University,[4] it is clear that Canadian literary historians have been incorrect in identifying her business as the first Canadian agency. In fact, the first professional agency in Canada was Hedges, Southam and de Merian, with offices in the Dominion Square Building in downtown Montreal. The company was conceived in 1946 and legally registered as a business on 15 January 1947. The agency's first advertisement appeared in the December 1946 edition of the *Canadian Bookman*.[5]

As a postwar enterprise, Hedges, Southam and de Merian was led by Doris Hedges, a woman dedicated to the promotion of Canadian literature during a period of literary scarcity. In addition to running her agency, Hedges was a public speaker, a radio commentator, a journalist, a social critic, a supporter of the arts, a poet, a short story writer, and a novelist. She published six books of poetry (three with Ryerson Press and another three in Boston, New York, and the UK) as well as three novels released in the UK and New York. Although she founded Canada's first literary agency and produced a considerable body of work, Hedges's career is not mentioned in the *Literary History of Canada*, the *Encyclopedia of Literature in Canada*, *History of the Book in Canada*, or the *Oxford Companion to Canadian Literature*. Before I began my research, I had never heard of her. Although Hedges's writing was not strong, it was no weaker than much of the work published by her male counterparts of the same generation. I suspect that her erasure from literary history had more to do with the fact that she did not embrace the academic high modernist aesthetic projects championed by the male critics of her era. As Carole Gerson observes, "the literary history that these projects constructed was based not on what the majority of Canadians had in the past written and read, but on the elitist vision that prevailed among Canadian scholars and critics."[6] After all, Hedges chose to found her agency in 1947, the same year John Sutherland published *Other Canadians*, an anthology celebrating socialist-realist values in contrast to A.J.M. Smith, who four years earlier had released his controversial *The Book of Canadian Poetry*, which valorized a "cosmopolitan" over a "native" conception of poetry. Controversy about the very nature of Canadian poetry was swirling around Hedges at the time she decided to establish her agency. How could she ignore those controversies, and what role would they play in her new business?

Faced with the erasure of Doris Hedges, I became determined to find her again. Who was this woman who pioneered literary agenting in Canada while pursuing her creative career in the period leading up to the Second World War and ending with the publication of her last novel in 1971, a year before her death? What made her decide to found a literary agency? How did she finance it? What relationship did she have with Canadian authors of her era? I began to think that Doris Hedges might open a door onto the values and debates influencing her times as a female writer. Perhaps we could see the historical events that affected her in terms of her own culture and upbringing, and perhaps by seeing things in those terms we might be able to see them in *other* terms than those reserved for the official histories. I began to think of a study that would place Hedges in the context of some of the literary, cultural, and political issues of her time and to examine those issues in relation to a figure who has barely been preserved in the country's literary archives. I wanted to explore the environments and institutions through which she moved. Although one might question Hedges's literary skills or business acumen, her career charts the revealing narrative of a woman who was striving to establish herself in an English Canadian literary marketplace and a literary culture that was dominated by men. Hedges was ultimately frustrated by her literary reception. Some might say that she does not deserve the title of Canada's first literary agent because her career in that role was so short-lived. But it is precisely her failure to achieve this success that merits commentary, simply because a study of Hedges's failure is also a study of her age, which was, after all, defined not only by those who succeeded as authors or ran successful agencies but equally by those who tried and failed. Another way of putting this is to say that we cannot understand success unless we understand failure.

Hedges was crafty. In 1953, she wrote to William Arthur Deacon, the book review editor of the *Globe and Mail*, to complain that *Dumb Spirit*, her most recent novel, had not been reviewed. She used the Hedges, Southam and de Merian stationery and said she would like to meet Deacon in Toronto when she came "to see publishers, editors, and our 85 clients from your fair city!"[7] It seems highly unlikely that Doris represented eighty-five Toronto authors in 1953. No, it is impossible. That would be a staggering number of writers to represent from any city, even by an established and thriving agency during the boom years of North American publishing. And if Doris had signed on eighty-five authors from Toronto alone, by 1953, where are their letters to and from her? No documentation can be found. This was a fabrication. No agent representing so many authors at that time (and even today) could have been so consistently ignored by writers and publishers alike. There was a deceptive, self-promoting side to Hedges that intrigued me. At some level, she was making herself up.

It seems more likely that when she wrote to Deacon, Hedges resurrected some agency stationery in order to give her complaint more credibility. When she received no response from the *Globe and Mail* editor, she wrote to his assistant on 7 October 1954, on letterhead now showing her home address in Montreal (9 Redpath Place), complaining that "it is irritating to be a Canadian writer and to be ignored in his own newspapers, so I am bothering you about this matter, although I hate to do it."[8] She provided a list of her five books and promotional material relating to *Elixir*, a novel which had been published earlier that year. It was, she said, "a long poem in book form."[9] Finally, Deacon responded at length, offering that "you may find some comfort in the fact that we have not, so far this year, reviewed a book of poems by any writer. Circulation figures for volumes of poetry – even the best-known poets of today – show that very few people have any interest in this type of literature. Fifty years ago, poetry found a good market in Canada. I can only suppose that the kind of poetry being written has lost the ear of the public."[10] Deacon was confused by Hedges's conception of her novel *Elixir* as a "long poem." In reality, the book had been reviewed in the *Globe* soon after it was published.[11] I was starting to see that Hedges's career, and her complaints, did indeed open a door onto the values and tastes of her age, not to mention the way her actions revealed her quirky personality traits.

Surely Doris Hedges, as a self-styled literary agent, would have understood Deacon's point about the declining interest in poetry. Yet she persisted. What drove her? I needed to find out more. But how to begin? There were multiple threads. I was fortunate enough to be working with some very dedicated students who got infected with the Hedges bug. We started collecting information haphazardly. We created a timeline and, piece by piece, began to fill in the blanks. Yet the more those blanks were filled, the more questions emerged. Hedges was frustratingly hard to follow, mainly because she left no children to tell us about her life. Passenger lists over decades show her departing from and returning to Canada, but the purpose of her multiple voyages remains unclear. What was she doing on all those trips, many of them overseas?

Hedges died in 1972. Her obituary in the Montreal *Gazette* describes her as a "well-known Montreal author" whose books "received critical acclaim in Canada, the United States, and Great Britain."[12] The *Gazette* also mentioned Hedges's mysterious wartime activities: "she held a post in the psychological warfare division of the U.S. Office of War Information."[13] How was Doris Hedges contributing to "psychological warfare"? I did find answers to that question. But there are scant traces left of her literary agency or her private life. She left few papers or letters. There are no business records. No manuscripts. No family albums. No memorabilia. Nor were there any family documents, and, as far as I could discover, only one person living in my own time had spoken with Hedges in person. That was the Montreal notary who had completed her will, a copy of which I obtained after exploring the labyrinthian depths of the legal records system in Quebec. He remembered Hedges, but he could not provide much information of value.

Hedges did not die poor. Where did her money come from? What kind of business activities was her husband Geoffrey involved in? Hedges's wealth could not have been the result of her work with the literary agency, since it appears to have ceased operation after about a year (despite her assertions to the contrary). Practically no client records can be found. Yet six years after it apparently ceased operation, Hedges was still writing letters on company stationery, as if the business were prospering. Why would she do that? Why would she pretend to be running an agency that did not exist? It would take me almost three years to get closer to an answer. But early in the investigation I began to wonder about Hedges's motives and her modes of self-representation.

At one point, one of my research assistants showed up with a document she had recovered from some deep data pool and announced: "I have a theory. Doris Hedges was a spy!" I did not rule out the possibility, given some of Hedges's obvious deceptions. But if that were true, exactly whom was she spying for, and to what end? We explored different scenarios. My imagination got the better of me. I began to picture Hedges in clandestine outfits. How did female spies dress in the 1940s? Then I came to my senses. I began to wonder what Hedges looked like. Although I had been amassing information about this elusive writer for almost six months, I had yet to see a photo of her. It was only when I decided to order all her works – held by obscure used-book dealers around the world – that some of my curiosity was satisfied. A copy of Hedges's poetry collection *For This I Live* arrived in the mail. There she was, pictured on the dust jacket: "Mrs. Doris Hedges" the caption read, under the photograph of a determined-looking middle-aged woman. The book was published in 1963. She would have been sixty-seven years old. But the woman in the photo was younger than that. Hedges wanted to project a youthful version of herself to her readers. Inside the book, there was a dedication: "To Margaret with love," in Hedges's handwriting. Who was Margaret? Nothing in my research about Hedges's contacts led to a person of that name. And none of the photographs I found could be trusted.

It was tantalizing to think that Hedges led another life beneath her public persona. Private relationships. A hidden side. Intimate friends. In another book I obtained – her collection of poetry suggestively titled *Inside Out* – I found a note to a nameless person: "This collection of poetry is my latest. It is published in England, but not available in Canadian bookstores. It is a gift from me to you. Let me know if you would like another copy." I would dearly love to have found the person Hedges was addressing a year before her death. I would also like to have known more about the person who wrote the back-cover copy for *The Dream Is Certain*, with its strong impression of Hedges: "To meet Doris Hedges is an exhilarating experience."

Clearly, I had discovered a woman of many dimensions who lived and worked in a city populated by some of Canada's best-known anglophone writers in the postwar period: Patrick Anderson, Leonard Cohen, Louis Dudek, Robert Finch, Mavis Gallant, Gwethalyn Graham, A.M. Klein, Irving Layton, Dorothy Livesay, Hugh MacLennan, Brian Moore, P.K. Page, Mordecai Richler, F.R. Scott, A.J.M. Smith, John Sutherland. I had to remind myself that Hedges's life in literary Montreal went back even further, for she was born in 1896. Although she was in close geographic proximity to the writers who formed the McGill Group (Leon Edel, John Glassco, Leo Kennedy, A.M. Klein, F.R. Scott, and A.J.M. Smith), Hedges seems to have had little interest in their work. I can find no correspondence between her and any other Montreal writer. Not a single letter.

When Hedges died, in 1972, she was residing at 9 Redpath Place, an upscale address not far from the fashionable stretch of Sherbrooke Street that is home to Montreal's Musée des beaux-arts. For many years she often gave as her home address the Ritz-Carlton Hotel, a couple of blocks east of the museum; this domestic arrangement must have cost the Hedges dearly. After all, who actually *lived* at the Ritz? Quite a few people, it turns out. In his history of the hotel, Adrian Waller notes that "each year, numerous moneyed Montrealers took Ritz-Carlton suites for several months at a time while their townhouses were being redecorated, or to escape a marital row. Most permanent guests moved in with their own paintings, furniture, even drapes, however, treating the hotel as a residence-cum-private club where they could luxuriate in Continental hospitality for as long as they could afford it."[14] One patron "died in bed at the Ritz, having been there for two decades."[15]

The Hedges inhabited this upper-class environment. One might expect that their lives were filled with glittering engagements, that the existing record would provide some evidence of their participation in the social and literary life of the city where they had lived, off and on, ever since their marriage in

Paris in 1926 (Hedges flirted with Europe and Paris on several occasions and would no doubt have seen her Paris marriage as an expression of her continental, romantic leanings). While Hedges did attend high-society events in the city, she never appears in writers' accounts of literary life in Montreal during that period, which is especially baffling given the fact that, after 1946, Hedges had established a literary agency in a prominent downtown office building. It was as if she existed as a ghost in a metropolis illuminated by its literature, during a period when Montreal was the cultural centre of Canada. Although Hedges gave several public speeches in the postwar years, she seldom appeared in the company of other writers, a curious stance for a woman whose profession as a literary agent was at least partially dependent on building strong relationships with fellow authors. And although she was active in the Montreal branch of the Canadian Authors Association, her participation in that organization was short-lived.

I wondered about Hedges's daily habits, living with Geoffrey in the Ritz-Carlton Hotel, sporadically, for years. Where did they eat their meals? Did Doris Hedges ever cook? How can you cook for yourself if your home is the Ritz? Or where would your housekeeper do the cooking? In your suite? I also wondered about her husband, Geoffrey Paget Hedges, who might well have been the breadwinner. But what did he do after they returned to Montreal following their Paris wedding in 1926? I discovered that he had been a stockbroker at the most inopportune moment: he was working at his Peel Street office in Montreal when Black Tuesday hit on 29 October 1929. What panic ensued for him and Doris? What effects did the crash have on his livelihood?

Geoffrey had the resources to absorb that kind of financial shock. I learned that he was part of the Benson and Hedges tobacco dynasty. His grandfather, William Hedges, founded the company along with Richard Benson in 1873. Geoffrey's father, Alfred Paget Hedges, managed the company after 1885, the same year in which Benson left the business. Alfred died in 1929, when Geoffrey was thirty-two years old. He had arrived in North America via New York on 2 December 1922, listing his profession on the ship manifest as "Factory Manager." In the 1924 Montreal telephone directory, he described himself as working for Benson and Hedges. By 1925, he identified himself as the vice-president and manager of the J. Hirsch and Sons Cigar Company. The following year, he added the title of managing director of Benson and Hedges to his directory listing. Benson and Hedges gained a strong foothold in Canada by purchasing Hirsch's company in 1927. On 7 September 1929,

Geoffrey returned to England, giving as his address "c/o Benson and Hedges, 13 Old Bond St. London." So, while one side of Geoffrey's career involved stock market trading (he was a member of the New York Stock Exchange in 1929), another side was devoted to the international tobacco trade. It was the heyday of a tobacco industry that equated smoking with independence and glamour. In New York that year, public relations guru Edward Bernays mounted a "freedom march" of smoking debutantes and fashion models who walked down Fifth Avenue during the Easter parade dressed as Statues of Liberty and holding aloft their Lucky Strike cigarettes as feminist "torches of freedom."[16]

Like Geoffrey, Doris was well connected. She was the daughter of William O. Ryde and Edith Sarah Dawes. William had immigrated to Canada from England in 1886 to work as a manager for Dawes and Company brewers in the town of Lachine, southwest of Montreal. The company was established by Thomas Dawes, who opened the brewery and a surrounding farm in 1811. The brewery became famous for its Black Horse Ale. Its operations contributed enormously to the industrial development of Lachine and are credited with the town's development in its small local museum.[17] The Dawes family owned 370 acres of land in the area. Edith's father was James Dawes, a well-known public figure who was actively involved in the management of the Dominion Bridge Company, whose headquarters he helped move to Lachine. Dawes's wealth led him to pursue various investments in horse racing and yachting. By the time Doris was born, in 1896, the Daweses were wealthy landowners with multiple business interests. Between 1868 and 1897 James and his wife Sarah had ten children, further expanding the reach of the Dawes family into the commercial life and culture of Montreal. Even today, one can drive along Lakeshore Boulevard in Lachine and see the imposing Dawes Brewery building, with a big poster of a black horse on its eastern wall.

I speculated that when Hedges founded her agency in 1947, she must have had some deep-pocketed backers. Perhaps the money came from her extensive family. Or perhaps some of it was provided by her business partners, who were almost as mysterious as Hedges herself. I have the legal documents regarding their business partnership. They are dated 15 January 1947. One of her partners was Donald Cargill Southam, who was described as a "Publisher." He was the grandson of newspaper magnate William Southam and the son of Wilson Mills Southam, one of Canada's wealthiest philanthropists. Donald had moved to Montreal in 1938. How he became involved in the agency is unclear, as is the exact nature of his role. Three other partners were listed: Jacques Teste de Merian, J.E.M. Hoare, and Spalding Black. This meant that the agency was founded by five people, although only three of them appeared on the company roster and official letterhead. De Merian was an exotic partner. His full name was Count Jacques Teste de Merian Roquevaire. De Merian's main claim to fame, aside from his aristocratic title, seems to have been his ownership in France of a 1937 Bugatti Type 57SC Atalante racing car, one of the most expensive cars in the world.[18] In 2008 de Merian's famous vehicle sold at auction for close to US $8 million.[19] This was a man with money. The agency's registration papers simply describe his occupation as "Gentleman." John Hoare was the owner of Burton's Booksellers and Stationery, which was also located in the Dominion Square Building. Later I would discover that the founding of the agency had a great deal to do with Hoare's plans to expand his bookselling business. Spalding Black was described as an "Industrialist" living in Montreal. His roots were in advertising, specifically with the Salada Tea Company and, later, Canadian Industries Limited, for which he managed the cellophane division.[20] One of his most notable achievements was the creation of a 1937 merchandising film titled *The Lady Who Couldn't Say No*, which was a guide to marketing products to housewives because "the great volume of buying in stores" is "done on impulse by women."[21]

It was an odd group of people to collaborate in founding a literary agency, and none of them had any prior experience in the agency business. But Hedges, who was the principal figure in the operation, seems to have seen herself as one member of an emerging international triumvirate of female literary agents who were active during the period. Hedges, Southam and de Merian would be working with the D.C. Benson and Campbell Thomson agencies in London and with the W.A. Bradley Agency in Paris. An overview of the William A. Bradley Literary Agency Archives, prepared by the Harry Ransom Center of the University of Texas at Austin, explains the importance of the agency:

> The William A. Bradley Literary Agency was founded by William A. Bradley and his wife, Jenny Serruys Bradley, circa 1923. At its height, it was the preeminent literary agency in Paris, representing major authors on both sides of the Atlantic, cultivating new talent, and bringing European literature to a larger American audience. Characterized by Gertrude Stein in *The Autobiography of Alice B. Toklas* as "the

> friend and comforter of Paris authors," William Bradley handled the majority of the "Paris exiles" in the 1920s and 1930s. The Bradleys influenced the shape of modern literature by taking risks on experimental writings at a time when both American and European publishers were hesitant to pursue new and different works.[22]

After William Bradley died, on 10 January 1939, Jenny continued to operate the agency, retaining William A. Bradley as the firm's name. Letters from the Hedges agency to Bradley indicate that the correspondence was with Jenny Bradley in Paris. At the same time, Hedges's agency had established a relationship with Christine Campbell Thomson, a literary agent who was running her own agency in London at the same time Hedges, Southam and de Merian was starting up. As Mark Andresen notes,

> Christine Campbell Thomson was a rare beast in the London of 1947; a woman, who ran her own thriving business, employing a second, Moira Curd, to act as her personal secretary … Having initially proofread authors' submissions for the publisher, Curtis Brown, in the Twenties, in 1930 she left to form her own agency, joining forces with D.C. Benson Ltd. in the summer of '38.[23]

As the first literary agency in Canada, Hedges, Southam and de Merian began with some lofty goals. They would become a respected literary agency serving a wide range of Canadian writers in the postwar years. They would sell international rights to Canadian works and would represent francophone Canadian writing overseas, with the idea of placing authors from Canada in foreign French markets. They would become the Canadian counterpart of literary agencies run by women in France and the UK. They would pool their considerable resources to establish an agency that was profitable, professional, and internationally respected. However, all indications are that the agency died after little more than a year. The last letter I can locate, sent to Jenny Bradley, is dated 17 March 1948.

Although she wrote poetry, Doris had already realized how limited the market was for poets, not only in Canada but internationally as well. This may explain why her agency did not prosper as a purveyor of verse. But there was another reason she might have found it difficult to get Hedges, Southam and de Merian off the ground: she had competition. Established Canadian writers had been seeking and finding representation with British and American agencies since the early 1900s. By the time Hedges founded her agency, several active Canadian writers had been taken on by Willis Kingsley Wing, a prominent New York agent who began to work with Canadian writers and gradually expanded his list of Canadian authors to include Ralph Allen, Pierre Berton, Ralph Connor, Robertson Davies, Robert Kroetsch, Margaret Laurence, Sinclair Ross, Jane Rule, and Adele Wiseman.

One could simply conclude that Doris Hedges was Canada's first professional literary agent and that as a literary agent, she failed. But this was only a small part of her life. It doesn't explain why she felt such a willingness to start that agency, how she managed to publish seven books, how she became a broadcaster and public speaker, or how she imagined herself as a woman writer and entrepreneur in postwar Montreal. Her life sheds light on the age in which she lived. The disappearance of Doris Hedges also illustrates how easy it was for a woman of her generation to be lost, to be deleted from the histories. As Janice Fiamengo notes, the kind of research involved in recognizing the work of forgotten writers can lead in interesting directions, but those directions are not always recognized by contemporary literary scholarship:

> We know, of course, that earlier authors lived lives as full and complex as our own; had a multitude of ideas and purposes for their work; sought inspiration in a variety of contexts, sources, and people; responded to the world at times subtly, passionately, conventionally, obliquely, unconsciously; wrote well and wrote badly; wrote for money and for pure aesthetic commitment; were influenced by their education, reading, literary community, childhood experience, publisher, spiritual longings, physical passions, social conscience, intellectual convictions, inner voice; and so on. We know in the abstract that the task of analyzing any of these aspects of the writer's work – the writer's processes, influences, and contexts – is significant. But a great many of us tend not to be compelled by such scholarship. We prefer instead to discuss our own contexts, influences, and commitments, examining past writers not for themselves but as an occasion to comment on our present moment, seeking the light they shed on our (we believe more pressing) concerns, projects, and preoccupations.[24]

What follows is my attempt to reconstruct Doris Hedges, to place her in her time, in the full realization that so many pieces in the puzzle of her life have been lost. I wanted to understand Montreal and Canadian writing through her eyes, to see her sense of frustration, to appreciate the odd combination of privilege and ambition that made her personality unique. I also wanted to understand how she managed to get into print, what constraints she faced as an author, and how she overcame them. Because there are so many gaps in her story, so many unanswered questions, Doris Hedges's career also invites us to fill in the blanks, to explore the city she inhabited, to ask questions about the nature of being a female writer when Canada's literature was coming of age.

CHAPTER 1

1896–1939

Doris Hedges was born Doris Edith Ryde in Lachine, Quebec, to William Osborne Ryde and Edith Sarah Ryde (née Dawes) on 10 April 1896. It is not clear why Doris's father immigrated to Canada in 1886. He may have been hired by the Dawes family to manage their Lachine brewery. In marrying Edith Dawes, in 1892, William entered the prominent Dawes family network. The following year, Edith gave birth to Herman Chellaston Ryde, who died a few months later. The child's burial record indicates that William had, by this time, become the manager of Dawes and Company. Doris was born on 10 April 1896. After Herman's death, she would have no other siblings.

For the next decade, Doris grew up in Lachine, surrounded by the prosperous members of the Dawes family. Her grandfather, James Pawley Dawes II, had been running the Dawes Brewery, along with his brother Andrew Joseph, since 1878.[1] By the early 1880s, the company owned several buildings and a considerable amount of land in Lachine. The city's museum notes that "the history of Thomas Dawes, his brewery and his descendants remained closely tied to the history of Lachine until 1922, nearly a century during which the brewery's growth and the city's growth were indissociable."[2] Joseph Pawley Dawes II established the first telegraph line between Lachine and Montreal in 1882. He lobbied on behalf of the Dominion Bridge Company to obtain tax advantages that would encourage the company to relocate to Lachine, which it did. Dawes became an active member of the board of directors and a major shareholder in Dominion Bridge. He was also a member of the board of directors of the Merchants Bank of Canada from 1886 to 1907. His wealth allowed him to indulge his passion for horse racing, yachting, curling, and golf. In his brief biography of Hedges's grandfather, James Pawley, Gordon Burr notes that

Figure 1.1
"Missie" Ryde, 1902

> James Pawley Dawes' career centred on Lachine, where his family had made extensive investments and the town's economic development was his main concern. Through his involvement in such sectors as banking, insurance, and, in particular, manufacturing, he was able to move beyond a purely local economy to become involved in ventures of national importance. His entrepreneurial success was probably the result of equal measures of readily available capital, personal initiative, and his standing as a member of a notable local family. As a successful manufacturer, on an equal footing with the élite of the Montreal business community, Dawes also had the opportunity to build another successful career as a sportsman.[3]

I have emphasized the prominence of the Dawes family in order to provide some sense of the economic privilege and social status that surrounded Doris as a child. Her mother, Edith Sarah Dawes, was involved in local benevolent societies and was the first regent of the Dollard chapter of the Imperial Order Daughters of the Empire. Her father, William O. Ryde, had become involved in the many activities connected with the Dawes family. Around 1906 – when Doris was ten years old – she left Canada for Europe. William must have returned to Canada during this period – or perhaps he never left – because he was active as the president of the Lachine Curling Club from 1908 to 1909.[4] William had three brothers and two sisters in England, so there were many family connections that might have accounted for these overseas travels. Although the precise details of the family's itinerary remain unknown, the biography on the dust jacket of *Words on a Page* claims Doris received a cosmopolitan education in France, Switzerland, and England (in a 1941 letter to the editor published in the *New York Times*, she indicated that she had also lived in the United States at some point). She seems to have travelled back and forth between Canada and Europe during the years leading up to the First World War. In a biographical note attached to the announcement of one of Hedges's lectures at McGill University, the *McGill Daily* said she attended private schools,[5] probably in Paris. In the typescript for a radio talk titled "Books Are Precious," Hedges recalls attending a production of *Chantecler* by Edmond Rostand with the famous actor Lucien Guitry starring in the title role, which debuted on 7 February 1910, at the Théâtre de la Porte Saint-Martin in Paris. Rostand's performance inspired Hedges's interest in acting. In "Books Are Precious," she quotes *Chantecler*'s inspirational lines: "My song jets forth so clear, so proud, so peremptory, / That the horizon, seized with a rosy trembling, / Obeys me."[6]

The Paris years had a formative effect on Doris and placed her right in the middle of the European arts scene. She was only fifteen, in 1910, when she met such personalities as Gertrude Stein and Isadora Duncan along with Duncan's brother Raymond, and the dancer Nijinsky. Doris was taking ballet lessons from one M. Raymond at the Paris Opera Ballet. In a 1957 article in *Maclean's*, she recalls visiting with Katrina Buell, a potter and painter who exhibited at the Paris Salon in 1911 and 1912. Doris notes that "Katrina was an associate member of that noted movement of Canadian artists, the Group of Seven," and that "she knew everybody in Paris."[7]

Public attention was highly focused on the art world during the years Hedges spent in Paris. The year 1911 marked the emergence in the Salon des Indépendants of the first official exhibition of Cubist works. In August of the same year, the *Mona Lisa* was stolen from the Louvre. Doris was surrounded by art controversies and was travelling in some pretty exotic circles for a fifteen-year-old, given her contact with figures such as Duncan, Nijinsky, and Stein. Yet for her, Stein "and the other famous people to whom Katrina introduced me impressed me, but not as Names or Figures. I accepted them as normal and ordinary. I thought that life was like that, and that my own would be studded with such encounters."[8]

At one of Katrina's dinners, in 1911, Doris was asked to come early to help in the kitchen and then to dance a tango during the party. For Doris, this was her "most memorable meal" although she actually consumed "very little food."[9] The real sustenance of the evening was spiritual, sensual, erotic. We see a side of the young Doris Hedges that emerges in her poetry and fiction. The evening revolved around Doris's encounter with one of the guests:

> Suddenly the curtain that separated the kitchen from the studio was pushed aside and a young man came into the room. He had dark skin and black hair, coming down in a widow's peak. He was thin and wore a rather shabby suit with sleeves a little too short, showing his hands. His eyes went up at the corners, and they were looking at me with amusement.[10]

She makes small talk with the man, who "seemed vaguely familiar," and then Katrina tells Doris that it is time for her to dance:

> I went into the studio and looked around. Everyone was eyeing me kindly, and the scent of fruit and wine and paint was intoxicating. Someone put a gramophone record on, and a tango came out. I took a rose from a vase, stuck it in my hair and started to do the tango. It was fun and I was enjoying it. Their eyes were still kind and they watched with interest. I forgot myself and danced to the pulsing rhythm. I was a Spanish lady in a mantilla, dancing without a partner.
>
> And then they were no longer looking at me, and I felt a hush. The young man had come silently into the room and I could feel his presence behind me. I turned toward him, still dancing. He was smiling. He made a quick movement, caught up one of Katrina's batik scarves from a chair and draped it swiftly around his very slim waist.
>
> Then he was standing in front of me and I was no longer a lady dancing alone. I have never forgotten that moment. We danced. I was fifteen and full of the pure thrill of dancing for itself alone. We moved across the room in the spell of the tango, our feet moving in unison and our bodies swaying. The record stopped.[11]

Only after the dance ends does Doris learn that her mysterious partner is none other than Nijinsky, "the Faun!"[12] The realization of whom she has been dancing with is a transformative moment: "He took my arm and piloted me to a corner. I was trembling. It seemed to me that I had gone through a miracle without being aware of it."[13] Nijinsky fetches a jug of wine and two glasses. "Drink with me to the dance," he says. And Doris does: "It was my first drink of wine and it gurgled into me like true nectar."[14] She had become the nymph to Nijinsky's faun.

Hedges's recollection of this sensual evening (she called it her "most memorable meal" even when she remembered it forty-five years later) also says something about her growing sense of herself at a historical turning point for women. The first International Women's Day, on 19 March 1911, was marked by protests and marches around the world (in 1913, the date of International Women's Day was changed to 8 March to commemorate an important strike by female garment workers in New York in the 1880s). What began as a labour protest initiated by the Socialist International in Copenhagen became a worldwide movement seeking the right for women to vote, hold public office, and obtain equal pay. By 1912, the protests had spread to Paris.

Figure 1.2
Nijinsky as "The Faun," Paris 1912

During her years in Paris, Hedges may well have attended French designer Paul Poiret's La fête de Bacchus on 20 June 1912, where Duncan, "wearing a Greek evening gown designed by Poiret, danced on tables among 300 guests and 900 bottles of champagne were consumed until the first light of day."[15] It seems unlikely that Doris, an educated sixteen-year-old with connections to artists such as Stein and Duncan, would have been able to ignore the radical currents swirling around her during those years. That experience stood in stark contrast to her life in Canada, where she had lived in a small community among her well-to-do family. At home, Canadians were reading historical romances and rural fiction. The best-selling book by a Canadian author in 1912 was *The Street Called Straight*, by Anglican rector Basil King.[16] The same year, at the Musée des beaux-arts in Montreal, the main exhibit was conventional oils and watercolour paintings by Mary Riter Hamilton. (Hamilton would become a highly respected artist, mainly because of her brilliant paintings of the First World War battlefields completed in France and Belgium between 1919 and 1922, but at this point in her career she was mainly known as a skilled landscape painter.)[17] Meanwhile, a month before the 1912 Women's Day march in Paris, patrons of the arts were flocking to see a revolutionary exhibit of Italian Futurist and Vorticist paintings at the Bernheim-Jeune Gallery, including works by Giacomo Balla, Umberto Boccioni, Carlo Carr, and Gino Severini. Such works were mostly scorned in Canada, where resistance to modernism and avant-gardism continued throughout the First World War. As Jonathan F. Vance notes, this was because

> many observers connected modernism with Germany; it was a fit of madness, a product of prewar excess and wartime upheaval that would wither and die once peace and stability returned. J.J. Shallcross, speaking to the Island Arts and Crafts Club in Victoria in 1917, derided the Cubists and Futurists as "the aftermath of a flood of Teutonic influence … [and the] unwholesome emanations of Prussianism." Estelle Kerr agreed, writing in *Canadian Magazine* that "ultra-modern art which had its birth in Germany has been killed by the war." Even artists from the Allied nations who practised these styles were condemned. The modernism of American poet Ezra Pound was full of "vorticist banalities," thought one critic, and could hardly compare to the "exquisite verse" of Rupert Brooke.[18]

By 1913 the Ryde family was in England. They set sail for Canada and arrived in Quebec City on 3 October 1913.[19] Doris was seventeen. Nine months later, Canada would be at war. During the Great War, she worked with the Red Cross and the St John Ambulance Brigade, for which she won a badge for her service (1916–19). She served as a voluntary aid detachment nurse and won the General Service Medal. When she returned home, she took up residence with her mother and father. The 1921 census gives the Ryde family address (135 Crescent Street, Montreal) and indicates that William Ryde was retired.[20] Doris was twenty-five.

For the next five years, until she married Geoffrey in 1926, Doris lived in Montreal but visited England often. Passenger records paint a picture of a young woman on the move, although I have had no success in determining what drove her interests in these years. She had expressed no particular interest in writing, and in fact, her first publication would not appear until ten years after her marriage. But it is worth noting that literary publication in Canada was a rare thing. As Lyn Harrington observes, "in 1917, Canada had published twenty-six books; in 1918, forty-three; in 1920, seventy. Other Canadian titles were published abroad or imported."[21] Many of those titles did not reflect the aesthetics of the Montreal Group of poets who were embracing modernism and mocking the Victorian values of authors aligned with the Canadian Authors Association, founded on the urging of Stephen Leacock in 1921. They also did not reflect the massive shift that had taken place in Canadian art in response to the war. As Brian S. Osborne writes, "for many Canadian intellectuals of the day, their personal experiences of the Great War caused them to rethink their personal identities and the definition of nationhood."[22] Part of this new sense of nationhood involved a reimagining of the Canadian landscape, as was so clearly demonstrated when the Group of Seven painters held their first exhibition at the Art Gallery of Ontario in May 1920. For Osborne, "their work was but part of a surge in political, artistic, and literary nationalism that has been associated with a network of intellectuals preoccupied with making Canada a distinct and better place to live."[23] Hedges's involvement with the CAA during this period was part of this nationalist ferment.

Although the CAA came under repeated attacks from the modernists, the organization was taking specific steps to promote and protect Canadian writing. For example, they were instrumental in the passing of the 1921 Copyright

Figure 1.3
Doris Edith Ryde, 1919

Act of Canada, which came into effect in 1924. The CAA was also responsible for originating the first standard book contract, in 1926. Eventually, Hedges became involved in the CAA. But I wonder how she spent her time in Montreal and overseas in the postwar years. I suspect that she carried on her work with the Canadian Red Cross, which had come to prominence during the war. The Red Cross remained a potent force for Hedges throughout her life. At her death, she bequeathed a significant portion of her estate to the organization.

We do not know where Doris met her husband, Geoffrey Hedges. They were married at the British Embassy Chapel in Paris on 28 September 1926.[24] They planned to spend their honeymoon in Switzerland and then sail to Canada for a brief visit to Montreal at the end of October. Then they expected to proceed to New York, "where they will take up their residence."[25] Lovell records that the Hedges were residing at several Montreal addresses from 1926 until their deaths,[26] except for a few years spent in Toronto during the war. However, it is also possible that the couple spent 1927 in New York, since Lovell does not record a telephone number or address for them in Montreal that year, and because the *Gazette* referred to her in 1927 as "of New York."[27]

Geoffrey served in both world wars. He entered the British Army through the Royal Military Academy in Woolwich in 1915. He was wounded, earned the Military Cross, and attained the rank of Lieutenant Second Major. In 1940, he was commissioned by the RCAF to draw up the plans for the Women's Division. He became commanding officer of the women's depot in Toronto, training the first 5,600 women in the RCAF.[28] During the Second World War Geoffrey fought in France with the Royal Horse Artillery. After the war, he came to Montreal to manage the Canadian division of Benson and Hedges. In 1928, he became the Montreal uptown manager of the L.F. Rothschild and Company, a stockbroker with international offices. By September 1929 – one month before the Black Tuesday market crash on 24 October – he was listing his profession as "broker," with offices at 1410 Peel Street.[29] There is no way of knowing how that crash affected Geoffrey's activities as a broker, but it seems difficult to imagine that the effect was not profound, especially because he was trying to manage a business in Montreal during the Depression. Between 1930 and 1933, one-quarter to one-third of the workforce in Montreal was unemployed.[30]

Figure 1.4
Geoffrey Hedges, 1929

At this time, Doris's passion was for the theatre. The Theatre Guild of Montreal's opening season was 1929–30 and she had roles in two plays presented at the Moyse Hall Theatre at McGill University. On 26 March 1930, she played Mrs Fulverton-Fane in *The Perfect Alibi* by A.A. Milne (Geoffrey played the butler).[31] Later that year, she played Martha Culver (the younger sister of Constance Middleton) in Somerset Maugham's *The Constant Wife*, which premiered on 18 December 1930.[32] When Hedges acted in a production of *The Constant Wife* in 1949 to celebrate the guild's twentieth anniversary, she "declined to repeat her young-girl part and took a smaller role more suited to her age."[33] The *McGill Daily* criticized this later performance: "Doris Hedges, unpardonably chewing gum, rather timidly measured up to the role of the masculine spinster. She was too obviously acting a part, which tended to disrupt the atmosphere of the play."[34] (Throughout her career, as it turned out, Hedges never shied away from "acting a part.") On 26 and 27 December 1932, Hedges played the Duchess in a major production of *Hamlet* at the Little Theatre in Ottawa. Her performance was described as one in which "grace and dignity were conspicuous."[35] The Governor General produced the play and the title role was performed by Viscount Duncannon.

Hedges liked to costume herself for these performances, but she was also devoted to dressing up for social occasions. Her outfits were frequently reported on by the *Gazette*. In December of 1926, at the ball in honour of Mr and Mrs W.P. O'Brien's daughter, Miss Patricia, Doris wore a "French gown of white chiffon embroidered in silver." In her hand, she carried "a large red ostrich feather fan."[36] On 12 June 1928, she attended the marriage of Elizabeth Olive; she wore "a three-piece costume, the coat and skirt of black crepe de chine worn with a hand-painted white blouse and a white hat."[37] To the races at Blue Bonnets on 23 June, she donned "a black crepe coat and skirt, a black and white blouse and a tight-fitting hat of white straw."[38] (Hedges was partial to black.) The 1929 race season found her wearing "a black crepe coat and skirt with a black and white printed crepe blouse"[39] and then another "black crepe ensemble with a beret"[40] to the races in 1930. At times, though, Hedges could be seen in colourful attire: the 1928 opening of the races at Blue Bonnets found her wearing a "three-quarter coat, pleated skirt of royal blue kasha with a white blouse and … a royal blue felt hat."[41] On 30 August 1930, Doris chose yet another colour by opting for "a frock of pastel green felt crepe with a straw hat to match."[42] On 23 January 1931, at the annual Charity Ball for the

Royal Victoria Montreal Maternity Hospital, she dressed "in black velvet, with a fitted sequin tunic, and black slippers with silver trimmings."[43] The fact that the *Gazette* chose to report on her fashions was an indication of her social standing.

Hedges's experience in the theatre would give her the performance skills necessary to succeed as a radio personality during the Second World War. Her interest in broadcasting and literary agenting may have been prompted by the discussions and presentations that took place at the CAA convention in Montreal in June 1935. Lyn Harrington provides a summary of the issues covered:

> One of the chief topics was discussion of a poetry magazine as urged by the Montreal Poetry Group. The most interesting speaker was Frank L. Packard on "Thrillers." However, the most valuable talk was probably given by Hector Charlesworth (Montreal) on "Writing for Radio," still a comparatively new medium.[44]

Charlesworth was the influential editor of *Saturday Night* magazine and the head of the Canadian Radio Broadcasting Commission (1932–36), the precursor of the CBC. In his speech, Charlesworth stressed how the broadcaster had "tried to do something to link up Canadian authorship with an audience which is far larger than that reached by any publication or group of publications."[45]

What is striking about the account of the convention provided in the CAA's convention number of its journal *Canadian Author* is the extent to which the organization's executive and membership were becoming aware of the material conditions surrounding literary production. In an introductory editorial to the convention issue, unsigned but probably written by the newly elected CAA president Pelham Edgar, considerable emphasis is placed on how "the most vigilant attention has also to be given to the channels through which our writings have to pass if they are to reach the public at all."[46] To this end, the CAA was considering the founding of a poetry magazine (established in January 1936 as *Canadian Poetry*) and other means through which writers could reach the public. The editorial also pointed out, in remarkably prescient terms, that

> one of our constant and most difficult tasks is concerned with the relations between author and publisher or editor. Another task, demanding increased consideration, is to stimulate and inform all who control the channels of circulation, including the various authorities from whom librarians draw their power of purchase, and the teachers, who, like the librarians, can do much by advice to readers.[47]

The minutes of the convention also record the fact that "questions have been asked, both at the Convention and in letters to the Secretary, as to the value of Literary Agents."[48] The issue concluded with a small section devoted to "Notes from Agents." One of these notes was provided by Paul R. Reynolds, perhaps the best-known agent in New York, who offered his interpretation of the effects of the Depression on the publishing industry: "I think things have improved and everyone hopes they are going to grow better and better."[49] Another agent from New York, Robert Thomas Hardy, said "I find the market quite good. Love stories always in demand; detective stories not so much in demand now, from pulp magazine standpoint, as the detective-horror slant. Westerns are popular."[50]

The CAA's involvement with the supply side of publishing also accounted for its renewal of the Association of Canadian Bookmen the same year as the convention. Harrington observes that "[Pelham] Edgar set about revitalizing the Association of Canadian Bookmen which had preceded the birth of the Association and re-surfaced for a few years in Toronto as a bookseller's association. The new version would be less commercial-minded, would embrace all phases of the book trade – authors, publishers, booksellers, librarians and readers. It would reach out to the 'unreading.'"[51] When the ACB began to run into financial difficulties in 1927, it did not shut down completely but entered a period of dormancy that lasted until Edgar took steps to revive it in 1936. After he assumed the presidency of the ACB, he sought out high-profile members of the literati to join him on the board. The organization held Canada's first National Book Fair during Canadian Book Week, 9 to 14 November 1936. Nationalism was in the air. A week earlier the CBC made its debut, replacing the Canadian Radio Broadcasting Commission with a new organization that would allow Canadians "to hear their own station," in the words of Leonard Brockington, the CBC's first chairman.[52]

Although CAA disorganization in Montreal forced the ACB to move the Fair to Toronto, the Montreal chapter of the CAA went ahead with a display of Canadian books for five days in the Sun Life Building. A year later, the second National Book Fair was held first in Toronto and a week later in Montreal on the top floor of the Mount Royal Hotel. A reception was also held at the Ritz-Carlton Hotel for visiting publishers and authors.[53] Although there is no direct evidence that Hedges was involved in the 1935 convention or the National Book Fair displays in Montreal in 1936, it seems unlikely that she could have avoided the impact of these events. They were well promoted and popular among the literary community in Montreal. Her earliest poem, "Apathy," appeared in the new CAA magazine, *Canadian Poetry*, four months after its first issue was published in January 1936. This indicates that Hedges was well aware of the CAA and its efforts to promote Canadian poetry to a wider reading public. It also means that she wasted little time in preparing her submission to the magazine, which she must have made soon after it was established towards the end of 1935. To what extent was her desire to write borne out of personal frustration? Hedges was channelling those frustrations into her poetry: the fact that her first published poem was titled "Apathy" is not without significance.

By her own account, Hedges published her first story in London's *Graphic Magazine*, although she does not provide the details of its publication and I have been unable to locate it. On the dust jacket of *For This I Live* (1963), we learn that "she began her writing career by submitting a short story to the *London Graphic* – which at that time published but one short story per issue – and having it immediately accepted." Much of her early work was inspired by frequent trips abroad. For example, in one of her radio broadcasts, titled "The Mind of the Poet" (1950), she describes a trip to La Baule, Normandy in 1935, in which she witnessed a beautiful scene on the beach that inspired her poem "Bittersweet," which she wrote around 1938.[54]

The publication of "Apathy" in the April 1936 issue of *Canadian Poetry* would have aligned Hedges with the bourgeois literary culture that would soon come under attack by the founders of *New Frontier* magazine, which was international and leftist in orientation.[55] By publishing in *Canadian Poetry*, Hedges briefly saw her work in the company of Dorothy Livesay's early socialist poetry, which had appeared in the first issue of January 1936, the same year as F.R. Scott's groundbreaking anthology, *New Provinces*. But by the time Hedges's "Apathy" was published in April, Livesay had moved on to *New Frontier*. Despite the changes taking place around her, Hedges was not prompted to alter her poetic affiliations. She was intent on writing about personal and private experiences and was trying to come to terms with the meaning of a relationship that was stalled:

Apathy

Into cold storage with love
For the winter, and wait, let us wait,
Let us wait, let us droop, let us never
Lift finger to pick up the pieces
And put them together. To gape at the fissure
Is all that we do, but to mend it
Or stop it from draining completely
Was never our business.
Come, substitute folly and mechanized pleasure
Let us dance, let us drink, let us spend
Of our vital, impassioned,
Our never-returning and exquisite loving
On shadows. On brilliant, on treacherous
Gaudy-hued travesties.
Into cold storage with love
For the winter, and wait, let us wait,
Let us wait for the Spring, let us never
Remember that Spring is behind us.[56]

Hedges begins her poem with an emphasis on the passage of time that is tied to a change in the seasons. The relationship has been put into cold storage, held in stasis, wilting like a doomed flower. And the people involved are rendered immobile, impotent in the face of the increasing coldness of their engagement. They understand that there is a divide, that a crevasse has opened up between them, but they are powerless to heal the rift. Instead, they divert themselves from the issues that separate them, focusing instead on distractions like "mechanized pleasure," or "dance," or "drink." They are not investing in something real; they are spending their love on "shadows" that are frivolous "travesties" that hide the true nature of their loss. Caught in a cycle aligned with the seasons, the speaker is resigned to putting love "into cold storage." There seems to be no relief from this cycle because it has happened before: spring will come, and perhaps the cold storage of emotion will end, but spring has come before, and the apathy in the face of this relationship has not faded or welcomed any warmth associated with the changing season.

The next year Hedges published "Loneliness" in *Queen's Quarterly*. The poem focuses on some of the issues she articulated in "Apathy":

Loneliness

If drunkenness would do it
I would sell my soul to Bacchus for a song.
If by some madness I could make you see
I would enclose myself within a maniac's cage.
Why should I care, why should my heart contract
That you can gaze at me with empty eyes
And calm acceptance when I nod at you
And say, "of course, my dear"? You are content
To look no farther. Who am I to dare
And dare again to hope that there are eyes
Covered as mine are, somewhere to rejoice
In meeting with my own, lips that are stern
When mine are, arms that will take
The burden of aloneness from my back
And shoulder it in yoke: no fairer bond
Than this could ever be, that we might know
Together when to pull, when to let laughter come,
When to be grave. If I were satyr full of wine
Or madman caught within a lucid moment, you
With pity in your eyes, perhaps, would never see
How sober was the sot, how sane the fool.[57]

It is tempting and admittedly risky to read this poem as a reflection on Hedges's marriage to Geoffrey. It focuses on the theme announced in "Apathy" – that of a cold relationship in stasis. One gets the sense that Hedges began to write as a response to personal pain and alienation. The speaker is willing to engage in extremes – drunkenness or mania – if it would break the stony gaze of her partner, who remains content to exist in this stagnant relationship while the speaker seeks an alternative, "to hope that there are eyes" that would meet hers directly and lift "the burden of aloneness from my back." She longs to be seen for what she is; she longs to find a partner who will share her emotional burdens in laughter and in seriousness.

For Hedges, eyes and sight are often equated with honesty and sexual discovery. The trope appears in her first story published in Canada, "Sleds," which appeared in *Maclean's* on 15 December 1938. The narrative, with its Christian moral compass, is reminiscent of Morley Callaghan's stories from the same period. The story focuses on Philip Trevor, a boy from a privileged family who is out on a winter day, pulling his shiny new sled to a nearby hill. But he is alone. He has no friends to sled with. Then, in the distance, he hears the sounds of boys laughing, and he finds that "there was something in the laughter that drew him irresistibly."[58] It is some kind of male siren song. Soon he joins the group of boys and is racing them down the hill on his sled. They make fun of him at first. He is not one of them, and he knows it, but he can't quite figure out why. Then one of the boys approaches him directly and Philip feels overwhelmed: "Something new in him seemed about to burst. The grey eyes studied him. They did not look at his clothes or his 'sissy sled,' they were looking right at him, into him. It was the first time Philip had ever been stared at like that."[59] Soon, this intimate stranger – his name is Dusty – has to leave, and although Philip knows he will be punished for coming home late, he longs to follow his new friend.

There is a current running between the boys, a latent sexual energy that finds them heading off together. Dusty stops. He stares at Philip. "Philip stared back. Both of them had stopped. It seemed that something had to be explained between them, but neither of them knew how to do it."[60] Philip is nine. Dusty is fourteen. He threatens to hit Philip if he follows him. But that only intensifies Philip's desire to enter the older boy's world. "Philip's hand dropped and his mouth opened. The boy was not much taller than himself and certainly looked no older. Premature trouble and not enough proper food had stunted him. But his eyes were fine, and Philip had seen nothing else from the beginning."[61]

Philip understands that Dusty comes from a different world, yet his electric attraction to the older boy's otherness only gets stronger as they head toward Dusty's house: "Here was this mystery again, the mystery of the difference in people that no one had been able to explain to him. He looked eagerly into Dusty's grey eyes, probing for the answer."[62] The boys had arrived in a part of the city unfamiliar to Philip. While he waits for Dusty to collect some boxes he will deliver for a belligerent employer, someone tries to steal Philip's scarf. Dusty defends him. Soon after, they arrive at Dusty's house, and Philip sees Dusty's mother: "She had a thin face, the cheeks fallen in, and grey hair, neatly arranged. She was all bent over, and she wore a shawl over a cotton housedress."[63] All of a sudden, Philip realizes that it is evening, that he will be late for dinner, and that he has been involved in an experience that will transform him: "The whole thing, the enormity of his adventure in disobedience, swept over him."[64] Dusty realizes that it's time for Philip to head home.

When he arrives home at the "great house," the contrasts between Philip's world and Dusty's become glaringly apparent. For the first time in his life, Philip Trevor has broken the rules. By engaging in this act of transgression, he has not only crossed a social barrier but also experienced a sexual awakening. His mother, seated in the living room, demands in an angry voice ("like a great iron wall, too high to climb, ever")[65] where he has been. Animalistic and monstrous, "She wore something that glimmered and had brown fur at the sleeves, and her hands came out of the fur, white, with red nails."[66] She demands that he be punished. But Philip's father senses that his son has experienced something that goes beyond punishment, and after the full story comes out, he realizes that the boy has had a transformative encounter.

They decide to help Dusty's family, to bring them some food because Philip realizes that Dusty's mother needs assistance: "She looked awful hungry."[67] Part of this story is glaringly moral: privileged child gains insight into the condition of those less fortunate and convinces his wealthy father to assist those in need. However, the other dimension of this story – what Hedges seems to be most interested in – is the energy generated by homosexual relationships. The Trevors' marriage is moribund. Philip's mother is other; she is soon left behind. "'Dad,' said Philip with desperation in his voice, 'please tell her I … There were things – oh, it's no use!'"[68] He knows that his father knows. "He could see that his son had had some important boy experience."[69] In this moment of recognition, Philip "looked at his father with that intent, serious expression that John Trevor felt in his own blood like a call."[70] His father points out that Philip is "different from Dusty." Philip understands why this is true. Dusty has no father. "'I guess it's because I've got you for a father,' said Philip. He said it quite simply, without affectation. John Trevor felt the slow color come up into his face from sheer emotion. He had not been so touched by any human wand for many years."[71] The story ends on a note of mutual adoration, with a final phallic trope.

In the three years leading up to the war, Hedges had established herself as a writer whose work could gain acceptance in several respected publications: *Canadian Poetry*, *Queen's Quarterly*, and *Maclean's*. Although it is true that the CAA and its *Canadian Poetry* magazine had become the subject of ridicule for modernists such as F.R. Scott, whose "The Canadian Authors Meet" (1927) satirized the CAA poets as stuffy, dated, privileged women devoted to what Candida Rifkind describes as "home, hearth, and Empire,"[72] the fact remains that Hedges's early poetry did not fit this description. It depicted relationships that were cold and broken in language that was direct and stark. Commentators ignored this starkness because they assumed that Hedges, like other CAA poets, could never embrace modernist standards. However, as Clarence Karr observes,

> It has been fashionable until recently for critics such as Frank Scott, from an arrogant, modernist perspective, to condemn the Canadian Authors Association as a group of self-congratulatory amateurs who eschewed standards and cared only about the commercial aspects of literary existence. Such criticism displays contemptible, condescending elitism and ignores the fundamental role which the association played in its early decades.[73]

Much of the poetry that appeared in *Canadian Poetry* demonstrates the extent to which the magazine's values are almost always misrepresented. As Dean Irvine observes, "literary historians have routinely omitted it from studies of Canadian little magazines, largely because of prevailing antipathies toward the CAA and its publications among critics and historians in the field of Canadian literary modernism"[74] but also because they represented the work of female poets who were aligned with local poetry groups. Yet, Irvine points out, magazines such as *Canadian Poetry* and *Contemporary Verse* were

> connected to an international modernist little-magazine culture that had emerged in the 1910s. That magazine culture originated with the

> work of women editors in the United States. *Contemporary Verse* was, like *Canadian Poetry Magazine*, not an avant-garde magazine in the tradition of Margaret Anderson and Jane Heap's the *Little Review* (1914–29), but rather a poetry magazine in the tradition of Harriett Monroe and Alice Corbin-Henderson's *Poetry: A Magazine of Verse*.[75]

As Irvine says, E.J. Pratt, the editor of *Canadian Poetry*, "published many of the poets in the 1930s who later developed their talents in the more fashionable Canadian literary magazines of the 1940s."[76] Livesay's leftist "Day and Night" was published in the first issue of *Canadian Poetry* in 1936. Her poems continued to appear as late as December 1938 and in the CAA's *Canadian Bookman* in early 1939. Yet women remained generally excluded from the modernist canon. After all, Livesay was not represented in the all-male *New Provinces* (1936), the first Canadian anthology to embrace modernism. The reason is clear. Modernism was considered to be a predominantly male aesthetic. As Carole Gerson notes, the modernists set themselves apart from female writers whom they saw as traditional, romantic, domestic:

> Scorning romanticism and sentimentality, they valorized detachment, alienated individualism, elitism and formalism over emotion, domesticity, community, and popularity, a binarism that implicitly and explicitly barred most of Canada's women writers from serious academic consideration.[77]

Gerson goes on to say that

> Canadian modernism's insistence on its own immaculate conception at McGill University in Montreal in the late 1920s led its proponents to pillory its female companions and precursors as "virgins of sixty who still write of passion" (to return to Scott's "Canadian Authors Meet"). The project of re-inscribing women writers into Canadian literary history challenges the self-fashioning of Canadian modernists.[78]

While Hedges may have resisted the modernist values being promoted at nearby McGill University, her early publications in *Canadian Poetry* did not place her in poor company. And while her first story was a moralistic tale designed to illustrate the boundaries between the rich and the poor, its realistic notes and its sexual subtexts set it apart from most of the Canadian short fiction being published in the late 1930s. It explored working-class life and represented it as something desirable to its central protagonist. Although the story can in no way be described as proletarian fiction, it does illustrate Hedges's awareness of issues surrounding the depiction of working-class people that had emerged during the 1930s. In this sense, Hedges was exploring literary realism and modernist forms of expression in ways that demonstrated her awareness of shifting aesthetic values that emerged during the Depression.

Canada declared war in September 1939. In many ways, the war became the catalyst behind the most productive phase of Hedges's career. The months leading up to the conflict crystallized many of the issues that would become points of tension in the city and the nation in the next few years. On 18 May 1939, King George VI and Queen Elizabeth visited Montreal and were driven forty kilometres through the streets on a route that came into contact with a variety of groups that represented the wide-ranging set of political and social values that made the city so diverse. In *City Unique*, William Weintraub reconstructs the royal visit, demonstrating the various forces at play along the route (I draw on his vignettes in what follows). There was widespread concern that too many people would crowd onto balconies and cause them to collapse. Would Premier Maurice Duplessis be drunk or sober when he was presented to Their Majesties? And what about the mayor – Camillien Houde – who had announced that if Canada went to war with Italy, Quebec would side with Mussolini? (Houde would eventually be arrested for advising Quebeckers not to register for military service.) How would the French Canadian population respond to British royalty, especially when people were being asked to buy and wave flags that they could scarcely afford? It was 1939; Canada was still coping with the effects of the Great Depression.

Weintraub follows the royal procession as it moves through the city, travelling past cheering crowds in Outremont while resentful labour movement members grumbled on its fringes, through the Jewish neighbourhood near Park Avenue whose factory workers were "plotting strikes and dreaming of social justice,"[79] past the *pure laine* districts of Montreal east and the Midget Palace on Rachel toward the baseball stadium on Delormier, where 45,000 Catholic schoolchildren waited to cheer the royals. The cortège headed west and proceeded downtown, past the expensive stores frequented by English clientele, then through the McGill campus up to Molson Stadium, where 14,000 English Protestant students waited to welcome them. Then the king and queen headed west again, into the Golden Square Mile and then farther into wealthy Westmount. Perhaps Doris and Geoffrey Hedges watched the cortège as it moved along Sherbrooke Street, right around the corner from where they lived. The tour ended at the Windsor Hotel, where a thousand guests honoured Their Majesties at a sumptuous dinner.

It was a day of excitement. But as Weintraub makes clear, it was also a day that highlighted a series of tensions defining the city – those between rich and poor, monarchists and Quebec nationalists, professionals and labourers, established landowners and immigrants, capitalists and communists. Those who inhabited the city at that time might have ignored these contrasts on a daily basis, but the royal visit, and the events leading up to Canada's declaration of war four months later, would have made it difficult for someone like Hedges to remain completely aloof. Yet, at the same time, it was difficult for her to escape the pull of her wealthy heritage. The Dawes family was rich and powerful, and their social standing was attractive to Doris, who struggled to come to terms with those who inhabited another world, or with those who embraced political beliefs that ran contrary to those associated with her family; she was no socialist, and she had trouble accepting those who would challenge the status quo. But, to her credit, she also understood that times were changing. Eventually, she would try to address the conflicts she faced through her poetry and fiction, and by engaging in activities that were designed to reconcile her sense of personal well-being with her recognition that she was living in a city that was increasingly divided between what she herself recognized as the "Haves" and the "Have-Nots."

CHAPTER 2
1939–1945

Although it might seem like an odd point of departure, Hedges's activities during the Second World War appear to have had their genesis in her involvement with the theatrical performances staged by the Montreal Repertory Theatre (MRT), which became active in Montreal in 1930. Most of this account of MRT is based on Philip Booth's detailed history of the company. Additional information is provided in Herbert Whittaker's *Setting the Stage: Montreal Theatre 1920–29*. Originally called The Theatre Guild of Montreal,[1] the company was founded by Martha Allan at a meeting held in Westmount in November 1929. Martha was the granddaughter of Sir Hugh Allan, probably Canada's richest man. Her father, Sir Montagu Allan, was president of the Merchants Bank of Canada as well as the director of eight other Canadian banks, according to his entry in *Who's Who in Canada* for 1928–29. He also co-founded the Ritz-Carlton Hotel in Montreal.

The Allans were well known to Doris's family long before her own involvement with MRT. Doris's grandfather, James Pawley Dawes, was a business associate of Hugh Montagu Allan. They were on the board of directors of several banks; in 1900 they worked together to revive steeplechasing at the Montreal Hunt Club. Doris's mother, Edith Sarah Dawes, was active in Montreal social circles until her death in 1947; she remained in contact with Montagu Allan throughout her life. Weintraub points out that the MRT "began as something of a hobby for members of the Square Mile elite."[2]

Perhaps it was Allan's connection to the Ritz that allowed Doris and Geoffrey to reside there for several years. That is pure speculation. But there is no doubt that Hedges's involvement in the theatre was prompted by her connection with Martha Allan and the Allan family's long-standing relationship with the Dawes. Although Hedges only performed in two MRT productions, she remained in close contact with Allan and witnessed the ways in which cultural organizations were developing national and patriotic responses to increasing tensions in Europe toward the end of the 1930s.

Six days after Britain declared war on Germany, on 3 September 1939, the MRT developed a wartime action plan. Booth points out that "the company had become officially affiliated with the Canadian Red Cross and would function as a unit of the organization for the duration of the war. All profits would go to Red Cross funds."[3] The MRT also developed a program known as the Tin Hats, which would be "responsible for a program of entertainment for soldiers under the Auxiliary War Services Department."[4] Over the war years, the Tin Hats entertained approximately twenty thousand soldiers and airmen.[5] I emphasize this particular connection between MRT and the war effort because it seems to have made a strong impression on Hedges, who was herself devoted to the Red Cross (the dust jacket of her novel *Robin* says that she was decorated for her work with the organization in the First World War and founded a Red Cross branch in Montebello, Quebec, during the Second World War). According to the Montreal *Gazette*, she later established her agency as a business that "specialized in the manuscripts of veterans of the Second World War."[6]

Hedges had been involved in the Montreal branch of the Junior Welfare League, albeit sporadically, for many years. The League, founded in New York in 1901 by Mary Harriman, was originally devoted to improving the living conditions and literacy of immigrants on Manhattan's lower east side. According to Nathalie Henderson, Harriman felt that "working through the church was too sectarian and hospital work too limited in scope. Her concept would be to organize young women from all religious backgrounds to go into the settlement houses and do frontline social work among the needy."[7]

The Montreal chapter of the League, established in 1912, was the first branch of the organization in Canada. At first it focused on social and educational issues; later, it became involved in providing health care and nutritional advice to underprivileged people. It also established nurseries and advised women about birth control.[8] When Canada entered the war, in September 1939, the League used its October newsletter to reflect upon the work done by its members during the First World War, and noted that "Mrs. Geoffrey Hedges received the Overseas Medal and the Allies Medal" for her service.[9] Four years later, in October 1943, Hedges contributed a short essay titled "A Time of Proving" to the newsletter, in which she reflected upon the fact that "most of us have been Privileged Women all our lives, without appreciating it."[10] Then she reveals that although "I resigned from the Junior League years ago without much thought" because she believed "it was time for me to turn it over to younger women," she had decided to return because "the League is in danger, as all organizations like it are in danger," and "when danger threatens, the clans gather."[11] By January 1944 Hedges had certainly made good on her determination to return to active involvement with the League. She is listed on the masthead of the newsletter for that month as head of the "Public Actions Committee."[12] Hedges's contributions to the League appear to stop after the founding of her agency in January 1947.

In the League newsletter, Hedges identifies herself as "a conservative in my thinking" who believes that "great movements forward have always been germinated first in the minds of single men of vision."[13] She rejects the idea of "reducing great art or great thought to a common denominator" in which "Utopia" might arise from "mass intelligence, and mass art, and mass government" because "a few fine artists and scientists and philosophers, with the fire of selflessness in their veins, will still set the tone of art and living for some time to come. A general levelling is repellent to me, because there must be a standard, and good taste must not be allowed to deteriorate past revival."[14]

Hedges was returning to the League mainly because of her clannism, her elitism, and her belief that its membership "represented the educated few." The League had always been associated with Montreal's wealthiest women (its headquarters had been located in the Ritz since 1934).[15] The pages of the League's newsletters were crowded with notices of meetings to be held at the hotel, along with advertisements for jewellery, elegant clothing, high-class travel, and the beer produced by Hedges's own family-run business at the Dawes Brewery in Lachine or the cigarettes manufactured by Benson and Hedges, which was managed in Canada by Geoffrey. Hedges wanted to preserve and expand the education of the chosen few so that they could remain in power: "We should at once revivify and revaluate our educational programme, with more emphasis on a study of politics, both local and national. We should have lectures and discussions for all members, together, on the Humanities, and on the questions that press upon our governments; such questions as the refugee and immigration problems, and the problem of juvenile delinquency, to mention only three."[16] For Hedges, the masses were a threat; she saw them, along with refugees and immigrants, as people associated with crime.

While Hedges expresses guilt over her status as one of the privileged "Haves" and observes that "many of the Have-Nots think we started the war in order to line our own pockets,"[17] her guilt does not last long. The idea that the war served the needs of the wealthy could only be countered through education, she says: "it is because of our education and gentle upbringing that we are fitted for leadership."[18] Hedges's article was a rallying cry to women of privilege who worried that the war would erode their social standing, particularly in the face of rising labour protests around the world.

In response to this socialist threat, Hedges argued, "we are now a group of women fighting for our right to exist" in a new order "heading dangerously towards mass production."[19] Explicit in this essay is Hedges's enormous sense of privilege and class-consciousness, along with her fear of the putatively uneducated working-class miscreants who might rise to power and displace the conservative capitalists who had masterminded their fate. As a Montrealer who was actively involved in the CAA, Hedges could not have ignored the 1942 founding of John Sutherland's *First Statement* magazine (1942–45), which Larry McDonald describes as "working class, nationalist";[20] F.R. Scott and Patrick Anderson's *Preview* magazine (1942–45), which McDonald calls "academic, theoretical, internationalist, and formalist";[21] or the influential 1943 publication by Scott and David Lewis of *Make This Your Canada*, which detailed the national program and socialist ideology of the Co-Operative Commonwealth Federation (CCF). Ian McKay notes that the book "sold 25,000 copies in less than a year – making it one of the most widely-read socialist texts in Canadian history."[22] In the same year, Montreal elected Fred Rose to the Canadian parliament. Rose was a Labour-Progressive Party MP (the LPP was the reorganized version of the Communist Party of Canada, which had been banned early in the war). Hedges had to recognize that many of the writers who were publicly affiliated with socialism lived in Montreal, including Louis Dudek, Leo Kennedy, A.M. Klein, Irving Layton, Dorothy Livesay, P.K. Page, John Sutherland, and Miriam Waddington, to name a few. How would she reconcile their arguments and aesthetics with the values surrounding her every time she attended the Junior League meetings, which were always held at the Ritz, or when she picked up the League magazine, with its advertisements for fine jewellery, expensive travel, and luxury furs?

Geoffrey had gone overseas in 1940. In a 1941 photo, Hedges is shown wearing an RCAF "Sweetheart" pin, probably sent to her by Geoffrey.[23] By Hedges's account, this was around the time that fighting in Burma intensified. It is uncertain whether Geoffrey fought at Burma, but Doris did follow the war in the papers. Her story "I Put Away Childish Things" was set in Burma. It appeared in *Good Housekeeping* in March 1943. In a radio talk she recounts that her readers wrote to ask if she had been stationed in Burma because the story felt so realistic.[24] Hedges responded that she had simply paid attention to the headlines, much as she encouraged the Women's Division of the Royal Canadian Air Force in Toronto to regularly read the papers in order to follow the war.[25]

Clearly Hedges believed that the arts could contribute to political change and that it was the responsibility of authors to get involved in the war effort. It was one thing to act in a play that entertained wealthy Montrealers or to publish self-conscious poems about love and loss; it was another to make literature relevant to the war. How could literature raise money that could be donated to the military? That question alone forced a consideration of the commercial aspects of literary production. The Tin Hats were raising money and entertaining troops. How could Hedges use her writing to contribute to the cause?

Hedges was determined to reach as wide an audience as possible. To this end, she turned toward radio broadcasting, a profession involving very few women at the time. Quebec culture, strongly influenced by the Roman Catholic church, left little room for women to advance themselves in the professional world. It is sobering to remember that women gained the right to vote in Quebec provincial elections only in 1940. In order to be recognized in this patriarchal system, Hedges would have had to pursue her ambitions aggressively; while she may not have become a regular on local or national radio, the fact that her commentaries gained acceptance by radio producers says a lot about her determination to succeed. Broadcasters' willingness to hire women owed much to the influence of Elizabeth Long, who had initiated Women's Interest programming at the CBC in 1938. As the network's first female executive, Long created programs on topics of interest to women and their advancement. But she also fulfilled a CBC aim during the war years – that of using the airwaves to encourage a sense of citizenship. As Barbara M. Freeman notes,

Figure 2.1
Doris Hedges, 1941

> The CBC's information programs, including talks for women, were government subsidized and designed to inculcate a sense of citizenship that was already laced through with increasingly flexible gender expectations. Like the women's pages in the newspapers, on which it was modelled, Long's Women's Interest niche reinforced women's domestic roles while allowing her programmers, broadcasters and listeners to explore more educative, feminist perspectives on their place in Canadian society. Her story is an instructive chapter on the links between the broadcast media and the women's movement in Canada, further illustrating the contention of Joan Sangster and other historians that feminism continued to have a life of its own between the "first" and "second" waves.[26]

Long's influence could not have been lost on Hedges, who was also interested in exploring the ways in which women could contribute to the strengthening of citizenship during the war. Meanwhile, the reality of the war had become increasingly present to Canadians, not only because of their involvement in the European front, but also because German threats often came very close to home. For example, on 11 May 1942, a German U-boat in the St Lawrence River torpedoed two British freighters off the north shore of the Gaspé Peninsula.[27] This was a catalyst for the Battle of the St Lawrence, an effort directed at stopping German forces from disrupting supply routes to Allied forces in the United Kingdom and Europe.

In her radio addresses and public speeches in the early war years, Hedges often commented on Canada's role in the conflict and on the condition of the country's soldiers. Between 1941 and 1945 she delivered five addresses for radio stations CBO in Ottawa[28] and CFCF in Montreal.[29] Her radio work sometimes involved live broadcast interviews with those involved in the war. The only existing recording of Hedges's voice can be found in a file containing a CBC interview she conducted with a British woman – Mrs Earle Smith – on 19 August 1945. This recording was difficult for me to obtain. There were delays and bureaucratic snafus. Once I knew that the recording existed, every day I waited for it only increased my curiosity about how Hedges would actually sound in conversation. When the file finally arrived, I played it with great anticipation. It was disappointing. The interview seemed staged, unspontaneous. Hedges and her interviewee were obviously reading from a script. Their voices sounded stilted, rushed, as if they were trying too hard to get through the dialogue. But there was Hedges's voice, more clipped than I would have imagined, somewhat British in intonation, clearly concerned with the public persona she was presenting to her radio audience.[30]

Much of Hedges's radio work focused on "Montreal's New Venture," a program established by the Junior League in a building the organization purchased on St Mark Street; it was colloquially known as the Jabberwocky Club. This was the first of several youth clubs that had been founded across Canada in response to rising delinquency rates and the need for more recreational activities for young people during the war. Tight budgets had forced many municipalities to cut back on recreational services. Charitable groups tried to step into the breach. According to Jeffrey A. Keshen, the Jabberwocky Club was an eleven-room house purchased by the Junior League for high-school-age adolescents:

> For a twenty-five cent annual fee, participants were directed into activities such as carpentry, painting, sewing, sketching [and] dress designing … Within a week of the club's opening, 600 young people had joined and nearly as many were placed on its waiting list, thus leading one local newspaper to comment that many more such venues were needed "as an answer to idleness and delinquency."[31]

In its account of Hedges's radio address on the club, the *Gazette* noted that it was delivered "under the auspices of the City Improvement League and the Municipal Service Bureau."[32] Hedges pointed out that the success of the club owed a lot to the fact that the young people involved were responsible for running it themselves. "They are aware, these children, that this is the first venture of its kind in Canada. That is a proud thing to them, and they are determined to make it a model for others."[33] The *Montreal Star* reported on a different aspect of Hedges's address, noting her observation that juvenile delinquency was still on the rise, and that the establishment of centres where young people could find innocent fun and entertainment was one of the most potent means for combatting it. "The men overseas expect us to look after their children. They expect, and rightly, to find their young sons and daughters grown into decent and lively manhood and womanhood on their return."[34]

Hedges seems to have given this same radio address earlier in the year in an 11 March broadcast titled "The Citizen and His Child." Hedges dwells upon the nature of democracy and emphasizes the role played by citizens in promoting liberty. Although democracy offers freedom, Hedges argues, it also demands responsibility, especially when it comes to child rearing. But rising delinquency rates show that "we have failed lamentably to take advantage of the best gift of democracy, the freedom to bring into the world, and to help into maturity, young men and women who are healthy, happy, and well adjusted to life."[35] Hedges cites delinquency statistics and argues that the rate of juvenile incarceration "has reached terrifying proportions" and that "in the wake of these young misdemeanours come worse offences, followed by disease, moral degeneration, and finally complete loss of a sense of citizenship."[36] Hedges believed that "a large percentage of the criminals in the world's jails, were once juvenile delinquents, who might have been saved."[37] She concludes by making a "special plea to parents"[38] to talk to their children about delinquency and the nature of citizenship.

Hedges links the importance of democracy and linking the future of democracies to the well-being of children. She argues that if the child suffers, the nation suffers, and if the future of the child is compromised, so is the future of the nation. The war has made the raising of children even more important, because in so many cases their fathers have gone overseas: "While our young men are overseas, getting killed, maimed, and nervously exhausted, we have their families, and their community to look after."[39] Hedges proposes several factors that can positively affect those families: "good family life," "adequate leisure-time activities," "better housing," "re-examination of the purpose of education," "protection of young people in employment," "enforcement of laws affecting minors," and "improved correctional facilities."[40]

Although Hedges's speech was well intended, it was also obviously written by a woman who had little direct experience with teenage children, for whom questions about citizenship are not often front and centre. While she was trying to meditate on the nature of freedom in response to the war, and while she saw in future generations the means of ensuring liberty, she was also responding to a widespread problem that prompted the Junior League to stage a "Delinquency Prevention Drive" during the week of 13–18 March 1944. The League even invited John J. McGuire, an inspector from the FBI, to be the guest speaker at a dinner marking the event. Although the League's Delinquency Prevention Drive was directed toward all children, the group took a special interest in young women who had contracted venereal disease. As Tamara Myers notes,

> Delinquent girls in Montreal may have elicited some sympathy being the "victims" of absent, immoral mothers, but they were also eyed suspiciously as the vectors of disease. Montreal had an ignoble reputation as a centre for prostitution and venereal disease, made worse during the war as statistics showed that rates for servicemen with VD were highest in Quebec. Adolescent girls became the target of delinquency workers concerned about the effects of their modern lifestyles. It was no accident that the opening session of Montreal's Delinquency Prevention Week (sponsored by the Junior League of Montreal, La Ligue de la Jeunesse Féminine, and the Jewish Junior Welfare League) began with the subject, "Juvenile Delinquency and Venereal Disease."[41]

Myers observes that educating young women about sexually transmitted diseases became a major focus for the League in response to the findings of a conference on female delinquency that was held in conjunction with a popular film that screened in 1944:

> A cautionary tale from the silver screen rivetted Montrealers in 1944. In March that year a Hollywood movie entitled *Where Are Your Children?* opened at the Snowdon Theatre in Montreal, coinciding with the city's Delinquency Prevention Week activities. Both the film and the well-advertised conference presented the problem of girls in wartime in overwrought style. In *La Presse*, ads for La Semaine de Sauvegarde de la Jeunesse délinquant began: "The father is in Italy. The older brother is in the navy. The mother works all day in a war factory." This situation inevitably produced delinquent teens, as the film pointed out. "Problème social exposé à l'écran" confirmed one paper. Others seduced viewers with sensational headlines: "This might be your daughter!"[42]

What is most striking about Hedges's activities regarding wayward youth was not her recommendations, which all make conservative sense, but her dedication to the treatment of children, given the fact that she had none of her own. It was as if, by embracing the cause of juvenile delinquency, Hedges allowed herself to assume the parental role she was never able to experience in her own home life; her efforts on behalf of children were a displaced expression of her longing for children of her own. It was as if, by focusing so intently on children and their home life, she was also focusing on the way her own home life seemed to be bereft of familial comfort, just as it was bereft of the same comfort in Hedges's story "Sleds," discussed in the previous chapter.

The desire to protect children, the dream of having children, the fantasy of a family organized around a child – these are familiar themes in Hedges's work. But so is the theme of the family as a constraining burden that is almost impossible to escape. The focus on childhood and the bonds of family that emerge in "Sleds" reappears in the 1943 story "I Put Away Childish Things," which is notable for its emphasis on dream visions and fantasies. The story revolves around Heebie, a young woman married to a fighter pilot who has returned from the war. The action takes place during a suspended moment while Heebie is descending a staircase at her parents' home. She is about to join the family and her husband, downstairs, for dinner, but in the pause between steps Heebie experiences a reverie of herself in another life. She is a nurse in Burma during the war. She has been travelling with a senior nurse called the Matron and an older man, an orderly, who is involved in the war effort. The Matron tells Heebie that if she follows a path through the dense jungle, she might escape the horrors that await her and find her way to the coast, where she might be rescued. The story returns again and again to Heebie's feverish imaginings, which she attributes to bouts of malaria contracted in the jungle. Fortified by quinine, Heebie makes her way to the coast and discovers a liberating "pale-fawn beach. It was a small beach, perfect in shape, like a woman's well-cared-for fingernail."[43] The simile seems misplaced in this jungle setting, but it is the expression of a protagonist, and of an author, who have lived in privilege. Heebie is capable of experiencing conflicting emotions that reveal her social status: "She felt helpless; but immediately she thought of money" because "perhaps now," in the jungle, "it might save her life."[44]

Although readers praised the story for its verisimilitude, it is in fact not very convincing as literary realism. The idea of a single woman making her way through a dense and threatening Burmese jungle fortified by a few quinine pills is stretching it, but the fantasy becomes complete when, emerging into the sunlight on the manicured beach, Heebie spies a seaplane piloted by a handsome man who soon whisks her away. Romance blooms; her physical and emotional rescue is complete.

The story is much more interesting when read as a figurative expression of Hedges's subtextual concerns. It is a symbolic story about the need to escape from childhood, from one's parents, and the final impossibility of doing so. By making it through the jungle to the open beach, Heebie is figuratively reborn. She is an only child whose parents objected strenuously to her desire to enter the war. She recalls that "there had been almost hysterical outbursts from her mother. There had been coldness from her father. It had been as though she had never really known them before."[45] They had not been able to grasp her desire for independence: "They had not understood her wanting to go into training as a nurse. They had not been able to get it straight." Her mother had said, "You are all we have," and Heebie wonders: "Why did I have to be an only child? Why do parents always say they 'gave' you everything, as though they wanted it back?"[46] Heebie conceives of parenting as a material arrangement, a loan to be repaid.

Hedges draws on her own experiences as a nurse in the First World War, and of her own status as an only child, to create Heebie's character. The title of the story, a biblical allusion,[47] suggests that this will be a coming-of-age story, one in which Heebie puts her childhood behind her and emerges from the shadow of her parents and the restrictions they have tried to impose on her. But the truth is that she is never really permitted to escape her childhood or the barriers of her past. The jungle in the story is metaphorical; it is the terrain she must navigate in order to obtain her freedom as an adult. Again and again we are reminded that this threatening landscape is imagined, not real. As if to confirm this, at one point Heebie recognizes that "all this suddenly seemed unreal. Perhaps it seemed so because of the Matron's habit of calling the greeny-purple mush that was the jungle, 'the woods,' as though she were describing a glade in Devon or Yorkshire, in her native England."[48]

In the real world, Heebie is descending the staircase in the grand home of her parents on the first night home since her marriage to Timothy Court, who has returned from the front and has now become a flight instructor. Tonight, she is wearing a gold dress and "the very beautiful topazes that Timothy Court had given her as a wedding present."[49] Heebie catches a glimpse of her own reflection in the long mirror at the top of the stairs. This is the narcissistic moment that seduces her, the instant that lulls her into a self-centred dream of escape and rescue. She imagines herself in another life that inevitably merges with her actual life. The staircase is the jungle. She is experiencing a "feverish daze."[50] The pilot who rescues her in her dream is another version of the husband who waits for her downstairs.

The privilege that surrounds Heebie also constrains her. Behind the narrative is a simmering resentment at her unalterable status as an only child, as if such children were forced to carry an unnatural burden, the parents to blame for their own curtailed fertility. But only at the end of the story do we discover that Heebie may be entering that same parental world. She herself is pregnant: "The child that was coming to Heebie and Timothy lay warm under her breast."[51] Perhaps because the story was published in *Good Housekeeping,* Heebie is cast as an American who is about to have a child at just the right historical moment: "This was the right time, the perfect time, to bear an American citizen. This was the right way to challenge life, and the future."[52] This sentiment appears to be an expression of Heebie's desire to celebrate life and the family unit at a time of intense national conflict. Yet somehow the final sentiment seems forced. The story closes on a picture of Heebie imagining herself locked in the confines of family. "Heebie stood there smiling, with her parents beside her and her eyes on her husband."[53] Her final gaze is a frozen gaze. Nothing will change. We understand that Heebie's symbolic jungle escape is really a fantasy about escaping her own family constraints. After all, the senior nurse who accompanies her is called the Matron and she speaks with Jerry, the orderly, in parental terms that cast Heebie as a symbolic child:

> Jerry said, "Well, ma'am, you and I, we're not so young as we was; and I for one am for stayin' on 'ere, on the off-chance the plane can get through once more and take us orf later. But the Miss 'ere, she's young, and if I was 'er, I'd take a chance on the blinkin' woods, I would!"[54]

No wonder Heebie thinks about her family as she is descending the stairs: "she was afraid of what she would meet below. There is a bond between parents and children, an emotional bond that nothing, no experience, no separation can break."[55] In other words, family locks you in.

Hedges's conflicted response to the nature of parenting and parents' influence on children necessarily informs her public addresses and explains her determination to become involved in causes like Delinquency Prevention Week. In "The Citizen and His Child," as in the address titled "A Time of

Proving," Hedges struggled to bridge the gap between her privileged position as a well-to-do Montrealer and her sense of the resentment toward that identity shared by the working class. She understood the social issues of the day and wanted to help those less fortunate than herself. The main focus of her benevolent activities seemed to be on youth. But at the same time, she distrusted precisely the group she wanted to help, mainly because she saw delinquency as the result of poor education, which she associated with poverty; yet poverty was a threat to her own social status as a wealthy Montrealer. It was up to people like her to ease the threat, to shine a light, to show a clearer path. And it was particularly writers like her who were charged with that kind of illumination and the growing but uncomfortable realization that literature had to be grounded in "red-blooded" reality or in what Hedges had called "the realism of modern life." The tension between the call to privilege and the recognition of everyday life, devoid of that privilege, remained constant for Hedges.

She delivered several public speeches during the war years. "The Place of Poetry in Modern Education" was presented to the poetry group of the CAA in February 1944. This lecture lauds the value of poetry and decries the world's devaluation of it. Hedges drew inspiration for the talk from Sir Richard Livingstone's *The Future in Education* (1941). Livingstone argued that although different forms of specialized education were becoming available to a wider group of people, the same people lacked the guidance necessary to make informed choices about the most useful forms of education to pursue. It was like being confronted with a restaurant menu that covered several pages instead of one "which used to offer a few old-fashioned dishes."[56] The problem with the new menu is that, faced with an abundance of choice, "there is nothing to guide the customer's selection."[57] As a result, people might order one item over another without fully understanding the ramifications of their decision. People have been seduced not only by materialism but also by their passion for scientific learning, even though "science has betrayed us, not by its own fault, but by our emphasis upon it as the ultimate arbiter."[58] A person who now had the opportunity to obtain different forms of education might choose one that led to material gain or scientific knowledge, but "a man must be more than a mere breadwinner, and must have something besides the knowledge necessary to earn his living."[59] That "something" is "the spiritual side," which has been lost as a result of the war. Hedges argues that the "human side" of learning "must be developed by a wider knowledge of history and literature." She believes that poetry is "a necessary curative to the mental, moral and nervous ills of the scientific age,"[60] yet few people are capable of appreciating poetry because poets "have been considered an esoteric, high-brow influence, rather emasculate and effete, and not part of the realism of modern life." Nevertheless, the poet is destined to lead because he or she has a deeper understanding of truth. Poets are, by definition, "people who are not ordinary."[61] But in order to connect with a modern audience, Hedges says, their work had to be "red-blooded and vital, full of meaning, for everyone."[62] Hedges's final plea is that poets find a way to make their writing more relevant to the common reader: "Poetry must find a place in the life of every human being. Poetry and religion, hand in hand, must be brought out of their dusty and somewhat craven corners, and made to work again as the leaven of the lives of men."[63] Perhaps she was thinking of Shelley's belief that "poets are the unacknowledged legislators of the world,"[64] or of Wordsworth's goal of focusing on "subjects from common life," which are conveyed through "the real language of men."[65]

Hedges's focus on the role of the author was probably a response to many of the contemporary discussions concerning the role of the author during the war, especially those prompted by meetings of the CAA during the war years. (My account of the CAA during those years is indebted to Lyn Harrington's commentary in *Syllables of Recorded Time*.) The 1940 CAA convention was held at Macdonald College in Ste Anne de Bellevue, rather than at a downtown Montreal hotel, in order to save money. Prime Minister Mackenzie King sent an opening message to the convention, in which he stressed that Canadians were engaged in "a defence of the customs, culture and values of our people" and that "anything which the Canadian Authors Association can do to strengthen the regard for the literature and poetry of our nation is a great contribution to our defence and our victory."[66] The message was clear: writers did have a role to play in the war. But it remained for those writers to clarify the nature of that role. An editorial in *Canadian Author and Bookman* noted that it was "a challenge, immediate and urgent for Canadian writers to keep alive spiritual aspirations, dreams of a larger democracy, to assist in battling defeatism, the insidious enemy within our gates, to demonstrate the value of a native literary tradition."[67]

The influence of this editorial on Hedges is suggested by its emphasis on the writer's duty to reinforce "spiritual aspirations" during the war, a point that Hedges makes in many of her talks. The CAA also stressed the role of writers in relation to young people, as was made clear by CAA president Madge Macbeth when she noted that "we have a clear and definite duty to the heroic youth who are giving their all that we might be spared. As I see it, it is our duty to keep telling them and those who stay at home – what they are fighting for."[68] Hedges advanced the same idea in her later essays, focusing on the importance of democracy in the face of the Nazi threat. At the convention, Watson Kirkconnell followed up on Macbeth's message by arguing that "the writers of the Third Reich are among the most dynamic instruments in the hands of the Fuehrer. Against such weapons, the best brains and pens of the free world must be devoted."[69] When he told the assembled writers that "the Front Line runs through our writing-desks" and that "our typewriters are machines of attack in a great cause,"[70] it was a call to arms. And when Kirkconnell emphasized the need for realistic literature that bore witness to the everyday issues of the age, he was also calling for a revolution in the kind of literature that writers produced. Perhaps this is what led Hedges to recommend "red-blooded" literature that would be "the leaven of the lives of men."

At its September 1942 convention, held in Montreal, CAA members heard an influential speech delivered by Carl Carmer, who was president of the Author's League of America. Carmer described the creation of the Writers' War Board in the US, an organization that was designed "to serve as a liaison between the writers of America and the government departments which want writing jobs done that will in any way whatever, directly or indirectly, help with the war."[71] The CAA delegates voted to establish a similar organization in Canada called the Writers' War Committee (WWC). According to Harrington, Kirkconnell

> and five other Canadian authors (Gibbon, Clay, Sandwell, Alan Sullivan and Eric Gaskell) sat in a smoke-filled bedroom of the Mount Royal Hotel, holding a bull session with Carmer. Together they drafted the resolution which was ratified by the membership next morning: that the Canadian Authors Association set up a Writers' War Committee aimed at providing the War Information Board with a Dominion-wide reservoir of Canadian writing talent, the WWC to be autonomous within the Association.[72]

Hedges's involvement with Canada's Wartime Information Board and the US Office of War Information was probably connected to the CAA's efforts to establish the WWC, although I have not been able to determine how she became directly involved with these organizations. Peter Buitenhuis notes that "when the Wartime Information Board (WIB), headed by Charles Vining, was finally established on 9 September 1942, Canadian authors were eager to offer their services."[73] He points out that "the WWC board drew on writers from across the country, not all of them CAA members, while the Société des écrivains canadiens created a separate French section under the wing of the committee."[74] As William R. Young explains, the creation of the Wartime Information Board (originally called the Bureau of Public Information) reflected the Canadian government's attempt to use data provided by the social sciences "as tools in its information policy,"[75] starting in 1939. Ivana Caccia notes that the Wartime Information Board was charged with investigating "how to improve industrial morale; how to engage consumers and producers in reducing waste by saving and recycling; and, last but not least, how to reduce tension in English/French relations for the sake of national unity."[76]

In his study of news management during the Second World War, Timothy Balzer observes that "the major agency creating propaganda for the Canadian public was not one of the military PR teams but, rather, a civilian agency, the WIB, which oversaw efforts to ensure that Canadians remained committed to the war effort."[77] The government's decision to rely on information transmitted by academics and intellectuals shifted the power base in the government bureaucracy. These educated specialists were relied upon to provide the government with data about Canadians' daily lives and they also helped the government to develop its domestic information policies when patriotic interest in the war effort began to wane. This led to charges that the government was manipulating the news at the expense of a free press, which also wanted influence over government policy. As Young observes, the "attack on centralized information activities" was also linked to Quebec politics under Maurice Duplessis, who presented Canada and its information-management activities as yet another means of muzzling Quebec.[78]

Duplessis's defeat in the 1939 Quebec election and Canada's growing involvement in the war prompted Mackenzie King to set up the Bureau of Public Information as a means of collecting and disseminating information that would be useful to the war effort, even though it continued to rile the press, who resented the government's propagandistic control of the war narrative.

As Young notes, King believed that "only by researching the political and social interaction in the country could the Bureau prepare material that would generate the required support for the war effort."[79] It was a question of managing how the war was presented through various news sources, and how the Allies' efforts could be framed to reinforce the government's wartime strategies. King was responding to a suggestion made by W.H. Brittain, the dean of Macdonald College, who argued that one way of generating such support was to enlist the co-operation of "an omnibus organization of educators."[80] He recommended that "the government hire a 'small but expert group of highly qualified specialists in economic, social and industrial questions'" who would "secure and summarize basic information."[81]

Although various forms of obtaining this information were tried, King remained unhappy with the approach to information gathering, especially when his advisers informed him that "the Bureau had failed to make an impact on French Canadian opposition to various wartime measures."[82] When the Bureau of Public Information became the Wartime Information Board in 1942, plans were begun to initiate the collection and analysis of domestic information relevant to government policy. John Grierson became the director in 1943. He believed that the education system had not kept up with the complex issues of the day and that, as a result, people had come to rely too heavily on the media to inform their judgment. Grierson argued that a revamped educational system should do more to encourage individual critical thought. Although he was aware that information provided by the government was always a form of ideology, he also felt that government could educate the people "in a world where the state is the instrument of the public enterprise."[83] Grierson believed that the government could best achieve its objectives "by studying public attitudes and then by preparing programmes that would relate the war effort 'to the larger matter of the reputation of Ottawa and the parliamentary institutions.'"[84]

Grierson's sympathy with left-wing organizations led to suspicions about his motives; he could not gain government approval for his program. As a result, he resigned in January 1944. Davidson Dunton, a newspaper man, replaced Grierson as head of the WIB in January 1944. He had previously served as the director of the reports branch, "the information gathering service of the Board."[85] Under his leadership, the WIB circulated information briefs to civil servants, making them aware of Canadian attitudes to various issues. The Board also distributed a more confidential document, the "WIB Survey," to individuals on a special list. According to Young, it was under Dunton's direction that "the Board's system of correspondents reached its peak ... Correspondents included clergymen, housewives, projectionists on the National Film Board's movie circuits and the writers' war committee of the Canadian Author's Association."[86] The Board also "acquired research facilities to survey the labour, American, foreign-language and daily newspapers, as well as to monitor public opinion."[87] "From these dispatches, the branch regularly prepared a confidential series of 'Field Reports' that topically analyzed the letters as a means of piecing together a picture of general attitudes, including areas of discontent."[88]

Hedges was probably recruited to the WIB during Dunton's tenure as the information branch director, since her reports span the period March to September, 1943. The connection between Hedges, the CAA, and the Wartime Information Board is suggested by the fact that her WIB reports are located in the CAA fonds. Her first report, dated 25 March 1943, indicates that she joined the WIB sometime after the CAA decision to found the Writers' War Committee in September 1942. Her last report, dated 6 September 1943, would have been submitted to the WIB just a few months before she became the director of the Public Actions Committee of the Junior League in January of 1944. Hedges had clearly decided to devote her skills as a writer to the war effort.

The series of eight reports that Hedges provided to the Wartime Information Board present a revealing picture of public responses to the war in 1943. The March 25 report begins by noting a "general feeling amongst professional and white collar people that the taxes do not leave enough cash on hand for emergencies, such as illness or other contingencies (the need to install a new furnace, for example)."[89] Hedges identifies a growing sense of resentment among this professional class towards those in "the higher brackets" because for those wealthier people "cash is easier to come by and taxes easier to pay without sacrifice."[90] She emphasizes that taxation of the professional class forces them to compromise the education of their children, a factor which hinders their ability to preserve the "leadership" roles they had obtained through their diligence and hard work. At the same time, she notes the dissatisfaction among "the lower income people" who fear that their investment in the war, through the purchase of government war bonds and savings, will never be repaid.[91]

Hedges was identifying a growing sense of class-consciousness during the period as well as growing tensions between income groups. But how accurate were her observations? Was she reacting to day-to-day events and inferring broader patterns from those events that had no real factual accuracy, or was she providing the WIB with trustworthy information upon which the government could base its policies? In fact, as Emmanuel Saez has shown, wealth distribution was generally stable in the period following the Second World War, and income and wealth inequality remained at record low levels in the decades following the war until the late 1970s, when it began to rise dramatically.[92] In other words, there was no real evidence that income disparities were increasing when Hedges wrote her report. What then would have prompted her to focus so intently on the relationship between income levels, education, and the stability of the state? The answer may well lie in a government document that was released just ten days before Hedges's report was submitted to the WIB. That document was *The Report on Social Security for Canada*, which was submitted to Parliament on 15 March 1943. The report, written by Leonard Marsh at the request of Mackenzie King, was similar in intent to the *Beveridge Report*, which had been prepared for the British Parliament in 1942. Both documents discussed the nature of the postwar welfare state and the need for social assistance programs to offset the negative impact of the war on personal savings and earnings.

Historian Michael Bliss has called the Marsh Report "the most important single document in the history of the development of the welfare state in Canada."[93] Antonia Maioni describes its impact:

> Drafted in less than one month in January 1943, this extraordinary document mapped out a dense and detailed plan for comprehensive social programs, constructed around the ideal of a social minimum and the eradication of poverty. The realization of this ideal, according to Marsh, meant the recognition that individual risks were part of modern industrial society, and that they could be met by collective benefits throughout the lifecycle. Full employment at a living wage would be the engine for this vision, supplemented by occupational readjustment programs. "Employment risks" were to be met through income-maintenance programs, such as unemployment insurance and assistance, accident and disability benefits, plus paid maternity

> leave (a proposal definitely ahead of its time). "Universal risks" were addressed through national health insurance, children's allowances, and pensions for old age, permanent disability, and widows and orphans.[94]

It would have been impossible for Hedges to bypass Marsh's report, given her involvement with the WIB. However, Marsh was promoting what was essentially a socialist vision, one that challenged her own sense of class division and privilege (Hedges's address on all the reports is "Ritz-Carlton Hotel"). At the same time, the introduction of welfare ideology during the 1940s had a profound effect on the socialization and interpretation of female identity. As Magda Fahrni observes, these new ideas about the nature of "political, social, and economic citizenships" were ultimately "gendered" because they were "frequently framed in the language of familial roles and responsibilities."[95] This meant that "women's social citizenship often depended on their roles as wives and mothers."[96] It also meant that "women claimed this right of citizenship as wives, as mothers, and as consumers, using what Susan Porter Benson has called the 'trope of the good manager.'"[97] Hedges's attention to rising food costs, to rationing, and to the treatment of young people who had lost fathers to the war, demonstrates her attention to this trope. Although she was childless, her efforts were still directed toward performing motherhood, performing household management, performing citizenship. In some ways, it seems as though this performance often displaced her personal life, of which we know relatively little.

What seems to have energized Hedges, in her creative writing as well as in her WIB contributions, is her engagement with the tension between opposing social models. But there is also in Hedges's reports a mounting sense of outrage over what she sees in the streets. Too many people are drinking. She reports

> a very real fear of a return to bootlegging, crime, and secret drinking, especially amongst young people and those in the Services. A general anger against beer restrictions (as being the "working man's" drink) and fear that lack of beer will force young people to drink hard liquor. A general condemnation of drinking in the streets, and of drunkenness in the streets, among troops.[98]

Many people had no accommodation. Wartime manufacturing had brought thousands to the city, but there was no housing for them. To make matters worse, prices had risen dramatically during the war, and in 1942 ration books had been introduced in order to regulate the sale of coffee, tea, sugar, butter, and meat. Hedges comments on the price of gas ("resentment and suspicion of so many cars on the streets at pleasure hours") and food rationing ("anger and bad feelings about black markets and a suspicion that not enough steps are being taken to prevent them").[99] In these short reports, she paints a picture of the human response to war-related issues that few newspaper stories were able to capture.

In her second report, dated 10 April 1943, Hedges again reveals her growing sense of frustration with labour movements. Montreal had been gripped by a transit strike called by the Canadian Brotherhood of Railways employees. Hedges drew attention to what she believed was "the wickedness of strikes in wartime, as a general principle" and called upon the government to "make people understand that strikes cause deaths on the fighting fronts."[100] Although the connection between local strikes and the fate of those on the fronts remained unclear, Hedges's main objection seemed to be that her opinion was not shared by most others, since only "the 2% of the intelligent folk" could really grasp the fact that "both labour and management in Canada are the dupes of outside powers."[101] In other words, Hedges believed that 98 per cent of the population could not really understand the threats posed by the labour unions.

Hedges covered such a variety of topics in her reports that it is difficult to understand what use she expected the government to make of her observations as they were transmitted to the Wartime Information Board, particularly because they seemed to be entirely subjective. She emphasized the importance of radio broadcasting, but noted a general "dislike of the preachy type of woman's voice in radio and general announcing" and "a growing tendency to turn off the newscasts, because of the 'dead' and inexperienced voices giving it out."[102] She complained about Americans entering Canada to buy groceries, defying rationing laws in their own country. Hedges thought of them only as "people who come across the border and buy our meat, or other supplies, and take them back."[103]

In her 12 May report, she objected to wartime fundraising efforts that were being promoted by Hollywood stars. Her sense of resentment towards

Americans seemed to inflect all of her observations. "Among educated people," she claimed, there was "a fear that we will resort to the American news analysis and commentary instead of straight news,"[104] suggesting somehow that Canadian news sources were untainted by the kind of propaganda that she saw characterizing the American broadcasts, a strange position to adopt in a report designed to assist the Canadian government in strategically refining its own propaganda efforts. Hedges recorded other complaints: resentment about job security, "resentment about the way the blackouts are being mismanaged," "a sense of shame about the potato black market, and the gasoline black markets, and the tyre black market," not to mention "no esprit de corps" and "general horror at the drunkenness in the streets."[105] All of this discontent was mixed with the observation that there had been much discussion "among all types of people" about "the Communist activities in Canada" and "a very general feeling that the Government is keeping the public in the dark about 'what is going on' in a subversive way, in Canada."[106]

On 28 May 1943, Hedges focused her report on the Bermuda Conference, which had been held from 19 to 30 April at Hamilton Beach. The aim of the conference was to discuss the fate of Jewish refugees who had been liberated and of those who still remained in European countries occupied by the Nazis. Although there was "fear of influx of Jews into Canada," according to Hedges, there was also a general recognition ("among a large number of educated people") that "we have no right to refuse to take refugees."[107] Here she was attempting to reconcile her sense of moral obligation with her recognition of the widespread anti-Semitism that continued to impact public sentiment; the country's immigration policies at the beginning of the war were often anti-Semitic.[108] But Hedges emphasized that refugees should not be admitted strictly on the basis of wealth. Rather, "the first tenet of his residence here should be gratitude and thankfulness." However, it was difficult for the public to focus on the issues because "we are 'punch-drunk' on horror and war" and, as a result, "newer and more forcible methods must be used, in the future, to put over any important news or announcement or call to action." Apathy was growing, she noted, even among "the thinking people."[109]

By 13 June 1943, Hedges seems to have reached a peak of dissatisfaction. Her report consists of nine subjects, with complaints ostensibly representing public attitudes attached to each. Radio: "Boredom with current Canadian entertainment on radio"; Housing: "it is a disgrace to us, this housing situation here"; Liquor: "If you hand over a dollar extra at any of the Liquor Commissions, you can get all the stuff you want"; Food: "I wish we knew how to manage things better in Canada"; Money: "in matter of distribution, are we lousy!"; Soldiers: "a feeling that we're an expense to the people, and an incumbrance [*sic*]"; Women: "They make no sacrifices. Why should we spend money in war services for them?"; Youth at headquarters: "The waste that goes on in my department burns me up"; Often heard: "I wish to God someone would drop a few bombs on the Province of Quebec. It's the only thing that would wake people up to where we're heading."[110]

Two weeks later, on 30 June, Hedges noted that there was a "general slackening of every effort because of over-confidence" and the sense that "the war is already won."[111] Hedges cautioned that "we can still lose the war if we slack" and advised the press to make every effort to wake up the general population to this reality. Meanwhile, people were complaining about high food prices (Hedges notes that many people "telephone and speak to me about finding out why these prices are so high" because "I have done radio broadcasts on hoarding and so on").[112]

Mixed with Hedges's comments about "too-high vegetable prices" and how "the weather here has damped enthusiasm about Victory Gardens"[113] is her response to the visit of Madame Chiang kai-shek, who addressed crowds in Montreal from her balcony at the Windsor Hotel on 17 June 1943. Mayling Soong, or "Madame Chiang" as she was popularly called, was an international celebrity whose American education and experiences with the reform of child labour laws in China had given her international prominence. Her marriage to Chiang kai-shek in 1927 only added to her stature, especially in her handling of various Chinese government portfolios. When Chiang was captured and imprisoned by anti-Japanese forces in early December 1936, Mayling Soong was reported to have secured his release by Christmas. Because she was a practising Christian, Americans saw in her interventions an affirmation of Christian faith in China (she was instrumental in Chiang kai-shek's conversion to Christianity in 1929). But she was best known for her humanitarian efforts to establish orphanages for children who had lost their parents. In 1938, Chiang kai-shek and Mayling Soong were named *Time* magazine's "Man and Wife of the Year."

Because Mayling Soong and her husband embraced Christian principles during a period of rising Japanese aggression, they were often seen by Americans as a means through which the Japanese could be resisted in China, especially after the start of the Second World War. Mayling Soong toured North

America in 1943 in order to enlist support for China's war with the Japanese. She was received with massive enthusiasm and treated as one of the world's leading humanitarians. Her presence on this North American tour raised a host of questions about how China was understood in the United States. In some ways, Mayling Soong was a figure who represented the perfect assimilation of a Chinese person to the American way of life, since she was a Christian who had received her education in the US and who had tried to introduce progressive policies into a country widely viewed as backward by Americans. As Karen Janis Leong notes, she was also seen "as a woman who fitted squarely within domestic ideas about gender roles" and so "could be viewed as the foreign equivalent of an American woman."[114] Her appearance in the United States also prompted debate about the treatment of Asians during the war and encouraged discussions about the nature of orientalism and otherness.

Soong visited Ottawa and addressed the Canadian Parliament in June. On 17 June she made a brief stopover in Montreal, en route to New York. Hedges's response to her brief visit begins with a complaint about the lack of a loudspeaker system that would have enabled more of the crowd to hear Mayling Soong's speech. Hedges notes "a feeling among the thinking people in the crowd that a good opportunity was missed."[115] But despite this failing, Hedges believed that Mayling Soong's charm "went over even at that distance, and in the silence."[116] Her words raised the issue of immigration, and the question of "whether or not we ought to open our immigration doors to Chinese settlers after the war."[117] For Hedges, the debate among the population concerning immigration fluctuated among apathy, racism, and anti-Semitism: "When Jews are mentioned, general repudiation of allowing them to come into Canada on the basis of fear for our pockets! It is difficult to get any Canadian to take a real interest in immigration problems. It seems to be a dead issue, having lain dormant for so long. Some propaganda and education would be a good idea," Hedges asserts, "as this is a basic postwar problem for Canadians."[118] Notable here is Hedges's casualness regarding the general attitude toward the Jews, and also her sense that, even in 1943, the war would soon be over, a feeling that was widespread.

The brief vignettes that Hedges provides of the political issues of the day illustrate the tensions of living in Montreal during this period. She talks about "the Lacombe allegation" and notes "a cynical acceptance of its probable truth, by every class of people."[119] Liguori Lacombe was a former federal Liberal MP representing the Laval-Two Mountains riding in Quebec. In September 1939 he had voted against the Liberal Party's support for entering the war and had introduced an amendment calling for Canada's non-participation. Lacombe had already earned the resentment of many federal MPs for his stance on the conscription debate. He had voted against the issuing of war credits and was a staunch defender of Québécois nationalist rights. Like most French Canadians, he did not support compulsory enlistment. In June 1940, soon after the evacuation at Dunkirk, Mackenzie King introduced legislation calling for conscription for the defence of Canada alone. However, many Canadians favoured full involvement in the war, which led to a dual-class military system: those soldiers who had volunteered to fight overseas were the A-level soldiers; then there were the "zombies" – soldiers who were caught in a strange limbo, part of an army for which they would not fight. In 1942, as the war advanced and fears of a Japanese annexation of British Columbia started to be voiced in the media, King held a referendum to reverse this Canada-only policy. Although a majority of Canadians voted Yes, the plebiscite was defeated in Quebec. Following the plebiscite, King's government passed Bill 80, authorizing overseas conscription if necessary. In response, several Quebec Liberal MPs quit the party in protest and joined the nationalist Bloc populaire canadien in Quebec.

Lacombe had been active in the movement against conscription since 1939. In the 1940 election he ran as an independent and was re-elected. In 1942 he formed the Parti canadien to protest the federal government's conscription legislation. He did not earn any friends in the federal parliament a year later when he asserted that three MPs in King's government had profited from the war. This is the "Lacombe allegation" that Hedges is referring to. Lacombe made his charge in French, but when it was translated into English, public confusion arose as to whether Lacombe was accusing particular Liberal MPs of profiting from the war, or whether he was saying that three members of King's cabinet had profited. Either way, there were calls for Lacombe to either prove his allegations or to resign. Instead of providing proof, Lacombe turned the incident into a language issue, arguing that he had been misunderstood because of a poor English translation of his words.

Hedges's comment suggests a general acceptance of Lacombe's assertion that federal MPs were indeed profiting from the war. But her interest in the Lacombe controversy probably had more to do with what he represented in terms of Quebec politics than it did with federal policy. Lacombe's anti-federalist stance, his alignment with nationalist forces in Quebec, and his arguments about his representation in an English translation all pointed to the increasing influence of separatist forces in Quebec, and of course such nationalism could never be divorced from questions related to language. In other words, while Lacombe may have been right about war profiteering, he also represented a threat attached to the idea that Quebec could go its own way, in defiance of the federal government.

This had always been the subtext of the anti-conscription movement, but Lacombe's comments about language, coming as they did one day after the St Jean Baptiste holiday in Quebec, prompted Hedges to reflect upon the nature of French–English tensions in the city. She includes a section of her 30 June report on the holiday, a commentary that reveals the stark lines separating English and French Canadians living in Montreal. For the first time, Hedges refers to "my Paris French, which they mistrust." On the day of the holiday parade, Hedges "went into the crowd to listen" and found that "the sentiment was quite antagonistic and unfriendly to the English-speaking element, and this came out because I moved about in the English part of the town, where the French people were obviously strangers, many of them looking about for the Ritz and the Art Gallery, never having seen either of these buildings."[120] Those institutions were very familiar to Hedges, since she resided in Montreal's Golden Square Mile, a tony downtown area encompassing both the gallery and the hotel. As Hedges's Wartime Information Board documents make clear, she was actually living at the Ritz-Carlton when she wrote the reports. What was home for her was entirely foreign to many of the city's francophone inhabitants, a difficult bifurcation to grasp from the perspective of anyone living in the city today. For Hedges, iconic buildings like the Ritz-Carlton or the Musée des beaux-arts were epicentres of desire, structures to be sought after by those who lacked the privilege and power to know and enter them. The masses "looked about" for these buildings in vain, as if they were made to be invisible to the French-speaking population in 1943 – *les autres* – others who came from what might as well have been foreign lands, the neighbourhoods east of Boulevard St Laurent.

Through Hedges's eyes, we begin to see the concrete manifestations of the modern forms of separatism that would emerge in Quebec in the 1950s and 1960s. As Magda Fahrni notes, "the Quiet Revolution was a much longer 'evolution' that began well before 1960."[121] Lionel Groulx's "Quebec first" ideology was at the heart of the nationalist journal *Action Française*, which Groulx edited between 1920 and 1928. The same period saw the founding of the secret and anti-Semitic Ordre de Jacques-Cartier, also known as "La Patente" (founded in 1926). Separatist ideology could also be found in Esdras Minville's publication of the pro-Catholic and nationalist *Invitation à l'étude* (1943); in the Refus Global manifesto (1948); in the right-wing politics of Alliance Laurentienne (founded in 1957); in the radical left-wing Rassemblement pour l'indépendance national, or RIN (founded in 1960); and in the militant Marxist-Leninist Front de libération du Québec, or FLQ (founded in 1963). The threat of separatism would remain ever-present for Hedges. She would live long enough to witness the formation of the Parti Québécois in 1968, four years before her death.

Hedges's account demonstrates that the resentment fuelling separatist sentiments in Montreal was perfectly apparent much earlier, catalyzed as it was by the conscription issues surrounding both wars, and mobilized further by the growing division between wealthy anglophones and working-class francophones. As Weintraub says, while everyone was being asked to "pull together" for the social good, the fact remained that "there was little blurring of Montreal's well-defined social barriers. In their sincere efforts to help win the war, the French and the English were not being brought any closer together and neither were the blue-blooded rich and the not-so-rich."[122] Hedges was concerned with this rift. In one of her reports, she complains that there is "anger among the English-speaking listeners, that so many French accents are used on the English networks."[123] Was this truly the anger of radio listeners (how would Hedges know?), or was it an expression of Hedges's own resentment at feeling excluded from a more active role as a female broadcaster because she did not possess the requisite French Canadian accent?

Hedges understood that by entering the world of broadcasting during the war, however sporadically, she had also begun to participate in a new means of reinforcing cultural hierarchies. The way her listeners perceived her had a great deal to do with her own sense of social standing. As Leonard Kuffert explains, the revitalization of the postwar world depended on the media. In this regard, Kuffert points to the influence of J.S. Thomson, the president of the University of Saskatchewan from 1937 to 1949 (with a leave in 1942–43 to become the general manager of CBC), who argued that "plans to recivilize the postwar world" depended on promoting a "new spirit" that was "first the possession of a few, almost a secret doctrine, but it spreads abroad and like leaven hidden in the meal, it works until the whole lump is charged with a new life."[124] Kuffert goes on to observe that for Thomson,

> using the relatively new technology of radio as a means to spur a "moral and intellectual revolution" would challenge "a culture that is very widely spread by modern technology, by the movies, by the radio, by cheap books, by music, dancing," on its own ground. Critics were not after a revolution but, rather, a shoring up of conventional cultural hierarchies. Thomson described the promise of radio outreach rather dramatically, declaring that "the whole question of artistic standards in music, in dancing, in literature, in pictures, in radio programmes, and in the religious life of the Churches is related to this venture we have in mind."[125]

Hedges was participating in a "secret doctrine" that would not only contribute to reconstruction but also reinforce her own sense of social status. Radio became a refuge from the world she witnessed on a daily basis in Montreal. The tensions noted by Hedges in her WIB reports are related not only to language but also to religion: Montreal encapsulated a Protestant/Catholic divide that aligned wealthy anglophones with money and prestige, set against working-class francophones who lacked the advantages experienced by the well-heeled inhabitants of the Golden Square Mile. Inevitably, the threat to anglophones posed by the separatist movement linked socialism with the labour movement. In other words, it was associated with Difference. As the wife of a wealthy businessman and a member of the Dawes-Hedges families, Hedges would have perceived this threat as a direct challenge to her own standing as a well-to-do Montreal anglophone whose family had deep roots in the province. In her report, she writes that "it is our job to get this great problem adjusted as soon as possible, and get on with the growth of Canada as a nation. Until it is put on a reasonable basis, we shall be a laughing-stock in the world."[126] Hedges did not say how this problem might be "adjusted," but she was determined to ensure that British people settling in Canada felt welcomed and secure.

Hedges's attitudes and her own position as a writer and infrequent broadcaster prompt one to wonder about the values shared by those who provided reports to the Wartime Information Board. To what extent were those reporters capable of conveying the sentiments of a broad-based representation of the public? How did their own values and ambitions colour their commentary? What were their specific qualifications for the job? What use did the government make of their findings and how did those findings affect national policies? In the case of Hedges's reports, what becomes clear is that her biases were capitalist, upper-class, anglophone, and Protestant. They reveal her to be a person who was fixated on class distinctions and who identified herself with an elite group she felt had the intelligence necessary to produce effective social and political commentary. At some point, one gets the sense that her reports were a form of personal complaint about her own frustrations and resentments concerning wartime conditions.

These complaints colour her one-page-long WIB report for 4 August 1943, which is peppered with words such as "suspicion," "apathy," "anger," and "resentment." She says the public does not trust the war news and notes "a very general feeling among all types and classes that the public is told nothing, except what is thought to be good for it," because "the Government does not trust the public reactions to the truth."[127] Although Hedges notes (twice) that this kind of suspicion is "very general," she can't seem to include herself in this description – even if it involves "all types and classes" – because the class she belongs to somehow transcends "all types." While doubts about the media sow "apathy" among the public, "real interest is found only in the thinking people," and "those are few."[128] The same can be said about the situation in occupied Italy, which the "unthinking" people and "the uneducated people" regard as a form of "amusement": they believed that Mussolini could be defeated easily, and that for the Allies, "taking Italy is a picnic" (the Allies had started bombing Sicily and Sardinia in May 1943 in preparation for a possible invasion, and by July the Allies had captured Palermo and started bombing Rome).

Hedges notes that "an antiwar attitude is growing daily" among French Canadians, and "open declarations [are] made that the war is none of our affair." Faced with this opposition, Canadian soldiers demonstrate "a patient sort of acceptance of abuse in the villages and towns, by French-Canada citizens." At this point, as if the connection between this "abuse" of Canadian soldiers and her own work were self-evident, Hedges adds that "I work in the War Services Information Bureau."[129] In other words, she saw herself as a metaphoric English Canadian soldier whose exclusion from French Quebec was part of the "abuse" suffered by the conscripted men when they were posted outside the city. The United States Office of War Information was created by Franklin D. Roosevelt in June 1942 to unify government information services and to disseminate propaganda in the US and overseas through various media outlets. Its purpose was similar to the Canadian Wartime Information Board. (I have been unable to locate any reports or documents prepared by Hedges for the Office of War Information.) Hedges's alignment with the Wartime Information Board in Canada and the Office of War Information in the US was a means of affirming her social position, since individuals involved with both units were, by definition, members of an elite who were contributing to a new paradigm of social engineering that depended upon the collection and dissemination of information by those who were deemed capable of manipulating it. In this sense, those who worked for the WIB were differentiated from the general public.

As Ivana Caccia notes, ideas about using "social technology as a modern means to conduct politics" were introduced in the early war years by writers such as Brooke Claxton, a Montreal MP who argued that governing needed to become "more and more a job of engineering."[130] Faced with the influences of Britain, Europe, and North America, he said, Canadians needed to be united in order to overcome "ignorance, apathy and difference – racial, political or economic"[131] and "for that purpose, the government should use propaganda to raise the country's morale and keep the public aware that all were part of a big national project."[132] Hedges was obviously a proponent of this model. Again and again in her journalism and broadcasting we see her equating "apathy" with a threat to democracy. She understood herself to be serving an educational role that allowed her to distinguish herself from the masses. As Caccia says,

> The rather vague concept of "the public" stood as a comprehensive reference to the class of people employed in different social activities such as workers, farmers, soldiers, sailors, office workers, tradesmen – and women, too (usually mentioned as a separate social group). It was sometimes replaced by a far less neutral term of "the masses" because of its added connotation of unruliness, street manifestations, and large numbers of labouring people demanding something or other or being manipulated by self-designated leaders. In short, "the public" was, for those in positions of political power, everybody except the governing "elite." The elite possessed the necessary tools to govern, legislate, educate, and acquire knowledge in order to govern, legislate, educate, and acquire even more knowledge more effectively.

> Among the elite were men and women who by birth, class, or education considered themselves fully prepared to express publicly their ideas and act upon them for the benefit of the country. The potential seemed great in the late 1930s and early 1940s to influence Canada's progress on its road to modernity. There was, as [Doug] Owram describes, a "community of intellectuals who were not only active in observing and assessing the changing nature of the state in Canada but were also the proponents of, and participants in, that change."[133]

Hedges's final report for the Wartime Information Board is dated 6 September 1943. She is still talking about public "resentment" directed at the government (the word appears three times in the one-page report), about issues like the absence of statistics concerning French Canadian enlistments (they are "unaware that they are not doing their fair share"), financial allowances in the air force ("the boys do not get enough to live on in a city like Montreal"), and the availability of liquor ("the looseness in rationing liquor at the Liquor Commissions has made many people very angry").[134] Despite these complaints, there is a sense that Hedges is losing interest in the reports. It appears that her involvement with the WIB terminated at this point. Looking back on the eight reports she completed between March and September of 1943, it seems that Hedges saw her documents as a means of expressing her own sense of frustration and alienation as the war presented a series of domestic and international incidents that challenged the security of her privileged status. After all, the reports lacked the kind of detail and factual evidence that would support many of her subjective impressions, and it is hard to imagine how the government might have made use of her opinions. Yet Hedges's involvement with the WIB did serve one important purpose: it reinforced her own sense of elitism, her own belief that she was a member of an educated class who understood contemporary issues far better than the working-class people she believed she was observing, if only occasionally and from a distance. The divide between rich and poor, English and French, was evident not only in the streets. Contemporary writers were focusing on the topic in eminently successful novels such as Gwethalyn Graham's *Earth and High Heaven* (1944), Hugh MacLennan's *Two Solitudes* (1945), and Gabrielle Roy's *The Tin Flute* (1945). As a Montreal writer, it would have been impossible for Hedges to ignore the social tensions depicted in these works, which were critical of the values associated with her Westmount and Golden Square Mile milieux.

The relationship between the Haves and the Have-Nots is a theme that Hedges returned to often. She discussed it in her 1943 article "A Time of Proving," and it was the focus of the central conflict in her early story "Sleds" (1938), which was, after all, a Depression-era story centred on class conflict and the disadvantages of poverty. As James Doyle notes, Canadian short story writers during this period often published realistic fiction "in their tendency to use the social crisis as a backdrop for exploring a variety of psychological and moral issues."[135] Hedges's use of realism was extraordinary, given her Quebec roots. As Doyle writes, "in Quebec, especially, writers of fiction tended to ignore the Depression."[136] Doyle quotes Emile Talbot's observation that "of the roughly 100 novels published in Quebec from 1930 through 1939 only two deal with the Depression in a substantive way and only three or four mention it. Writers interested in the theme of the struggle for economic survival, furthermore, tended to focus on rural Quebec rather than on the urban society that is the usual setting of Marxist or other socialist fiction."[137] This was because "they saw the basic conflict to be not between capitalism and some socialist alternative but between materialism and religion."[138]

In June 1945, Hedges published a short story in the *Milwaukee Journal* that again explored the relationship between social classes (how Hedges ended up in a journal originating in Milwaukee is a mystery I have been unable to solve). The story, "The Murdered Rose," opens on a scene of two soldiers – Sil and Larry – who are recovering from their war injuries in an unnamed town. Their convalescence is tied to some new hobbies: Sil carves a picture frame "with his girl's initials"[139] while Larry digs in the garden. A nurse's aide asks if they'd like to see *Going My Way*, the film showing at the local theatre. (Neither of the men is apparently interested in seeing a film about singing priests.) Then the focus shifts. The aide hands Larry a letter he has received from someone he has never met – a woman named Verity Warde. She has written to Larry because she wants to leave him her modest property and a small income. Verity is eighty years old. Larry decides to visit her in order to find out whether the offer is a hoax. Why would Verity choose to leave her estate to a man she had never met? How did she even discover Larry's name?

These questions are never answered, a fact that strains the credibility of the story, if we see it in realistic terms. But perhaps this story is more of a fantasy, and the relationships in it more symbolic than mimetic. Verity has little in the way of real family left. She is being visited by her niece and grandnephew who, we learn, have designs on her estate. Verity is unaware of their intentions until she learns that the grandnephew has stubbed out his cigarette in the heart of a rose in Verity's garden, a rose that symbolizes a long-gone but powerful love affair associated with her youth. In a rage, she heads indoors to confront him about the dead rose, only to overhear him talking on the phone about his plans to swindle her. Verity is determined not to leave her niece or grandnephew a thing. The story closes with Larry's arrival. His sympathy for Verity and his shock at the violated rose guarantee that he will come into his surprise inheritance, and there the story comes to a close. What this story shares with Hedges's other short stories – aside from its focus on people of different social classes interacting – is its concern with the deficiencies and tensions of family life. Perhaps it also imagines a relief from these tensions through new relationships that can be magically established through the power of narrative, or through random encounters that end up verifying the idea that meaningful relationships can still be found by Hedges's characters, despite all the barriers they face.

"The Murdered Rose" is such an improbable story that I wondered whether there might be other factors accounting for its conception. Here I can only speculate, but it may be that an essay she published in the *Montrealer* in the same month as "The Murdered Rose" provides some insight into Hedges's interest in using a symbolic flower as a central motif in her story. The *Montrealer* piece begins with what Hedges calls "a true story."[140] In it, a young woman enters a flower shop during the war. The smell of the flowers makes her cry, and her tears fall on the flowers around her (much as Verity Warde's tears fall on the rose that symbolizes her youthful love). Although she had that very day received flowers sent by her husband, he had in fact been killed in the war two months ago. They had had an argument "about a family matter," and when he sent the flowers her husband attached a note saying, "all my trust and love,"[141] his way of indicating that he wanted to resolve their differences. But now it was too late. It had taken two months for the flowers bearing that message to arrive. The saleswoman in the florist's shop is saddened by the story, and after her customer leaves she, too, sheds tears. But she realizes that "flowers were fighting this war, and she was proud to be a part of it."[142] At this point Hedges enters the narrative, which becomes an account of the laborious process of sending flowers to loved ones during the war. She says, "It is a war story, but why should it not be used to remind us that there are times in all our lives when we need the tangibly beautiful to tide us over?"[143] Flowers become a symbol of courage, of sustenance, of resistance, and of love. If Hedges had simply stopped with that symbolic representation, "Flowers Have Fought" would fall flat. But what redeems it is the remarkable account that Hedges provides of florists' efforts to deliver flowers during the war.

She points to "the magnitude of the job done by flowers in this war, the almost mystical communion they evoke."[144] And she reflects on "the millions of lonely rooms, brightened by the one living bit of beauty, sent on the wings of the heart to loved ones."[145] However, to "say it with flowers" was no simple feat. When the war began, there were "six points of delay" involved in sending flowers from the front to Canada: (1) The soldier ordered his flowers via a cable that was sent from the cable company to a government censor; (2) the censor examined the cable request to ensure its compliance with regulations; (3) the request was sent back to the cable company; (4) the cable company sent it on to a central point in Dundee in the UK; (5) the cabled orders were sent to a florist in Canada from Dundee; (6) the flowers were delivered, at very little profit to the local florist. Hedges learned that "the whole arrangement was unsatisfactory and unwieldy":

> The delays were irritating and destructive to sentiment, and during the many processes, mistakes were bound to occur by the thousand. The business of tracking down the persons to whom the flowers were supposed to be sent was a colossal one for the Canadian florists. There were mistakes in the address, mistakes in names, people had moved, initials were mixed. It was all too complicated.[146]

As a result, the Floral Telegraph Delivery Association collaborated with various charitable organizations to design a new way of sending flowers from the battlefronts to Canada. Soldiers marked their orders on a printed form that was given to their canteen manager, who sent the form on by airmail to The Florists Association in Canada, which allocated the distribution of the orders to local florists. Hedges notes that for Christmas, Easter, and Mother's Day, a total of 126,000 orders had been placed in the last year alone. Much of her information on the sending "flowers by wire" was gained by interviewing Montreal florist Leo McKenna in his office behind his store. She concludes the piece by reflecting on the idea that

> flowers are strangely intimate. Walk along a road in spring, and you suddenly remember times and people not thought of for years. The clover in a nearby field had brought them back. Passing a florist's window, a blaze of colour meets your eye, and reminds you of the time you graduated from college, and your friends sent you flowers, or of the time you were so ill, and your room was kept bright with the symbols of interest and love.[147]

The proximity of Hedges's story "The Murdered Rose" to this account of flowers is remarkable. It suggests that the story is a narrative exploration of some of the observations that Hedges made in her article on the florist industry during the war, published in the same month. For Verity Warde, as for Hedges in her article, flowers represent a powerful means of evoking the past and personal memories. In some ways, flowers keep personal experiences alive; they make them present. Perhaps this is why Hedges named her flower-loving eighty-year-old character in "The Murdered Rose" Verity Warde, since her name suggests that in her love of a particular rose she is a keeper of truth, a warden of verity.

Toward the end of the war, Hedges became involved with the Royal Empire Society as the chairwoman of its Veteran-Civilian Committee. During a meeting on 17 February 1945, Reverend Doctor F.W. Norwood addressed the society, discussing among other topics why more French Canadians should be encouraged to participate in the Society. At this meeting Hedges suggested the formation of a junior council that would discuss the subject of "what the value of the British Empire meant to us all."[148] An article in *The Maple Leaf* took note of Hedges's leadership of the Society's Veteran-Civilian Discussion Group, describing the attendees: "the veterans are French and English-speaking men and women of all ranks, and include prisoners-of-war and heroes of the Battle of Britain."[149] This group was a forum for guest speakers, veterans, and rehabilitation workers to discuss their experiences. Hedges received praise for this initiative from the Royal Empire Society headquarters in England, which expressed the hope her program might be extended across the Commonwealth. Hedges became the chairperson of the Education Committee of the Montreal branch of the Royal Empire Society. It was her job to announce the winners of an annual essay-writing prize given to students who had written effectively about the benefits of empire. In a short *Gazette* opinion piece on 9 March 1946, she argued that these contests were held "to

Figure 2.2
Doris Hedges, 1945

stimulate thought on the part of young people and to awaken a more dynamic conception of the British Empire and Commonwealth in the minds of its sons and daughters."[150]

Hedges was concerned about the fate of soldiers returning from the front as the war drew to a close. The *Gazette* reported on an address she gave to the Professional and Business Women's Club of Montreal on the subject of returned veterans. Hedges argued that returning soldiers were "uneasy and dissatisfied with conditions in Canada – the land for which they had been fighting" and that their condition had been worsened by what Hedges said were "psychiatrists and other specialists who have 'converted the whole thing into something really terrifying.'"[151]

Hedges was also involved in helping British brides settling in Canada to integrate into Canadian life. The Acorn Club had founded a British Wives Committee, to be known as the Oak Society, under the auspices of the War Service Coordinating Council. On 5 July 1945, Hedges led a discussion series for British wives on the topic "What do you hope from your new life in Canada?" In November, she gave a radio address titled "Our British Brides" on the same topic.[152] Her involvement with the settlement of war brides was a response to the influx of women who were arriving daily on designated trains (the "Diaper Special") from Halifax. There was a real need for assistance: between 1942 and 1948, some 43,000 war brides and their 21,000 children arrived at Pier 21 in Halifax, where they boarded trains destined for various locations throughout the country.[153] This was called "Operation Daddy." The women were presented with copies of the *Canadian Cook Book for British Brides* (1945), designed by the Women's Voluntary Services Division (WVS), which had been established by Margaret Konantz in Winnipeg in 1938. It introduced the new brides to Canadian food and customs ("treacle is molasses, scrag end of lamb is neck of lamb," and "raiding the ice-box" is "a national sport").[154] The gift seemed innocent enough. But even in this case, French nationalist politics intervened. As Fahrni notes,

> The Association catholique de la jeunesse canadienne-française (ACJC) argued that English women were morally unworthy of young French Canadian men, despite their often superior education. The ACJC warned that French Canadian families would not necessarily extend a warm welcome to these brides, and it wondered aloud whether the children of these unions would be "French" or "English."[155]

It seems that no matter where Hedges turned, even in her benevolent activities, she was always reminded of the gulf that separated the anglophone and francophone communities in Montreal. Given her lifetime involvement with the Canadian Red Cross, Hedges may have been inspired by the efforts of the WVS: in collaboration with the Red Cross, the WVS collected garments, bedding, and food to be distributed to families who had been evacuated or who had lost their homes. Hedges may also have been involved in the efforts of the Canadian Wives Bureau, which was established in 1944 by the Department of National Defence and the Canadian Red Cross to assist foreign wives in relocating to Canada.

Germany surrendered on 7 May 1945. The *Gazette* announced the Allied victory in a massive headline the following day. The paper reported that on news of the surrender, "the city's million poured from offices, stores, factories and homes to unite in the streets in a riotous celebration that had its focal point at Peel and St. Catherine streets and its tentacles stretching out to the 16 suburban municipalities that surround the city proper."[156] But the city's inhabitants had been celebrating in numerous ways in the months leading up to V-E Day. The pages following the headline provide snapshots of what Montrealers were attracted to at the end of the war. The paper provided listings for ten theatres showing English films, two theatre productions, and six cabarets, not to mention the Hamid-Morton trained wild animal shows at the Forum.

Although Hitler's death had been reported on 1 May, the Soviet Union, in order to destabilize the Allied forces, openly claimed that he had not died. The UK's MI5 Security Service notes that even in June 1945, "the Soviets announced – falsely – that Hitler's remains had not been found and that he was probably still alive. This announcement caused a predictable flurry of 'Hitler sightings' across Europe. Allied officers sought to establish beyond possible doubt that Hitler had indeed died in his bunker."[157] As late as August 1945 there were still rumours that he was alive. The *Gazette* published pictures of what he might look like if he had adopted an alias, changed his appearance, and fled Germany. So the spectre of Hitler's return was still there. And the war in the Pacific raged on. But Montrealers were eager to embrace the war's end. Hedges's family was certainly invested in making its relief widely known. The Dawes Brewery was being managed by Doris's uncle, Norman J. Dawes. On 9 May, the *Gazette* ran an advertisement paid for by the brewery, picturing a woman with upturned eyes clutching a newspaper with a simple headline: "Peace."

Montrealers felt festive, yet there was a strain of anxiety in the air. One level of anxiety had to do with concerns about the rise of communism in Canada. When Fred Rose – the only Communist federal MP – was arrested on 30 March 1946 and charged with being a Russian spy, those concerns increased further. But some theorized that Rose had been set up by Igor Gouzenko, a cipher clerk at the Russian embassy who had defected to Canada on 5 September 1945, bringing with him documents from the embassy safe about Russian espionage activities in the West. The Gouzenko Affair dominated the headlines for months. The information he provided resulted in the arrest of dozens of people suspected of being Soviet spies and is often credited with triggering a Cold War mentality that fundamentally altered Canada's approach to security intelligence. There was concern that Gouzenko had revealed attempts to steal secrets about nuclear bomb technology, which Canada had been involved in developing as part of the Manhattan Project. Those concerns were undoubtedly heightened as a result of Japan's surrender after the bombing of Hiroshima and Nagasaki. Canadians were flooded with information about the devastation wrought by the atomic bombs. In response, on 29 June 1946, Hedges presented a talk on the topic of the atomic bomb. She emphasized the value of responsible citizenship in controlling the proliferation of nuclear weapons.[158]

While she was consistently engaged in writing about events related to the status of postwar Canada, Hedges was also beginning to think about how she could become more involved in promoting Canadian literature (and her own work). She had been speaking about the possibility of starting a business in partnership with John Hoare, an experienced editor who was also the owner of Burton's bookstore in downtown Montreal. She had also been working on her first Ryerson chapbook, *The Flower in the Dusk*. It seemed like the right time to make a career move. The next chapter examines Hedges's postwar writing and the circumstances leading up to the founding of Hedges, Southam and de Merian.

CHAPTER 3

1946–1948

What were the circumstances that led Hedges to become the central figure in a literary agency that was established so soon after the war? She must have had very little time to spare. She was still giving public talks and attempting to publish her poetry and fiction. In 1946, Lorne Pierce, the book editor at Ryerson Press, included twelve of her poems in *The Flower in the Dusk,* which appeared in the Ryerson poetry chapbook series that year. Sandra Campbell notes that the series, launched by Pierce in 1925, was designed "to come up with some big financial successes in his publishing program to offset unprofitable titles which stimulated Canadian cultural nationalism."[1] The idea was to promote Canadian poetry in a cheap and accessible format. The quality of the poetry published in the series was often secondary to the author's ability to contribute to production costs. As Gillian Dunks points out, "most emerging authors contacted Pierce directly in order to publish a chapbook. If authors could afford to cover the cost of printing a chapbook, they frequently were included in the series."[2] Print runs seldom exceeded five hundred copies. Authors were often asked to purchase a certain number of copies in order to offset expenses, even as they sometimes complained about the brevity of the chapbooks (most were eight to twelve pages) or about the fact that their publication in softcover made them seem like substandard objects, since paper covers were associated with low-brow commercial publishing at the time.

After the publication of 120 titles, the Ryerson chapbook series was in the midst of a transformation when *The Flower in the Dusk* appeared in 1946. That transformation was a reflection of shifting literary values that developed in response to the war. Dunks argues that the series can be read as "a subfield of literary production" that encapsulates broader trends in the Canadian literary field in the first half of the twentieth century:

> The struggle between late-romantic and modernist producers to determine literary legitimacy within the series constitutes the history of the field in this period. Pierce's decision to orient the series towards modernist innovation during the Second World War was due to late romantics' loss of their dominant cultural position as a result of shifting literary tastes. Modernist poets gained high cultural capital in both the Ryerson series and the broader field of Canadian literary production because of their appeal to an audience of male academics whose approval ensured their legitimacy. Late-romantic poets, by contrast, lost cultural capital due to their inability to captivate an audience of academic "tastemakers" and, in some instances, due to their gender, as editors frequently framed female poets as opposed to emerging modernism to dismiss their work.[3]

Dunks asserts, following Pierre Bourdieu, that the chapbook series should be "read in light of the struggle between late-romantic and modernist producers within it, whose various attempts at gaining 'legitimacy' characterize this temporal period."[4] If this is the case, then Hedges's *The Flower in the Dusk* occupies a kind of borderland between the late romantic and modernist impulses of its author, who was drawn to two worlds: the sentimental and religiously inspired poetry she inherited as a reader who came of age at a time when modernism was just beginning to make an impact in Canada, and the tougher, less lyrical, and more cynical poetry that was being promoted by the modernist poets who were living and writing in Montreal in the years leading up to the war, particularly those associated with the McGill group. Hedges's chapbook occupies a liminal space in the Ryerson series itself, torn as it was between romantic and modernist impulses at this transitional moment in Canadian writing.

Pierce may have seen Hedges's poetry as a bridge between these two worlds, as a form of mediation between a disappearing past and a troubling present. His decision to emphasize modernist verse corresponded with the beginning of the war. Pierce's newfound embrace of modernism could also be seen as an expression of the idea, shared by many authors, that modernist writing was equated with liberty and freedom. As George Hutchinson explains regarding the American view of the relation between poetry and politics,

> The Writers' War Board, founded two weeks after Pearl Harbor as an independent propaganda agency, spotlighted modernist books as the targets of Nazism. American publishers gladly joined the crusade. To buy a book, particularly a "modern" book, was to defend liberty. "This book, like all books," read the back of the dust jacket to Muriel Rukeyser's volume of antifascist poetry *Beast in View* (1944), "is a symbol of the liberty and the freedom for which we fight. You, as a reader of books, can do your share in the desperate battle to protect those liberties – Buy War Bonds." The front of the dust jacket featured an abstract rendering of the inside of a rifle barrel.[5]

By the end of the war, Pierce was consistently emphasizing the importance of poetry that eschewed romantic subject matter and focused on realistic detail. Dunks quotes from Pierce writing to Eugenie Perry in 1944, noting that "the tendency in verse today is toward ultra-modern, hard-bitten, and realistic. I think perhaps it will have a salutary effect, for the Canadian artist in both words and paint is reluctant to look into the faces of the people about him."[6] In his brief comment on *The Flower in the Dusk*, E.K. Brown articulated the shift in poetic sensibility rendered in Hedges's poetry when he noted that "sharp pictures of many sorts are drawn in Mrs. Doris Hedges's *The Flower in the Dusk*, but feeling is not so aptly rendered."[7]

It is significant that both Pierce and Brown equated modernist writing with realism in painting as well as literature. The war had brought profound changes to the conception and purpose of art. As Lora Senechal Carney observes, "more and more voices were speaking for *art vivant*" or "living art" which was "based on French art from Cézanne to Picasso – and the term *art vivant* rather than 'modern' was the one used most often in francophone Montreal."[8] In English Montreal, a similar impulse to embrace new artistic forms was initiated by John Lyman, who founded the Contemporary Arts Society along with Paul-Émile Borduas and Robert Élie in 1939. That same year, the group curated the "Art of Our Day" exhibition, which brought Montrealers into contact with works by Wassily Kandinsky, Franz Marc, Diego Rivera, and other well-known painters whose work was obtained from Montreal collectors.

Carney notes that this shift in artistic values delineated a profound break with the status quo: "By the beginning of the war, the ruptures with old conservative values were growing more and more obvious."[9] Because many famous artworks had also been moved to Montreal for safekeeping during the war, Montrealers had the opportunity to see local exhibitions of many of the modern European masters, an experience that further served to undermine existing conservative ideals. Painters came to believe that they were responsible for using their artistic skills to bear witness to the war. Carney quotes Arthur Lismer's succinct description of this shift away from conventional assumptions about the purpose of art: "Teachers of art repeat the histories and the principles to students whose minds, ears and eyes are turned only to thinking, listening and seeing the things of the moment – the news of battles and heroes, the ebb and flow of conflict."[10]

As a result of this shift toward painterly documentation, realistic painting gained prominence during the war as a number of artists grappled with the challenges posed in rendering the horrors of the battlefield. In March 1944, the Canadian army organized its first exhibit of paintings in Ottawa, displaying the realistic canvases of thirty-three artists.[11] Many of them were involved in the Canadian War Records effort, which brought them into the centres of military conflict. Female painters "lived and worked closely with the armed forces, spending a great deal of time close to the front lines. Wherever they found themselves, they were expected to produce accurate images of fighting men, machinery, and the landscape of war. This they did by sketching in the field and later developing the sketches in watercolour or pastel."[12] The "Operational Instructions" for these painters highlighted the importance of achieving realistic detail in all regards, and provided specific instructions regarding the importance of capturing data: "After field sketches and notes have been completed, lose no time in securing additional details of topography, uniform, equipment, weapons and vehicles portrayed; and arrange for participants to pose as models."[13] While Hedges was not a painter, she was no doubt acutely aware of the changes that had taken place in painting during the war years.

In this kind of environment, verisimilitude became a value associated with the war effort itself. Perhaps it was the "sharp pictures" in Hedges's poetry that prompted Pierce to publish her poems. He did not seem to be concerned about the financial viability of printing her book. The Ryerson contract makes it clear that unlike many other chapbook authors, Hedges was not required to contribute to publication costs or to purchase a set number of copies. In other words, Pierce must have felt that her work might actually pay for itself, that it had commercial potential. Or perhaps he was persuaded to take a chance on Hedges in response to her enthusiastic self-promotion, captured in a letter she sent to Pierce on 23 January 1946. I reproduce the letter in full because it provides such a clear expression of the ways in which Hedges had begun to understand the interface between writing and business. She was a relentless self-promoter.

Hedges's address at the bottom of the letter is also indicative of her privileged social standing: she wants Pierce to know that she lives at the "Ritz-Carlton Hotel." She begins the letter by invoking her history as a professional writer and her acquaintance with Harry Burton, the well-known owner of what was Montreal's premier bookstore at the time: Burton's Ltd. More self-advertisement follows in the second paragraph, in which Hedges reviews her career "during the past ten years or so."[14] She notes that insofar as her poems are concerned, "very few of them have been published" because "my agent in New York does not handle poetry"[15] (she had published three poems by this time). This agent appears to have been Willis Kingsley Wing. Wing had taken on a number of Canadian writers and was the first agent to understand the potential rewards of selling rights to Canadian authors' works in the American market. While there is no remaining record of the extent to which Wing represented Hedges's work, and no record of any contract between them, a single index card in the holdings of the *Toronto Star Weekly* fonds at the Fisher Rare Book Library indicates that Wing counted Hedges as one of his clients in 1945. The card indicates that Wing sold Hedges's story, "The Murdered Rose," once in 1945 and again in 1948. Perhaps it was her early association with Wing that provided Hedges with another reason to set up her own agency the following year. Wing's successful career might have convinced her that she could find similar success from a Canadian base.

Clearly Hedges was not above making some questionable statements in order to bring credibility to her profile as a writer. In fact, she had produced very little publishable work over the last decade. When describing her own career, she did not say that she had published occasional stories in *Good Housekeeping*, *Cosmopolitan*, and *This Week*. Instead, she says "my stories appear" in these magazines, as if such publication was an ongoing event. Then she invokes Sir Andrew Macphail, a prominent intellectual, physician, and writer who became the first professor of history at McGill University in 1907. Apparently Macphail liked her poetry enough "to make gramophone records of them."[16] Those recordings cannot be found. In her address titled "The Mind of the Poet" (1950), Hedges explains why: "He made it into a recording

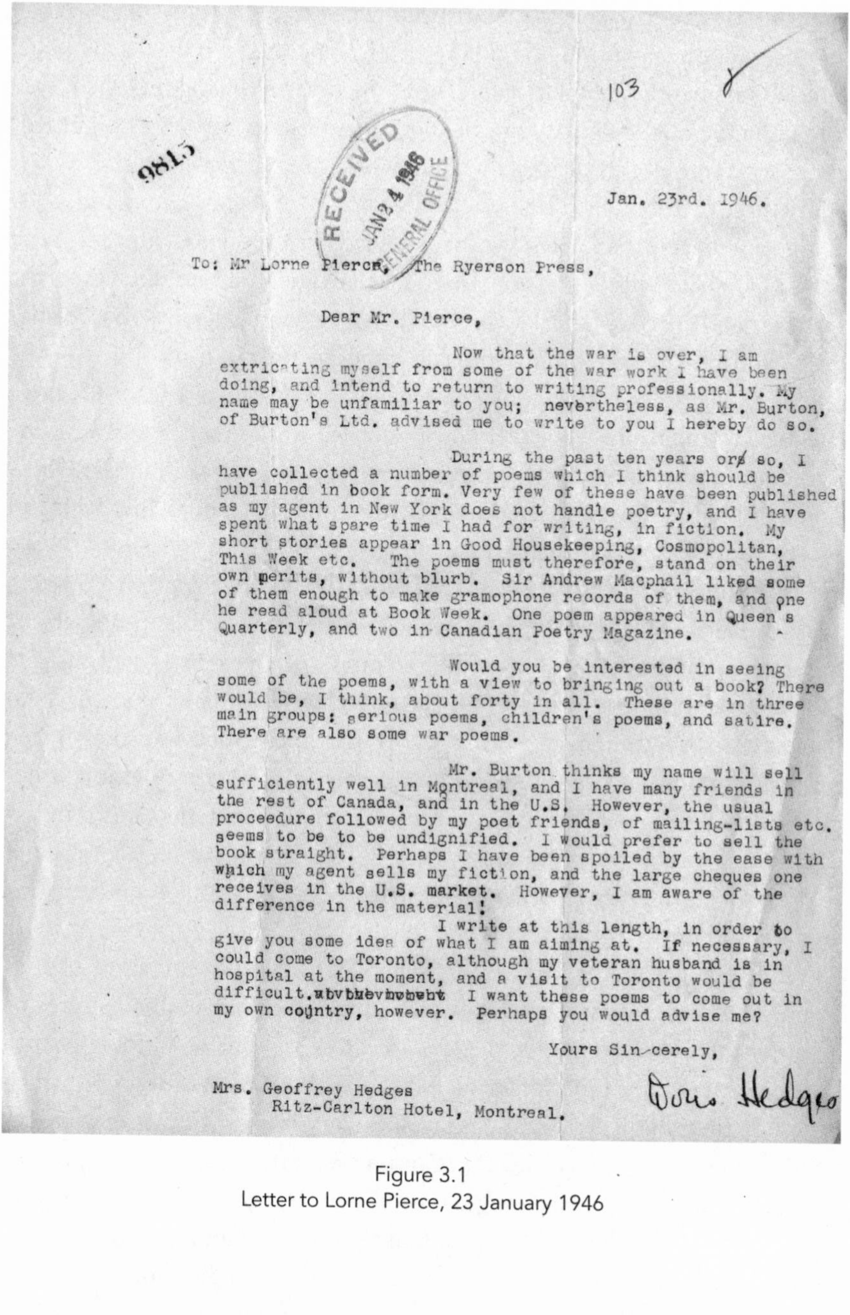

9815

103

RECEIVED JAN 24 1946 GENERAL OFFICE

Jan. 23rd. 1946.

To: Mr Lorne Piercm, The Ryerson Press,

Dear Mr. Pierce,

Now that the war is over, I am extricating myself from some of the war work I have been doing, and intend to return to writing professionally. My name may be unfamiliar to you; nevbrtheless, as Mr. Burton, of Burton's Ltd. advised me to write to you I hereby do so.

During the past ten years or so, I have collected a number of poems which I think should be published in book form. Very few of these have been published as my agent in New York does not handle poetry, and I have spent what spare time I had for writing, in fiction. My short stories appear in Good Housekeeping, Cosmopolitan, This Week etc. The poems must therefore, stand on their own merits, without blurb. Sir Andrew Macphail liked some of them enough to make gramophone records of them, and one he read aloud at Book Week. One poem appeared in Queen's Quarterly, and two in Canadian Poetry Magazine.

Would you be interested in seeing some of the poems, with a view to bringing out a book? There would be, I think, about forty in all. These are in three main groups: serious poems, children's poems, and satire. There are also some war poems.

Mr. Burton thinks my name will sell sufficiently well in Montreal, and I have many friends in the rest of Canada, and in the U.S. However, the usual proceedure followed by my poet friends, of mailing-lists etc. seems to be to be undignified. I would prefer to sell the book straight. Perhaps I have been spoiled by the ease with which my agent sells my fiction, and the large cheques one receives in the U.S. market. However, I am aware of the difference in the material!

I write at this length, in order to give you some idea of what I am aiming at. If necessary, I could come to Toronto, although my veteran husband is in hospital at the moment, and a visit to Toronto would be difficult. I want these poems to come out in my own country, however. Perhaps you would advise me?

Yours Sincerely,

Doris Hedges

Mrs. Geoffrey Hedges
Ritz-Carlton Hotel, Montreal.

Figure 3.1
Letter to Lorne Pierce, 23 January 1946

in his own voice, which was very precious to me. But sadly enough, it was amongst others in the collections of Martha Allan, and when she died it became mislaid, or lost, and has never been recovered."[17]

The sales pitch continues with a return to Burton, "who thinks my name will sell sufficiently well in Montreal" (another way of saying that she is well known in the city's literary circles), and to her disdain for the "undignified" promotional methods of other writers who use "mailing-lists, etc."[18] Why adopt those methods, Hedges argues, when her work already commands such a large audience? As she says, "perhaps I have been spoiled by the ease with which my agent sells my fiction, and the large cheques one receives in the U.S. market."[19] Hedges speaks as if these "large cheques" arrive on a regular basis, proof of her ongoing popularity among American readers. But the only way Hedges's writing could have generated a regular stream of "large cheques" would be if she had actually published work that had a continuing appeal to American readers throughout the war years. In fact, she had published only four stories in magazines by the time she approached Pierce in 1946,[20] along with three poems.[21]

Hedges closes the letter by saying she would be willing to come to Toronto to meet Pierce, but for the fact that her "veteran husband is in hospital at the moment." Here, Hedges plays the veteran's card in order to demonstrate the war sacrifices made by her family (an appeal to Pierce's well-known Canadian nationalism) and by affirming that "I want these poems to come out in my own country," a closing patriotic statement.[22] The letter demonstrates Hedges's determined attempt to promote herself in the literary world by exaggerating her achievements and by drawing on contemporary political and social currents in order to enhance her self-proclaimed status as a widely recognized and professional writer.

While Hedges seemed to be comfortable engaging in this kind of self-promotion in her surviving correspondence and in her public lectures or letters to the editor (mainly of the Montreal *Gazette*), she does not appear to have been part of the circle of writers so active in Montreal at the time, which is odd considering her plan to operate a literary agency, a business that depends heavily on social connections and networking. There is no record of her corresponding or socializing with some of the major writers who were active in Montreal when Hedges, Southam and de Merian was established in early 1947. Hedges could be assertive and opinionated in her public persona, yet there was another side to her that was retiring and reclusive; she was a public figure who came home to a sheltered private life in the privileged confines of the Ritz or to her large home in the Golden Square Mile. But even in those pampered settings, she must have been lonely in the months leading up to the opening of Hedges, Southam and de Merian, with Geoffrey in the hospital. To make matters worse, his mother died in London on 27 January 1946. He would have to get there to see his family as soon as he recovered and was discharged from the hospital. He might well be gone for a while. Faced with the prospect of spending a considerable amount of time alone, Hedges looked at the year ahead and focused on her plans to expand her writing career.

The poems in *The Flower in the Dusk* reflect Hedges's concerns at this turning point. The title poem focuses on a rose – identified as female – that can be seen as a symbol of the isolated poet who is unknown, her power associated with night and darkness. With "petals wrung / By sorrow and by pain" the lonely flower survives, "head unbowed." The descending darkness wraps her in shadow and hides "all her loveliness" and "all her scent." This hidden flower is clearly erotic, all the more so because its opening and closing petals attract the attention of passersby who gaze at it in the daylight, full of "marvel and in hope" that such a beautiful flower could bloom and thrive after "the terror of the night." But no one stops to consider the flower's hidden life in that dark night. To recognize the rose's extended symbolism, the viewer needs to understand that the flower represents "the eyes of youth." It becomes a metaphor of how youth survives, even in the enfolding dusk and darkness. Hedges opens her chapbook with a poem that tells us about hidden beauty, beauty in darkness, beauty that thrives in the face of pain and sorrow. The poem invites us to see the speaker as a version of the flower, enacting its own release.

The second poem in the chapbook also directs us to the poet's struggles with herself. "Poet's Protest" records an inner argument between two sides of the poet. One side believes that "you cannot / Prison beauty in a word," as if reducing beauty to the status of language robbed it of its ephemerality ("Ephemeral things are sacred"). But the other side argues that "a string of words" in a poem can work "Like finest jewels" that allow the poet to share "infinity's meaning." The speaker here is not sure which side wins. On one level, Hedges feels that poetry itself is a kind of betrayal, a poor substitute for what should actually be a prayer, or a religious form of expression meant to recognize the eternal and the infinite; in other words, God. This is why she ultimately disavows the very words she has written: "This is not poetry. / It is a chant, flung skyward / Heavy with challenge." But then she reverses herself: "Words were meant / To catch meanings in." The poem articulates the same debate that involved Lorne Pierce during the war years: Is poetry an expression of a higher order, and does it function as a spiritual vehicle, or is its value attached to the here and now of "ephemeral things," a form that allows the poet to "pour the moment" into a "mould"? Should it capture a transitory essence "written for one eye to see" or should it embrace a larger significance that exists in an atemporal realm aligned with "infinity's meaning"?

While some of the poems in *The Flower in the Dusk* struggle to reconcile romantic and realistic values, others are clearly expressions of an earlier sensibility. "The Wave" is a love poem that figures water in terms of female sexuality, "Rising and falling with the beat of the tides" and "bubbling" until it "spends itself" beating against the hard rocks of the shoreline. It knows "no purpose, no integrity" because its main goal is "to wind unceasing beauty at your feet."[23] The romantic subject figured here at her lover's feet adopts a sensibility quite unlike the one that emerges in "The Flower in the Dusk." Similarly, "You Must Listen" seems to be a later poem, inspired by imagist aesthetics, with its short, stark lines and its sparse, lean landscape:

I am tired
Of the moon shining
On the glittering snow. I weary
Of the silver ice
Lying inexorable
Upon the laughter
Of the summer water.[24]

Once again, the speaker wants to persuade herself that this starkness is a thing of value, that it is worth casting aside the comforting vision of a romantic backdrop that is reassuring in its figurative fullness and its longing for spiritual release. She reminds herself, twice, that "I am tired / But I must listen / To the singing notes of winter."[25] Hedges did not abandon her romantic inclinations easily. Even when she cut back the language in her poems in an attempt to achieve more concision and precision, she often found herself using that condensed verse to express moral and religious thoughts. For example, "Alloy" was first published in 1946 in *Canadian Poetry*, under the editorship of Earle Birney, a sign of its more modern appeal. It appeared the same year in *The Flower in the Dusk* chapbook, but despite its denuded lines it still pursues Victorian mores: "chaste simplicity" will keep a man "innocent / Of ill intent"; "the world is free" but "man can never see / His own ineptitude / Before God's mood"; "Man is but a shapeless mould / Without love's shining grace / Upon his face."[26]

Although the slim chapbook opens with an image of the "sorrow and pain" endured by a lonely rose (a sexualized rose aroused by sunlight that "warmed its blood" and invaded the "darkness" of "her scent"), it ends on a much less sensuous note in a poem revealingly called "Prayer," in which the speaker reminds herself that "the path of nature" must never stop "my heart and soul from contemplating the heavens."[27] In the chapbook's implied narrative, we move from the dark eroticism of the dew-petalled rose to a final surrender to God. The last word of the chapbook is "Amen." Hedges's Lord is her final lover.

Many of Hedges's poems invoke God or a higher authority. In *The Flower in the Dusk* (1946) she informs her readers that "man can never see / His own ineptitude / Before God's mood";[28] she ends the short collection with "Prayer." Twenty-five years later, in *Inside Out* (1971), she was still invoking God and attributing her worldly possessions to his beneficence:

> Nothing belongs to me,
> clothes, furniture, money,
> friends, children;
> nothing belongs to me
> and I'm glad!
> It's all a loan
> from God.[29]

Given the religious themes in her work, it seems logical to conclude that Hedges was devout, or that her benevolent work might have placed her in relation to Christian philanthropic communities that shared her values. Was she involved with religious organizations or church congregations that might have extended her social networks or shaped her views as a writer? There were two prominent Presbyterian churches near her residences in the Golden Square Mile, along with the Unitarian Church and several nearby Anglican congregations. But Hedges might have developed a strong sense of spirituality without any larger investment in a particular church. In his *Modernity and the Dilemma of North American Anglican Identities, 1880–1950*, William Katerberg suggests that between 1920 and 1950, "the diversification, perhaps fragmentation, of Anglican identities was apparent in both churches [the Protestant Episcopal Church in the United States of America and the Anglican Church of Canada], even if it was covered over with the ideology of comprehensiveness."[30] Katerberg notes that "the world of leisure industries, mass entertainment, spectator sports, and consumerism expanded between the wars, creating new forms of competition for the churches and undermining Victorian standards of 'proper' Christian morality."[31] According to Katerberg,

> Women, adolescents, and members of ethnic-religious communities found that they had more identities than ever available from which to choose, as institutional and communal restraints on individual behaviour continued to erode. These interwar centrifugal trends inspired countermovements by the state, churches, corporations, and social-service agencies to reorder society. The Ku Klux Klan was active in Canada, as in the United States. But despite such efforts the social context of identities became more diverse, and spirituality grew more individualized in Canada.[32]

While Hedges seems to have been quite steadfast in her Christian faith, her movement through various social identities (wife, poet, commentator, novelist, literary agent, etc.) perhaps coincided with an evolving or fragmenting spiritual identity that failed to conform to any specific institution. It seems telling that both her marriage and funeral service took place in chapels rather than churches. I cannot imagine Hedges vocalizing anything contrary to the status quo regarding the church, but I do think that in her poetry, such as in *The Dream Is Certain*, she is exploring her own spiritual values through a blending of themes: motherhood, redemption/salvation, gender/sexuality, and – of course – faith.

M.E. Reisner's *The Measure of Faith: Annals of the Diocese of Montreal, 1760–2000*, John Irwin Cooper's *The Blessed Communion: The Origins and History of the Diocese of Montreal, 1760–1960*, and Joan Marshall's *A Solitary Pillar: Montreal's Anglican Church and the Quiet Revolution*, offer glimpses into the growing diversification of Christian communities in Montreal over the span of Hedges's career. The Quiet Revolution may also have impacted Hedges's faith. Marshall suggests that the Anglican Church's historical alignment with wealthy anglophone Canadians of British heritage meant that during the 1960s and 1970s Montreal Anglicans felt "cut off from the mainstream of events and powerless to influence them."[33] Marshall notes that church attendance in the Anglican Diocese was declining during these years.[34] Perhaps Hedges felt increasingly voiceless within the church, though in Hedges's case I imagine that her extensive travelling in the 1960s affected her churchgoing more than the socio-political changes in Quebec. In any case, there seems to be some precedent during this period that explains why Hedges may have felt her poetry presented a better medium to express her views than any formal institution or ancillary group would allow. Despite searches of the Anglican Diocesan archives and other Montreal church records, I can find no mention of her involvement with any particular place of worship. The war may also have affected her views about religion. The title of her second Ryerson chapbook – *Crisis* – says a good deal about her state of mind in the immediate postwar years.

Crisis bears a copyright date of 1947, but a letter from Hedges to Pierce on 26 January 1947 makes it clear that it was published in late 1946. Hedges complains that "it was exceedingly unfortunate having the previous Chapbook appear as it did, ten days or so before Christmas, without a possibility of proper reviewing or advertisement, and after most people had bought their Christmas gifts."[35] In characteristic fashion, she draws attention to her status as a Montreal author: "It is only because I am well known in this city, that any notice has been accorded the book at all."[36] Hedges continues her typical hyperbole: "I have received a great deal of fan mail."[37]

She had come to believe in her own celebrity and was proud of any event that lent her more credibility as a writer. On a trip to New York, for example, Hedges claims to have heard one of her own poems being quoted to her at a dinner party. Apparently, certain American newspapers had pirated her poem "Glass Houses," a comic short poem about a goldfish, first published in *Toronto Saturday Night*.[38] In her letter, she also reminds Pierce of her status as a literary agent: "I am too busy with the agency (Hedges, Southam, & de Merian) to attend to the selling, reviewing, or publicity end of my own work."[39] Hedges did manage to get *The Flower in the Dusk* reviewed in the *Gazette*,[40] she says, but that was futile because "I have checked at two of our largest book counters, Morgans and Eatons, and find that no salesman has offered 'The Flower in the Dusk'"[41] to its customers. (In fact, such an offering could hardly be made, since, as Hedges notes in a handwritten marginal comment,

"No salesmen in Montreal since War.")[42] She adds that even in Halifax, the book was "not for sale at their best book store."[43] Although Hedges expressed her frustration at the chapbook's lack of availability, she had no concerns about reduced royalty income due to lack of sales, for the simple reason that she never expected to make a cent from the book. The contract for *Crisis*, dated 21 July 1947, states clearly that Hedges would receive sixty free copies of the chapbook "in lieu of royalty."[44] In other words, her complaints about the scarcity of the book were mainly about the way it affected her literary status and the degree of her celebrity, particularly in local circles.

Her complaint to Pierce provides an interesting commentary on what had and had not changed in bookselling. Hedges thinks of books as something that must be sold, by salesmen, like cars. The idea of an individual employee pitching a poetry chapbook to his many customers at a large Montreal department store in the month before Christmas seems like a fantasy from another age; it reveals Hedges's profound sense that poetry had value that could be promoted by effective salesmanship. At the same time, like many authors today, Hedges sought out her books in stores and was disappointed to find them absent from the shelves. That absence spoke convincingly of the department stores' assessment of the chapbook's potential, which was weak to non-existent (Hedges also comments on this in the margin: "No bookstores carry Chapbooks unless author is known well as a *friend*").[45] In the Christmas season, especially, the stores would have stocked mainly those titles that had the greatest appeal during the holiday season. In this business context, they had implicitly reviewed Hedges's chapbook, and rated its potential sales value as low. Or perhaps she did not have "a *friend*" in the bookstore business, even though she was about to start a literary agency, a venture that depended to a certain extent on established connections in the bookselling industry. If Hedges could not place her own books in the stores, how could she place those of others?

Of course, Hedges was not alone in being ignored by bookstores. In 1946, few people were interested in poetry, and even fewer in buying it. In an article published in the *Manitoba Arts Review* that year, Earle Birney asked two important questions: "can poetry become a significant art form in this nation? – is the making of poetry an activity of consequence in Canada today?"[46] His answer to both of these questions was "No." Birney argued that "poetry is the least influential of the arts in Canada" and that "there still does not breathe in this land a magazine of poetry with a quality or following anything like

4624

Jan. 26th. 1947

Dr. Lorne Pierce
Ryerson Bress, Toronto

Dear Dr. Pierce,

I received acknowledgement of the arrival of my new collection of poems, "Crisis", from Ryersons some time ago, but as it was dispatched during the Christmas holidays, I write to remind you of them. I shall hope to hear what you think of them in the near future.

It was exceedingly unfortunate having the previous Chap-Book appear as it did, ten days or so before Christmas, without a possibility of proper reviewing or admertisement, and after most people had bought their Christmas gifts. Through the kindness of the Gazette, I managed to get it reviewed very well, during Christmas week, but since then, I have checked at two of our largest book counters, Morgans and Eatons, and find that no saleaman has offered "The Flower in the Dusk" to them.

No book, it seems to me, can be expected to sell itself without benefit of publicity and timing of reviewing and saleamanship. It is only because I am well known in this city, that any notice has been accorded the book at all. As it is, the poems have been read at various groups etc. and I have received a great deal of fan mail. However, I do think it strange that Morgans and Eatons were not offered it. If a similar treatment was accorded it, by Ryersons, in other cities, how is it expected to have any chance whatever? I might add that friends of mine in Halifax have told me that it was not for sale at their best book store.

Naturally, I am most disappointed about this. All I ask is fair treatment for good work. Nothing more. No special publicity, no extra pushing, no spurious blurbing. If you like the second collection enough to accept it for publication, I sincerely hope that it will have a more even passage: I am too busy with the Agency, (Hedges, Southam, & de Merian) to attend to the selling, reviewing, or publicity end of my own work. I feel that the "Flower in the Dusk" should have further press advertisement from Ryersons, after the book can be bought at local book stalls.

Hoping to hear from you,

Yours Sincerely,

Doris Hedges

Figure 3.2
Letter to Lorne Pierce, 26 January 1947

Figure 3.3
Doris Hedges, 1947

that achieved by *Canadian Art*."[47] The only poetry magazine worthy of mention, according to Birney, was *Contemporary Verse*, but very few people read it. Even in the daily newspapers, Birney wrote, poetry is ignored: "The amount of rhythmic utterance hidden within the voluminous folds of a Canadian daily ranges from nothing to one-tenth of one per cent; of this, most are the trashiest sort of rhyming and the rest are generally pirated extracts from current anthologies."[48] Books of poetry fared no better in Birney's estimation. Although thirty-five new volumes of poetry were published in 1942, Birney notes, half were "tiny chapbooks printed at the author's expense, limited to two or three hundred copies, and circulated only at further cost to their begetters."[49] In making this observation, Birney no doubt had the Ryerson chapbook series in mind. He went on to note that publishers invested very little in promoting the poetry they did publish because there was no real market for it. On the other hand, they were happy to advertise a novel because "there is always a possibility that a novel might become a best-seller" while this would never be the case with a book of poetry: "The poet is permitted, at the most, a *succès d'estime*."[50]

Hedges's complaints about the availability of her chapbooks simply reflected the reality of the meagre Canadian appetite for poetry in general. Readers tend to forget that decisions about literary taste and value are often the result of this kind of material response to supply and demand. It was probably not the content of Hedges's work that prevented it from appearing on bookstore shelves; rather, it might have been the chapbook's physical packaging – its slim paper-bound appearance – that influenced the department stores' decision to bypass the title. Ultimately, the "real estate" occupied by any title on a bookstore's shelves is the product not simply of its content but of the way it is packaged and commodified. There was also the question of genre. People were not buying much poetry in the postwar years, and Pierce did not expect to sell many copies of his chapbooks (print runs were typically in the five-hundred copy range). On the other hand, readers in 1946 were magnetically drawn to war stories. The bestselling Canadian title in that year was Ralph Allen's *Home Made Banners*, the story of a prairie boy who eventually fights with the Canadian forces and experiences many of the horrors experienced by the troops during the war. Another 1946 bestseller was Edward Meade's *Remember Me*, also a war story, set in Europe, with a documentary edge. James Benson Nablo's immensely popular *The Long November* also focused on the war.

To get a sense of how the book buyer might see Nablo's novel in relation to Hedges's chapbook (if it were on the shelves), it is useful to consider some of the publishers' blurbs on the two books. *The Long November* was released in six different editions over nine years. It was republished in a new edition as recently as 2014, with the following description:

> *The Long November* is the story of Joe Mack, son of the grittier side of Cataract City – Niagara Falls – and his struggles to make something of himself; all for the love of well-to-do blonde beauty Steffie Gibson. It's about rum running booze, Chicago beer trucks, Bay Street sharpshooters, the mines of Northern Ontario and fighting the Nazis in Italy. It's also about the women, the many women – married, unmarried and widowed – who share Joe's bed. But they mean nothing – it's Steffie he wants.[51]

Now here is Ryerson's blurb for *Crisis*:

> Has the stamp of distinction. Mrs. Hedges has the touch of a craftsman and the sensitive mood of her work shows human insight.[52]

If Ryerson wanted to entice book buyers to purchase Hedges's work, they would have to use language that was a bit more compelling than that. But the fact remains that even if they had created better blurbs, they were promoting poetry books at a time when realistic fiction was becoming increasingly popular, with the recent publication of novels such as Irene Baird's *He Rides the Sky* (1941), Gwethalyn Graham's *Earth and High Heaven* (1944), Philip Child's *Day of Wrath* (1945), Hugh MacLennan's *Two Solitudes* (1945), and Lillian Beynon Thomas's *New Secret* (1946). Hedges also had to compete with poetry that responded directly to the war, including works by Patrick Anderson, Earle Birney, A.M. Klein, Dorothy Livesay, E.J. Pratt, Raymond Souster, and Bertram Warr, to name a few of the more prominent poets of the day.

Hedges did not always fare very well when reviewers compared her work to that of some of these more established poets. Writing in the *Dalhousie Review*, Alfred G. Bailey noted that *Crisis* is "dominated by [Hedges's] passion for social justice" and that "she usually attempts a more 'modern' idiom."[53] Still, he complains about "the didactic emphasis, the rarity of the concrete visual image" and "the tonal poverty of so many of the lines" which "all contribute to the lyric weakness and the consequent prosaic effect."[54] Bailey compares *Crisis* to Pratt's *Behind the Log*, where "we encounter the hand of a master."[55] Writing for "Letters in Canada," E.K. Brown also had reservations about *Crisis*. He noted that although "there is unusual breadth of mood" the language is "rhetorical rather than finely poetic" and "the poems seem to have been set down in a rush, and the poet to have believed that the force of feeling would blind the reader to the frequent thinness of realization."[56]

It would be unreasonable to expect to see a dramatic shift in Hedges's style or subject matter in the one-year period that separates her first and second Ryerson chapbooks. What is remarkable is the fact that Pierce chose to publish a second work by Hedges in such close proximity to the first. He would have had little time to assess the sales of *The Flower in the Dusk*, since the contract for *Crisis* was signed in July 1947, barely six months after the release of the earlier chapbook. There must have been other reasons accounting for Pierce's enthusiasm. Perhaps it was his desire, as a publisher, to maintain a foothold in the Montreal market. Perhaps he was swayed by Hedges's exaggerated claims of her local celebrity. Perhaps he was drawn to poems that tried to make sense of the war's devastation. Or perhaps he was interested in the way that Hedges mingled religion and spirituality with observations about modern life. The chapbook provides a series of glimpses into Hedges's attempts to retain her religious faith in an increasingly secular age. It also shows her willingness to reveal her own inadequacies in the face of this skepticism. Could poetry written by someone who occupied her social status claim authenticity, or did that social status undermine the writer's ability to see things from the perspective of those who were less fortunate? Hedges had begun to interrogate her own credibility.

The narrator of the chapbook's title poem wonders about her status as an observer of the "hunger" and "pain" she sees around her. Can she judge the condition of those who face "the empty kitchen drawer / And the gaping forage store" from the privileged vantage point of those who rest in "silken beds" while for others, "Hunger stalks at eventide"?[57] In "The Bridge of Words" the speaker becomes self-reflexive. She wonders about the power of language to bridge extremes. She has placed her faith in words as a means of carrying her across a chasm, but the words themselves fall into emptiness because there was "no hand" to "make them fast." The metaphoric bridge of words begins to crumble in the absence of God. Only when those crossing the bridge joined hands "and prayed / In silence" did the words release their power: "The bridge of words grew strong / And bore us safely past."[58]

In "For Every Man, the Choice," Hedges dwells on a central conflict: whether to believe in "a nameless Whom" who answers no prayers, or to embrace the tangible world of nature, "thrusting like Northern Lights / Into the dawn."[59] Hedges has no doubt about which side of this conflict attracts her: "spirit," we read, "Is more encumbrous, more alive" than all of our "temporal troubles."[60] The same dichotomy appears in "Courage," which paints a picture of two worlds that seem to stand apart: a symbolic city associated with the divine, or the corporeal realm of "the city's filth." Seduced by Mammon, the urban denizens walk the streets with "Hands in their pockets clenched / Upon corroding coin."[61] Meanwhile, "Above Is God." Hedges returns often to the questions that seem to plague her: What mobilizes people in this postwar world, and where can one still find God? Is a human merely "dream, or fantasy, or whim," as she writes in "Otherness," or is that human actually "God Himself"?[62] She wonders equally about the role of the poet. In "The Helpless Poet" she laments the destruction wrought by war and asks, "Have I the right to make a verse of this?"[63]

Hedges's poetry is preoccupied with choices between here and hereafter, pain and deliverance, suffering and redemption. These are her conservative compass points. But Hedges's poetry and fiction often show a completely different side, an attraction to sensuality and erotic imagery that suggests a desire to break the bonds of her own conservatism by taking a sexual plunge that is often tied to images of violence and penetration. Take, for example, "The Blade":

> Once, there were kisses everywhere
> Soft kisses, like a shaft of sun
> Across the daffodils.
> Others there were, more downward into me
> The blade of passion feeling for its mark
> Before the plunge.
> Kisses resting like dew were mine
> Dew in the moment of its vanishing
> Which in a breath
> Conceals the dancing footprint in the grass.
> Under those lips, the eagerness

Of thrusting hopes
I yielded smilingly, a fool
Until your glances entered me
Like golden anger.
The blade of passion held between your teeth
Cut ruthless path, now would be stayed
Within a kiss.[64]

One wonders who this "ruthless" lover might be. We have no idea. So little is known about Hedges's private life. She never mentions her husband except to note that she is married to him, or to observe that he is ill or away. He might well be that lover whose glances enter her. But I imagine, without evidence, that it is another lover whom she could only address publicly through her poetry, as in "Warning," which pledges that "I will be yours, my dear / Forever and a day,"[65] or "Invitation à la Valse," where the speaker tells us that "I liked what I saw in your eyes / It had nothing to do / Nothing whatever / With what was going on at the time."[66] (*La Valse dans l'ombre*, a 1940 film, was showing in Montreal in 1945.) This does not sound like a poem written to her husband. It sounds like a poem written in response to an extra-marital attraction:

Your hands moved restlessly
And your eyes looked at me
With a look I liked.
It had to do with me
Quite definitely with me
With you and me only
There was plenty going on at the time
But our charming mood
Met and matched
As though we had kissed warmly
Alone and happy in an empty room.[67]

While *The Flower in the Dusk* ended with a prayer, *Crisis* ends with a love poem that equates the disruption of the poem's ending with the departure of her lover. When he leaves, the words stop, as if writing could not exist without this romance. But then he returns and so do the words, the stars rise, and now "the cruelty / Is gone, and you, returned."[68] Hedges's poetry seems preoccupied with the effects of the war, but it also keeps returning to the theme of romance and seduction, as if she had become involved in a relationship that was allowing her writing to become more direct and revealing. The poems render this lover as a powerful force who can never be named or seen.

Unlike her poetry, Hedges's broadcasts and her social commentaries were well documented in newspaper listings, letters to the editor, radio addresses, and through her contribution to public assistance projects. She maintained her busy schedule of writing and reading her work on radio shows after the war. And, of course, she was intent on reminding her various audiences that she had become a literary agent. When the *Gazette* reported her 1 November 1947 radio address on the topic of writers who "are suffering from a sense of frustration and from defective education," she was identified not as a poet or writer but as the director of Hedges and Southam.[69]

Hedges continued her work with returning soldiers through the Veteran-Civilian Discussion Group in the months following the end of the war. The group was praised for its rehabilitation efforts and its contributions to facilitating the reintegration of war veterans into Canadian life. The last record of her meeting with the group was in December 1945.[70] A little more than a year later, she and her business partners founded Canada's first literary agency. What was it during that period that inspired the trio to conceive of that business? What made them believe that the time was right to establish such an agency in Montreal? And what former experience led them to believe that they could develop a successful agency in a country lacking any precedents? After all, the publishing industry in Canada was at a low. As Roy MacSkimming observes in *The Perilous Trade*, "the Depression and the Second World War cast Canadian publishing into a state of suspended animation."[71] To make matters worse, "Canadian publishers enjoyed neither American-style income from the sale of paperback, book club, broadcast, or movie rights, nor latter-day grant funding from government programs."[72]

Although the arts community had met at Queen's University in June 1941 to lobby the federal government for increased support to the arts, and although a group of prominent artists had participated in a historic "March on Ottawa" in June 1944 to demand additional support, the creation of the Massey Commission – a cultural turning point in Canada – was still five years away.[73] The Canadian Arts Council – the forerunner of the Canada Council for the Arts – would only be established in December 1945. This meant that in founding their agency in December 1946, Hedges and her partners had to rely mainly on private funding at a risky period for the Canadian publishing industry. In an article titled "Has Poetry a Future in Canada?" Earle Birney reflected upon the state of publishing Canadian poetry in 1946, noting that "some of those whose names appear in every honour role of contemporary poets have yet to see any one of their books sell five hundred copies."[74] This was not simply a result of the public's response to Canadian writing. It had a great deal to do with specific material conditions affecting literary production during the war years. Those conditions influenced the kind of books that could be produced and their physical and aesthetic design, which became less appealing to consumers. As Jonathan Vance explains, "the problem was not demand but supply":

> Paper was an increasingly scarce commodity (thanks to the enlistment of many men from the lumbering industry), printing machinery became more difficult to maintain, and binderies found it hard to retain the skilled workers who assembled books. Later in the war, the Wartime Prices and Trade Board issued guidelines to conserve paper: publishers should use the lightest paper possible, and should buy only the quantity that was needed immediately; margins should be narrower and the size and style of the typeface should be chosen to conserve space; and fly leaves, paper linings, slip sheets, backing boards, and special covers should be dispensed with for the duration of the war. Then came a new directive to book publishers (there was a difference of opinion as to whether it was mandatory or compulsory): 75 percent of each publisher's output had to be school textbooks, leaving only 25 percent for all other kinds of books. Publishers protested and complained, but generally complied.[75]

Clearly this was not the best time to pursue a business centred on literature and the printing and distribution of books. Perhaps there were other reasons that explain the desire to found a literary agency during such a challenging period. While Hedges did have wealthy backers in Southam and de Merian, she may well have viewed the creation of the literary agency as an extension of her outreach work with veterans and their families. The only evidence I have found to support this idea appears in Hedges's obituary in the Montreal *Gazette*, which notes that her agency "specialized in the manuscripts of veterans of the Second World War."[76] Or perhaps, from a more cynical perspective, she might have believed that, with no other big money yet invested in Canadian literary agencies, she and her backers would be the first and most profitable players on the block.

In late 1946, advertisements announcing the formation of the agency appeared in the *Dalhousie Review* and *Canadian Bookman*, along with notices in Ottawa's *Evening Citizen*.[77] A promotional piece issued by the agency articulated its aims:

> First, the wider and more consistent distribution of Canadian writing in the home market, in the United States, and in Europe. Secondly, the establishment and maintenance of the best possible relations between author and publisher on a basis equitable to both. Thirdly, to provide expert criticism and analysis of any work submitted by an author for this purpose.

The partners stressed that "their considerable experience in the publishing field, both at home and abroad, will make this service a useful one to Canadian authors generally." They also emphasized that "the firm is associated with a well-known literary agency in London and with another in Paris," those being D.C. Benson and Campbell Thomson (London) and W.A. Bradley (Paris). The claims to experience in publishing were no doubt exaggerated. The team's "experience" seemed to be more connected with finance than with the actual business of book publishing. The founding partners knew little about producing or marketing books.

Donald Cargill Southam, born in 1912, was thirty-four years old when the agency was founded. His main exposure to publishing would have been through his family connection to the Southam publishing empire that was consolidated by his father, Wilson Mills Southam. It may well be that Cargill Southam saw the agency as a means of expanding his family's widespread holdings in the Canadian newspaper industry after the war and was able to convince his father to invest in the fledgling business venture.

As I have noted, Jacques de Merian was a wealthy French aristocrat with a passion for rare sports cars. His life remains a mystery. He eventually married Marthe Marie Pineton de Chambrun, whose first husband was Prince Alessandro Edmondo Eugenio Ruspoli. This was a prestigious union. De Merian was a French marquis, a member of the distinguished Roquevaire family. Marthe was an Oxford-educated French princess whose aunt was Alice Roosevelt Longworth, the famous Washington socialite and the daughter of President Theodore Roosevelt. She spoke six languages. I have been unable to determine whether the couple had met by the time de Merian became involved in the agency or how he knew the other partners.

Two other names are mentioned in the partnership declaration filed on 15 January 1947: Spalding Black and J.E.M. Hoare. Little information is available about Black. He worked in advertising for the Salada Tea Company and later for C.I.L. – Canadian Industries Ltd. His photograph appears in an advertisement for the Advertising Club of Ottawa in the *Ottawa Journal* for 18 December 1937, where he is described as a "prominent Canadian advertising executive" who would be presenting "the recently completed merchandising sound film, 'The Lady Who Couldn't Say No,'"[78] a film about female consumers and what Black felt was their unquenchable penchant for impulse buying.

The most knowledgeable member of the group in terms of publishing was undoubtedly John Hoare. Born in Montreal, Hoare was educated in England and Germany. In the years leading up to the war he worked with the London publishing firm Constable in sales and foreign rights. After serving in the Fleet Air Arm of the Canadian navy in the war, Hoare moved to Canada and became the distributor for Penguin Books after Sir Allen Lane and his brothers had launched Penguin Publishing in 1935. In 1946 Hoare purchased Burton's Ltd from Harry Burton, who had founded the store in 1925.[79] Notably, Burton's Books in Montreal was located in the very building that housed Hedges, Southam and de Merian; his involvement with the agency began in the same year he took ownership of Burton's. The agency's decision to rent office space in the Dominion Square Building no doubt had something to do with the fact that Hoare was already a tenant. The firm had offices in room 333 of the prestigious building, an expensive property to rent, but they likely had no lack of financial resources, given the backing of Geoffrey Hedges's family, de Merian, Black, and Southam. Hedges herself, of course, was also part of the extensive and wealthy Dawes clan. If she had enough money to live in the Ritz, she had enough money for the pricey office space in the landmark Dominion Square Building.

The letters preserved at the Ransom Center shed light on the rationale behind the agency's creation. On 6 May 1946, on Burton's Ltd stationery, John Hoare wrote to Jenny Bradley to establish an initial connection with the

French agency. He reminded her that they had met "when I used to go over to Paris for Constables before the war."[80] He writes that he would like to translate "two excellent children's books – The Complete Bécassine and the Poupée Belge."[81] *Bécassine*, written by Jacqueline Rivière and illustrated by Joseph Pinchon, was a very successful comic strip that was eventually produced as a book series. *Journal d'une poupée belge pendant la guerre* (1918) was an illustrated French work of fantasy by two Belgian sisters – Jeanne and Laure Hovine. The sisters went on to enjoy highly successful careers as comic book authors and illustrators.

George L. Parker draws attention to an important change that took place in the publishing industry in Montreal after the war:

> Montreal's publishing industry received an important economic boost after the Fall of France in 1940. The Berne Convention authorities permitted the reprinting of French copyrighted works for distribution to the Francophone world for the duration of the war. This situation ended in January 1946, but helped foster the cultural maturity that led to the Quiet Revolution in Quebec after 1960.[82]

Hoare wanted to sell the popular French books in Canada. He noted that "I cannot find that either of these books has been published out here and I believe that I could interest a publisher in handling both these titles. Perhaps you could send me a copy of each if the rights are still available?"[83] Although Hoare was making this request as an established bookseller, the business of finding a publisher "if the rights are still available" was not something booksellers did. Those tasks were typically handled by literary agents. But because there was no Canadian agency handling such rights in Canada, let alone Quebec, Hoare had stumbled into a potential new venture. It soon occurred to him that in the absence of any Canadian agency "out here" that could handle his request, he might profitably set up his own. When Jenny Bradley responded to Hoare's request on 11 July 1946, she did so in terms that would have reminded Hoare, once again, that he was not yet in a position to handle the foreign rights to the titles he wished to translate. Although Bradley noted that the North American rights to *Bécassine* were free, she also posed two standard agency questions: "The French publisher would like to know the approximate size of the first printing and the approximate price the [book] would be sold."[84] Hoare had no way of answering these questions. So he asked

Bradley to send him one or two copies of *Bécassine* ("I need these in order to interest a publisher in them") and inquired whether she could secure "a provisional option for translating and publishing out here."[85] In making these requests, Hoare was already falling into the role of agent. Perhaps this communication made him feel that there was a pressing need for a professional agency in Canada, and that his involvement with such an agency might be a logical extension of his profession as a bookseller. The sample books were mailed to Hoare in early August.

At the end of the month, Hoare acknowledged receipt of the books but noted that he had received no answer concerning the translation option. This was not surprising, since translation options are seldom granted to individuals. Bradley understood what Hoare was gradually coming to realize – that in order to obtain that option a Canadian publisher would have to be secured. It was probably this realization that encouraged Hoare to think even more deeply about the founding of a literary agency that would act as a liaison between Canadian and foreign publishers. By 26 August he was writing to Bradley again, thanking her for the books and issuing a crucial proposal: "I should now like to approach a subject which has been on my mind for some time; namely, that of our working together between France and French-Canada."[86] Then he went on to note that

> by January I shall have organized the first serious Canadian literary agency. It will be managed by Mrs. Hedges, who is on the executive of the Canadian Authors Association and is very well known in publishing and literary circles. I shall also be a member of the firm, as will Mr. D.C. Southam, whose Southam Press controls newspapers across Canada. We would like opportunities to place French books with Canadian publishers, and vice versa, and also to place good short stories in the same way. I believe that, whilst there are only near five million French-Canadians, there is, nevertheless, a reasonable market for good French material out here, and I should be very pleased if we could work on fifty-fifty basis for what we place.[87]

This request forms the basis for the foreign rights program of Hedges, Southam and de Merian. On 11 October 1946, Hoare tells Bradley that "we are launching in a month or two."[88] Bradley agrees to co-operate with the new agency in terms of "the handling of French Canadian books on the

French market." On 30 October Hoare writes again to Bradley, explaining in more detail the role that the mysterious Jacques de Merian will fulfill in the agency: "I have given your letter to the Marquis de Merian, who will be looking after the French end for the firm."[89] Hoare observes that one limitation on the book market in Quebec is the influence of the Catholic Church: "the French market here is still rather hampered by the control of the Catholic church, which is much more determined in the limiting of literature than it is anywhere else in the world; consequently, at first, I shall be looking primarily for history, biography, detective fiction, children's books and straightforward, simple romantic fiction, of the type which could be sold for serial if not in book form."[90] The comments provide an unusual glimpse into the climate of publishing in Quebec at the end of the war and make it easier to understand why realistic fiction, particularly in French, had such difficulty making headway in the postwar years. It also allows us to understand, from the perspective of a newcomer to the field such as Hoare, the extent to which literary agents necessarily respond to the literary values of their ethos, and how difficult it is to break with that ethos when it is connected to long-standing authoritarian structures and values.

Hoare does not write to Bradley again until the end of 1946. On 30 December he notes that "the first Bécassine book is now translated and in type script. We shall be sending it off to the States next week."[91] Apparently, he'd had no luck in selling the book to a Quebec publisher, perhaps because he simply did not have the contacts to make that happen or because he'd overestimated the interest in the series in French Quebec. And even without a commitment by Bradley or the Paris publisher to grant Hoare an option on the translation, he took it upon himself to submit the book to American publishers. The only explanation for this would be that, in the event he received an offer from a US house, he could then present that offer to Bradley through Hedges, Southam and de Merian, whose founding as a formal business entity had been announced at exactly the time Hoare was writing to Bradley at the end of 1946.

Although Hedges, Southam and de Merian were not legally registered as a business until early 1947, it is clear that they were actively promoting the agency in late 1946, with the help of the Canadian Authors Association. In November 1946, a letter was released by the Executive Office of the CAA in Toronto, announcing the imminent formation of the agency. The letter explains why the CAA supported the enterprise:

Executive Office
7A Forest Hill Road
Toronto, Canada

Dear Member:

In the near future, announcements will appear in the Press, regarding the forthcoming establishment, on January 1st, of a firm of Authors' Representatives.

That such a service is necessary in Canada, can be judged from Gwethalyn Graham's statement at the C.A.A. Annual Meeting, to the effect that: "For the past twenty or thirty years, book contracts have become steadily more and more complicated. The Authors' League of America recently listed eighteen different possible markets for any one book at the present time, where a generation ago, there was usually one. No one writer can study all these markets, learn all he needs to know, and still have enough time, or a sufficiently free mind, to do his actual writing."

It is indeed a tiresome and distracting task for any writer, to market his own work. It is hoped, therefore, by rendering this service as authors' representatives, to serve and protect the interests of Canadian writers, as well as to establish and maintain better relationship between author and publisher. Undoubtedly, a real and practical service can be performed by a Canadian agency, towards developing the wealth of as yet largely untapped talent in Canada. The home market is a growing one, in both our languages, and it should be more fully supplied from home sources.

Hedges, Southam, and de Merian are fortunate in having excellent connections both on this continent and in Europe, where Canadian authors are achieving an increasing measure of recognition. They are associated in London with D. C. Benson and Campbell Thomson Ltd., and in Paris, with Mme. W. A. Bradley, both agencies of the first importance.

All types of manuscripts, with the exception, for the time being, of poetry and radio scripts, will be handled, on the basis of the customary agents' commission on all M.S.S. sold. No reading fees will be charged.

Hedges - Southam - de Merian
Registered
Authors' Representatives

Doris Hedges
Cargill Southam
Jacques de Merian

Figure 3.4
Promotional letter from CAA executive offices, 1946

One of the recipients of this letter was Canadian author Gladdis Joy Tranter, who had published several works by this point in her career.[92] Soon after receiving the letter, Tranter wrote to her friend Charles Clay, complaining that it was "a very sloppy communication indeed." She adds: "I have no idea who Doris Hedges is – yet she is the foremost member of the firm. I have never heard of her. Does she write, etc?" Tranter also wonders about the fact that the CAA letter was unsigned. "Not being on the letterhead of the organization and not being signed by anyone, I wonder whether our own organization is holding back – That it has been forced to send out the letter, but is not sponsoring it. Is it that, or is it simply lack of knowledge that made it like this?"[93]

The idea that Hedges and her colleagues could somehow force the CAA executive to send out a letter it did not really endorse raises tantalizing questions about the kind of influence the fledgling partners were able to wield. At the same time, the letter testifies to how thoroughly unknown Hedges was in the years following the war. She may have been recognized in Montreal circles, but her reputation had not made it to Toronto. In his response to Tranter, Clay tried to fill in some of the blanks, informing her that "Doris Hedges is a member of the Montreal Branch of the CAA, does writing and radio work, and now has joined forces with two very good people to operate a literary agency."[94]

The partnership agreement behind Hedges, Southam and de Merian is dated 1 January 1947. In it, Geoffrey Hedges authorizes Doris to conduct business. The male partners required no such authorization from their wives.

Even before the official documents were signed, Hedges had been pursuing her overseas contacts in the hope of obtaining new manuscripts and clients. Soon after the agency was officially registered, in January 1947, Hedges wrote directly to Jenny Bradley about the autobiography of Emily Carr ("perhaps Canada's current sensation, although her work has not been recognized until her death"),[95] for which Hedges, Southam and de Merian hoped to sell the French rights. To establish Carr's credibility for a French audience, Hedges stressed that "her paintings were hung in the recent French exhibition of U.N.E.S.C.O." and added that "we consider her autobiography to be a masterpiece."[96]

The book in question was *Growing Pains*, which was completed just before Carr's death in 1945 and published by Oxford University Press (Canada), under the direction of William Henry Clarke. Clarke had published many

CANADA
PROVINCE OF QUEBEC
DISTRICT OF MONTREAL

PARTNERSHIP DECLARATION

HEDGES, SOUTHAM & deMERIAN REGISTERED

We, the undersigned, DAME DORIS HEDGES, residing at the Ritz Carlton Hotel, Sherbrooke Street West, in the City of Montreal, wife separate as to property of GEOFFREY HEDGES, and the said GEOFFREY HEDGES to authorize his said wife; D. CARGILL SOUTHAM, Publisher, residing at No. 22 Granville Road, in the Town of Hampstead; JACQUES TESTE deMERIAN, Gentleman, residing at No. 1864 St. Luke Street, in the said City of Montreal; J.E.M. HOARE, Publisher, residing at No. 1898 Dorchester Street West, in the said City of Montreal; and SPALDING BLACK, Industrialist, residing at No. 17 Parkside Place in the said City of Montreal, hereby certify:

THAT we intend to carry on trade and business in co-partnership as Literary Agents, at Room No. 333, Dominion Square Building, in the said City of Montreal;

THAT the said partnership has subsisted since the 1st day of January, 1947; and

THAT we are and have been since the said day the only members of the said partnership.

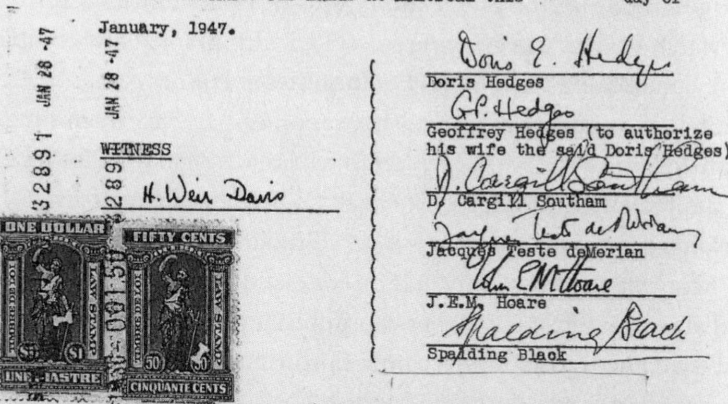

WITNESS our hands at Montreal this 15th day of January, 1947.

32891 JAN 28 -47

WITNESS H. Weir Davis

Doris E. Hedges
Doris Hedges

G.P. Hedges
Geoffrey Hedges (to authorize his wife the said Doris Hedges)

D. Cargill Southam
D. Cargill Southam

Jacques Teste deMerian
Jacques Teste deMerian

J.E.M. Hoare
J.E.M. Hoare

Spalding Black
Spalding Black

Figure 3.5
Partnership registration, Hedges, Southam and de Merian, 1947

Canadian authors and was determined to promote Canadian writing. Oxford owned the rights to Carr's books and had published *Klee Wyck* (1941), *The Book of Small* (1942), and *The House of All Sorts* (1944). Clarke's decision to allow Hedges, Southam and de Merian to market the foreign rights to Carr's autobiography represented a strong vote of faith in the fledgling agency, but it also was a recognition of the fact that in seeking out an agency to represent Oxford University Press Canada abroad, Clarke had little option but to turn to an agency in Montreal, for the simple reason that it was the only Canadian agency prepared to handle foreign rights at the time. In fact, it was the only Canadian agency prepared to handle *any* rights.

In February 1947, Hedges wrote again to Bradley, asking her to send a copy of *Bécassine* to D.C. Benson and Campbell Thomson in London, "where we have a good chance of selling the English rights."[97] The same month, Hedges was promoting a French translation of *Jealousy and Medicine*, a novel by Michał Choromański, a well-known Polish author. The book, translated into fifteen languages, was based on a clinical study of the relationship between medicine and sex. When war broke out, Choromański fled to South America and then to Canada with his wife, Ruth Sorel, a prominent dancer who established Les Ballets Ruth Sorel and the Ruth Sorel Modern Dance Group in Montreal after the couple settled there in 1943.[98] According to Hedges, Choromański had arranged for one of his earlier works to be published in France, but the publisher had died, and now he had empowered Hedges to renew negotiations for the publication of his work in France.

By 6 March Hedges was growing frustrated with Bradley. She complained that there had been no response to her inquiries about *Bécassine* and Choromański. She announced that "we now have another extremely interesting book in English, for which the author wishes to sell French rights."[99] Hedges's letter had the desired effect. Bradley wrote back a week later to apologize ("I have been absolutely swamped with work").[100] Bradley notes that she has sent a copy of *Bécassine* to "Miss Benson, London," and wonders whether Hedges has been able to interest any American publishers in the series. Hedges responded that "the translation was only finished at the end of January" and that "we have high hopes for it."[101] She also notes that she is sending "a book by a Canadian writer, the French rights for which are available."[102] A note at the bottom of the letter indicates the title: *Reach Me Your Hands* by MacCallum Bullock, an obscure Ottawa author.

The spring of 1947 brought challenges beyond those posed by the business. Hedges's father died on 10 March; her mother died sixteen days later. As an only child, the responsibility of arranging two funerals in a single month fell mainly to her. All of this was happening at a time when international communications had been seriously disrupted by extreme weather. England was experiencing heavy snowstorms and its wettest spring in more than three hundred years. The same was true for France. This caused massive disruptions in energy supplies and the loss of close to 10 per cent of industrial production. Domestic and international mail delivery was severely restricted. Widespread fuel and food shortages contributed to a business slowdown. By June of 1947, Hedges was getting impatient. She wrote again to Bradley, asking about the various titles she had submitted over the past six months. The response she received could only have increased her frustration. Bradley reported that the French publisher who was supposed to have been interested in Choromański's work knew nothing about it. The manuscript by MacCallum Bullock had not arrived. Neither had a copy of Carr's *Growing Pains*, despite the promises of Oxford University Press. No response had been received to the British submission of *Bécassine*. Then Bradley threw cold water on Hedges's suggestion that the Montreal agency could work with hers to submit French novels to American publishers for translation into English. Bradley was blunt about this: "I have given some thought to the idea of presenting French books in novelette form in the United States. I do not think French authors are very much in favour of such a diffusion of their works."[103]

The increasingly intermittent correspondence between Bradley and Hedges suggests that the more experienced French agent was also growing impatient with her novice Canadian counterpart. And Hedges must have felt rebuked by Bradley's curt dismissal of her proposal for American translations, especially because it conveyed Bradley's sense that Hedges did not understand the somewhat protectionist attitudes held by French novelists regarding the translation of their works. What Hedges certainly did not understand is how slowly publishing works. No deals had been concluded. Correspondence was intermittent. Books and manuscripts failed to arrive. The Canadian agency was virtually unknown when it came to foreign representation. Implicit in these problems was a central issue confronting Hedges and her business: There was no established agency tradition in Canada and no single author's representative who had enough clout to draw the attention of foreign agents and publishers. As Janet B. Friskney and Carole Gerson point out, "the big decisions, editorial and commercial, are made in New York and London and in the interest of his author a Canadian editor dare not forget it."[104] Name recognition also counted, and Hedges and her backers were simply not known.

The correspondence of Hoare and Hedges with Bradley is not the only communication that took place in the first six months of the agency's founding, but I have been unable to locate many other records to suggest that Hedges had built up even a modest list of client authors since the beginning of 1947. Without clients, there could be no revenue. Those authors who managed to appeal to foreign audiences (including Morley Callaghan, Sinclair Ross, Hugh MacLennan, and Mordecai Richler) often bypassed the Canadian market by first seeking publication in London or New York. Such publication was often facilitated by agents in those cities who dealt directly with Canadian authors. In such an environment, it was very difficult for Canadian publishers to profit by publishing those Canadian writers who had not bypassed them in favour of foreign houses. As Friskney and Gerson explain, by way of quoting John Morgan Gray of Macmillan Canada,

> the Canadian book publisher did not derive "any important part of his revenue (or *any* net profit) from Canadian general publishing"; the only reasons to engage in original Canadian trade publishing were those of "pride and prestige." Before 1960, neither Canadian literary fiction nor poetry had much international appeal; consequently,
> only Canadian publishers with a substantial nationalist commitment engaged in these areas of trade publishing, often entirely at their own risk.[105]

In the hope of appealing to American publishers, Hedges began submitting the translated version of *Bécassine* (*Becky's Childhood*) to companies in New York at the rate of one submission per month. She did not understand that agencies could make simultaneous submissions. As a result, she waited for each publisher to make a decision before submitting to the next, a cumbersome process that accounts for the fact that between January and July 1947 only four submissions had been made, each of which was rejected, in turn, by Simon & Schuster, Macmillan, Oxford University Press, and Random

House. At this point, Hedges simply abandoned the book. On 8 August she wrote to Bradley, saying "we are sorry that we have not been able to do anything with this book."[106] Meanwhile, the manuscript of MacCallum Bullock's *Reach Me Your Hands* had still not arrived in Paris. Hedges mailed a second copy to Bradley, noting that "the author is very anxious about it."[107]

As the end of the year approached, Hedges had still not received any word from Bradley about Choromański's work, which had been submitted to the French publisher Edgar Malfère. Choromański's manuscripts had also been sent to Société Française d'Éditions Littéraires et Techniques, who had also rejected the material because "with the present shortage of paper they cannot undertake the publication of these books."[108] It would appear that by the end of 1947 Hedges, Southam and de Merian had not inked a single deal. Somewhat pathetically, in March 1948 Hedges resumed her correspondence with Bradley, asking again about the fate of Choromański 's books, "which you have had for over a year." She added that "I think it would be best to send these books back to us if there is no hope for them."[109]

The response to this request on 22 March was not heartening. Bradley's office said that "the situation in the French publishing field is terrible and difficulties are growing every day, which makes publishers very cautious in their purchases. On the other hand, a number of firms have disappeared completely, or have had to cut down their output very drastically. All this makes the placing of foreign books much less easy than it had been for some time."[110] Bradley was not exaggerating. Newsprint and paper production in most countries had fallen dramatically after the war. While production in Canada increased dramatically, paper supplies in France had decreased by more than 50 per cent and in the United Kingdom by 60 per cent (see table 3.1).[111]

Writing in July 1947, Christine Campbell Thomson, Hedges's London subagent, told Bradley that

> Conditions here are so terrible that at the moment I have been able to do nothing; I hope that they may improve in the next few weeks but we have just had another paper cut and the news to-day of the fuel situation is so awful that it is small wonder publishers are afraid to take on new commitments; we reckoned in the old days six months was an average time to get a book out after the contract was signed; now we say two years and eighteen months if you are lucky![112]

Table 3.1

World newsprint production (*in short tons*)

	1939	1946
Canada	2,869,000	4,143,000
United States	939,000	771,000
Newfoundland	305,000	363,000
United Kingdom	848,000	330,000
Sweden	305,000	290,000
Finland	519,000	259,000
Soviet Union	210,000	200,000
France	276,000	133,000
Norway	226,000	121,000
Japan	436,000	83,000
Germany	415,000	80,000
Netherlands	104,000	39,000
All others	280,000	271,000
Total	7,732,000	7,083,000

In fact, Canada was the only country in the world in which paper production had increased in 1946, the year before Hedges's agency started. This might have given Hedges a misleading sense of optimism about the health of the publishing industry. Yet the stark figures related to a worldwide decrease in paper supplies during and after the war provide a potent reminder of the extent to which publishing companies are subject to material circumstances beyond their control. Added to the shortage of paper was a devastating rise in interest rates, which made it very difficult to borrow money:

> The 1946 inflation rate of ~20% was the highest yearly inflation rate of the entire 1920–1981 period. Inflation had not exceeded interest rates since the onset of the Great Depression, but did take off during and after World War 2; and did not do so again during the entirety of the 1950s, 1960s, or the early 1970s. Only near the very peak interest rates of ~1981, as well as near the very trough of ~1946 did the inflation rate meet or exceed rates on long term interest.[113]

Those who failed to consider the effects of these material circumstances on business did so at their own peril. While idealism might tempt people to enter the world of publishing, those entrants are seldom fully aware of how interest rates, exchange rates, paper and printing costs, and office overhead can dramatically affect profitability. The challenges of succeeding in the publishing business are also amplified by the negative effects wrought by bad weather, disrupted supply chains, legal issues, or rising tax rates. While literary agents do not have to make the same up-front investment in book production costs as book publishers, they typically generate revenue only on the basis of commission fees that are charged on author royalties or other book licences. If there are no clients there can be no royalties, and, even in the most optimistic scenario, the revenue generated through commissions does not usually flow to the agency all at once but tends to be spread over the stages of book production and publication. In other words, new literary agencies without an established backlist find themselves in the same position as new publishers: they must capitalize their businesses for a considerable period of time before any revenue comes in. Hedges also faced another hurdle: most aspiring Canadian writers in 1947 simply did not understand how agencies worked. Only the most successful writers were capable of attracting agents in the United States and Britain. Unestablished writers still thought of the publishing process in terms of the relation between author and publisher, rather than as a chain that linked author, agent, publisher, and bookseller. In order to build up her clientele, then, Hedges also had to educate potential customers about how agents worked. Yet there is very little material in print to suggest that she pursued an active advertising strategy or that she consciously sought out new writers from across Canada or from Montreal.

One way Hedges did promote herself and her agency was through public speaking events. On 1 November 1947, in a broadcast "planned to inaugurate the Second Post War National Book Week in Canada," Hedges argued that Canadian writers "are suffering from a sense of frustration and from defective education."[114] This may not have been the most effective means of attracting new clients. Hedges went on: "I believe our authors' lack of self-confidence and their sloppiness are the main reasons the markets of the world are not teeming with Canadian works."[115] What could account for such sloppiness among Canada's budding new authors? Hedges answered: "Literary style today is a sort of careless individualism of expression rather than an esthetic formula. This is an age of hurry and worry. We are all tired, frightened of the future and prone to use reading as a drug."[116] She ends her diagnosis with a complaint: "Editors in every market are asking for modern Canadian fiction, but a mass of fairy stories of supernatural material, and of historical romance is being offered. Canadians are not writing about the present and the future scene but about the past."[117]

In December 1947, Hedges accepted an invitation to address the McGill Writers' Club, as recorded in the *McGill Daily*. The announcement of her campus visit provides a good summary of her career at this point:

> The McGill Writers' Club announces that Doris Hedges, well-known writer, critic and poet, will be guest speaker tomorrow night at their meeting in the Union Board Room. The meeting begins at 8 p.m. and is open only to members and those wishing to join the club. Doris Hedges is an authority on writing, her stories having been published in such magazines as "Good Housekeeping," "Cosmopolitan," "This Week," "Macleans," "Montreal Standard," "The Toronto Star Weekly," etc., as well as in such famous English magazines as "The Strand Magazine," "The London Graphic," "The Woman's World," "The Royal Magazine," etc.[118]

In its coverage of the event, the *Daily* reported that attendance had been low because of "pressure of mid-term examinations," but this did not stop Hedges from speaking about her experiences as a literary agent.[119] At the event, it was also revealed that Hedges had lost the partnership of Jacques de Merian, since she was introduced as "one half of the firm Hedges & Southam Registered." According to the *Daily*, Hedges "stated that her offices often received requests from American editors for good Canadian background stories. While the majority of Canadian writers have the freshness of viewpoint that makes for a real quality of writing … the greatest fault in many of the stories which she receives is a lack of sound short story form."[120]

Hedges was promoting realistic fiction and, as a literary agent, was complaining about its absence in the submissions she received. Yet critics such as Colin Hill have traced the origins of realism in Canadian fiction to the 1920s. It was as if Hedges had missed two decades of profound changes in Canadian fiction. Much of the new fiction could hardly be described as "fairy stories." And, as Hill notes, "there are about three dozen 'core' modernist-realist novels" that appeared earlier, in the 1920s and 1930s.[121]

What could explain Hedges's sense that such works were rare? The contrast between the clearly identifiable inception of realism, as demonstrated by Hill, and Hedges's complaints about its absence indicates that although realistic fiction had existed in Canada since the 1920s, it had not yet made enough of an impression on writers to alter the opinions of a well-connected literary agent, even in the immediate postwar years. More than twenty years after the initial appearance of realism in Canada, the commercial perception of its presence suggested that it had not gained widespread recognition as a new and saleable literary genre among aspiring writers.

What this demonstrates is that our perception of literary trends can be significantly altered when they are seen through the eyes of those who make their living by trying to sell those trends. Canadian writers themselves may well have understood that writing in Canada was undergoing a profound shift in the years between the wars, but they failed to translate this understanding into the kind of material that would have allowed agents such as Hedges to recognize the presence of the shift. And because agents were increasingly responsible for identifying potential authors to American and British publishers who were demanding more modern forms of writing, it remained difficult for Canadian agents to promote Canadian material outside the country. One of the problems affecting the development of Canadian literature was a lack of literary agents who could inform Canadian writers about new trends in publishing (as Hedges tried to do in her address of 1947). But the absence of literary agencies was symptomatic of a lacklustre publishing industry that had failed to encourage the creation of a competitive Canadian book market. Canadian authors needed Canadian agents in order to become more saleable in foreign markets, but Canadian agents were few; Canadian agents needed Canadian authors in order to support their business model, but such authors were few, mainly because most authors still did not understand the benefits of literary representation, while those who did often sought it outside Canada. This situation persisted well into the 1970s. In the absence of Canadian agents, authors were forced to turn to independent business managers who acted as agents (Gabrielle Roy retained Jean-Marie Nadeau in this capacity in 1945) or to American agents (Hugh MacLennan signed with American agent Blanche Gregory, while Morley Callaghan worked with Ann Watkins and Harold Matson in New York).

In 1947, Hedges had taken on one Canadian author with strong potential. Hugh Garner had selected her to represent him for some of his short stories and for his well-known novel, *Cabbagetown*. The novel had been making the rounds of Canadian publishers since April 1946, when it was first submitted by Garner directly to John Gray at Macmillan, where it was reviewed by editor Peggy Blackstock. In response to comments provided by the publisher, Garner revised the manuscript and resubmitted it in December 1946. A month later, they returned it for more revisions. Macmillan was still not satisfied after the second resubmission and a review by Ellen Elliott in January 1947.[122]

Garner became impatient and turned to C.J. Eustace at J.M. Dent and Company in March 1947. Hedges was representing Garner at this point or soon after. Eustace, representing Dent, wrote to Garner on 7 November 1947, indicating that the publisher had asked Hedges to provide "the name of the American publisher to whom they have sent the manuscript" since Dent believed that "it would be most satisfactory to us if we could interest an American publisher in this book to share joint publication costs with us, as we feel that we should like to be sure of the support of an American publisher first before making any publishing offer."[123] Dent also wanted revisions and wrote to Hedges in an undated letter (probably mid-November 1947), asking to see the manuscript again once revised, and reiterating their conviction that "it should find an American market."[124]

Garner was frustrated and decided to try yet another house. On 5 February 1948, he turned to Robin Ross-Taylor of William Collins & Sons, summarizing "the story of CABBAGETOWN to date" and enclosing the most recent version of the manuscript. He mentioned his frustration with Dent and noted that while they were considering *Cabbagetown*, Hedges had also been "trying, unsuccessfully, to market some of my short stories."[125] Garner asked that any suggestions for revisions be sent directly to him, along with the manuscript: "I am sure that Mrs. Hedges will not think that I am usurping her prerogatives if you mail the mms. directly to me at the address on the letterhead. I will write to her and explain that it will save time and money for the book to come to me direct."[126] This was not correct protocol. Garner was indeed "usurping her prerogatives." Since Hedges was Garner's agent, the correspondence should have gone through her office and Garner should not have been dealing directly with Collins. When the manuscript and accompanying comments were returned to her with collect postage, she expressed her dissatisfaction with Garner by forwarding the manuscript to him again, also by collect post. In an undated letter to Ross-Taylor, Garner recounted Hedges's response:

> I picked up my manuscript of CABBAGETOWN on Saturday from the express office where it had been forwarded by Mrs. Hedges from Montreal. Accompanying it I received a terse note asking me what my reaction was to the turn of events. I am not sure whether she was prompted by exasperation with me or whether it was because you had sent it to her "Express Collect." She sent it to me the same way so I suppose that it evened things up. It is the first time that I ever received a manuscript back this way, and all I can make of it is that somebody is mad as hell about something.[127]

It is not surprising to imagine that Hedges was "mad as hell." She had obviously been working on Garner's material, and now he was bypassing her to deal with a publisher directly. Nothing undermines an author–agent relationship more than that kind of end run. But Hedges should have done more to communicate with Collins on Garner's behalf, and the fact that Garner wrote to the publisher directly is also evidence of her inexperience as an agent. Most agents will advise an author to stand back from all negotiations until a book contract is signed. Not surprisingly, Garner decided to terminate his relationship with Hedges. In his letter to Ross-Taylor, he notes that "Hedges and Southam are no longer acting as my literary agents. From here on in I will do my own huckstering, and I hope that you will allow me to let you see some of my stuff in the future."[128]

From this point on, Garner developed a direct relationship with Collins, who eventually published the novel. Later, he established a relationship with two New York agents: briefly, with David Lloyd, and for a more extended period with Willis Kingsley Wing, who was eager to represent Canadian authors and who recognized that his American counterparts had generally ignored them. Wing discovered that the contract Garner had signed with Collins gave them world rights to his first novel, *Storm Below* (1949), and options on his two next works. Wing convinced Garner that relinquishing such rights had been a mistake. Marc Fortin writes: "Although he felt confined by this agreement, Garner learned to manipulate the contracts to his benefit as much as possible, and went on to sell three more works to Collins."[129] In his study of Garner's correspondence, Fortin makes some important observations about the ways in which Garner came to understand author–agent relations:

09

109 Uno Drive,
The Queensway,
Toronto 14, Ont.

Mr. R. Ross Taylor,
William Collins & Sons,
70 Bond St., Toronto.

Dear Mr. Taylor:-

I picked up my manuscript of CABBAGETOWN on Saturday from the express office where it had been forwarded by Mrs. Hedges from Montreal. Accompanying it I received a terse note asking me what my reaction was to the turn in events. I am not sure whether she was prompted by exasperation with me or whether it was because you had sent it to her "Express Collect". She sent it to me the same way so I suppose that it evened things up. It is the first time that I ever received a manuscript back this way, and all I can make of it is that somebody is mad as hell about something.

From the above, and from your letter of last week, I gather that you are not interested in the publication of my book. I am sorry that you have decided not to bring it out. I was looking forward to receiving from you a more detailed summary of your criticisms and suggestions, and of working on CABBAGETOWN for the next couple of months with the hope that it would be published in the fall. I am not sure just what I am going to do with the book now, but I am unwilling to go ahead with the amount of work involved in carrying out your suggestions unless I receive more assurance than I have of your intentions toward it. Perhaps your outside reader's reactions were unfavorable, or perhaps you decided that it was not good enough for publication. Whatever it was I would have appreciated your telling me. During my sojourn among the publishers I have built up a protective screen against the things they say and write to me, so that sometimes it is hard for me to distinguish between a pat on the back and a kick in the nuts.

However, about CABBAGETOWN, de mortui nil nisi bonum. Let me take this opportunity of thanking both you and Mr. Sweeney for your courtesy and understanding in my meetings with you. I well realize that my manners and appreciation of what you have tried to do for me have not been of the best; I assure you that it is an aquired trait.

Hedges and Southam are no longer acting as my literary agents. From here on in I will do my own huckstering, and I hope that you will allow me to let you see some of my stuff in the future. This summer I intend to finish my book about the navy, and I am seething with ideas about a novel dealing with the decline and apprehension of a sexual psychopath. (Don't tear this up yet, I have not turned existentialist or anything).

I hope to see you again soon and until then, my thanks for your interest, and my best regards.

Hugh Garner

Figure 3.6
Letter from Hugh Garner, 1948

Garner employed two New York City author's agents in his early career, starting with David Lloyd, with whom he severed ties in July 1949, and then quickly moving over to Willis Kingsley Wing, who wrote Garner requesting that he have Collins keep the Canadian rights to *Storm Below*, so that Wing could negotiate for British and American publishing contracts. Collins, however, had British and American rights to *Storm Below*, and Garner wrote Wing on October 10, 1949 stating that Collins had not found British or American publishers for the book, and how disappointed he was with the sales of his critically acclaimed work. Garner explained how he would prefer "American publication first, or in conjunction with Canadian publication" (Garner). In his letter to Wing, Garner outlined the terms of his agreements with Collins, pointing out that Collins had an option on the next two novels written by Garner, although Garner now realized he was unhappy with this situation. Garner spoke with Charles Sweeney at Collins, and in a further letter to Willis Kingsley Wing, it can be seen how Garner was slowly coming to see how the publishing industry worked from the inside. Wing responded to the ongoing disagreement by arguing for complete control over all American rights for Garner's works, not only if Collins failed to find an American publisher. Garner's response was that he had offered Collins his latest book, was completely destitute, yet despite his financial situation, would not sign any new contract with Collins until Wing had read it over. Garner makes it very clear that he is uncomfortable with this proposal, and the dispute between American and Canadian publishing rights. Wing read through Garner's first contract, and explained to Garner that Collins, in fact, had all the rights to his first book, as well as his next two books in Canada, the United States, and Britain. Wing pointed out the problems with the contract, and Garner responded by claiming that the only reason he signed it was from "inexperience," and a few weeks later called his contract with Collins & Sons a "bondage."[130]

By the spring of 1948, Hedges's agency was slowing down. On 22 March of that year she received a letter from Xenia Seriabine with the Bradley agency in Paris, informing Hedges that "after all this time, I have no good news to give you about your books. All the publishers who saw them declined them so far, and I am afraid we shall be unable to do anything."[131] Seriabine concluded her letter by noting that "the situation in the French publishing field is terrible and difficulties are growing every day."[132] To add insult to injury, this bad news was conveyed to Hedges by an employee of the Bradley Agency, rather than by Jenny Bradley herself. In other words, the French agency had determined that Hedges and Southam no longer merited direct communication from the top.

This may have been the message that prompted Hedges to close her agency. But it did not stop her from pursuing her own career as a writer. In fact, Hedges redoubled her efforts as an author and soon began to turn her attention to writing fiction that might sell. To this end, she was gratified to learn, in March 1948, that one of her stories, "The Boxing Lesson," had been chosen by the CAA and La Société des Écrivains Canadiens to represent Canada in the 1948 arts competitions at the Summer Olympic Games in London.[133] This was indeed an honour, although few readers today are aware that there was once a literary component to the Olympic Games. From 1912 to 1952 the Olympic Games included an arts component that ran along with the sports competitions. The idea was originated by Baron Pierre de Coubertin, who conceived of the modern Olympic games, which began in 1896 under his direction. By 1906, de Coubertin was promoting the arts competitions to the International Olympic Committee. He encouraged the members of the committee to endorse his plan "to reunite in the bonds of legitimate wedlock a long-divorced couple – Muscle and Mind."[134] As Richard Stanton explains, de Coubertin was influenced by the work of John Ruskin, "who was one of the first art theorists to link moral and social reform with the idea of aesthetics and art education."[135] He was also inspired by Dr Thomas Arnold, the headmaster of England's Rugby School, who promoted "an educational system that incorporated sport and athleticism as part of its institution of learning."[136] After years of lobbying, de Coubertin managed to establish an arts component for the 1912 games in Stockholm, with submissions in architecture, music, painting, sculpture, and literature.

All entries to what was commonly known as the "Pentathlon of the Muses" were required to incorporate the theme of sport in one way or another. Although the arts competitions were often seen as a sideshow to the main event, the exhibition of arts entries became a popular part of the Olympics from 1912 to 1936. The Olympics were cancelled in 1940 and 1944 as a result of the Second World War. They returned in 1948, but the new IOC president, Avery

Brundage, wanted to retain a sports-only focus. Brundage prevailed, and the Olympic Arts Competitions were phased out after the summer 1948 games. However, this did not lessen the prestige of those artists who had been selected to represent Canada at the Olympics in London that year.

In the case of Hedges, the question was how she would use that success to bolster her profile as a writer and businesswoman. One also wonders whether nepotism had anything to do with Hedges's success in this competition. After all, her uncle, Sidney Dawes, was a member of the Olympic Committee the year that Hedges was awarded the prize, and she and Geoffrey had visited with Sidney and his wife in Murray Bay in August 1947, at precisely the time that the committee was determining who should be awarded the prize.[137] In an article announcing the selection of Hedges's story as Canada's literary entrant for the 1948 games, the *Gazette* provided a short summary of the author's career, based in part on an interview with Hedges. She was not modest. "Inspiration is all right, Mrs. Hedges said yesterday, but it must be poured into a technically perfect medium."[138] Hedges also argued that the contemporary writer needed courage: "In the writing field, courage is the key to success: courage forces the writer to think of and interpret the present which is his highest duty toward the reading public."[139] Hedges was keen to establish a link between her success in the arts competition and her experience as a literary agent. She used the opportunity to link her "cosmopolitan education" to Hedges and Southam. And then she made an eyebrow-raising claim: "The year-old Hedges & Southam venture has already handled some 2,000 manuscripts sent by approximately 1,000 clients, a large number of whom are veterans of the Second World War."[140]

This is a revealing statement in many ways. In order to understand the extent to which Hedges wildly exaggerated the success of her agency, as she did other aspects of her career, it is useful to stand back and put the nature of that agency in perspective. By April 1948, Hedges and Southam had been in business for sixteen months. They had placed two advertisements regarding the agency since its founding. A new business does not operate at full capacity overnight. It might take years for a literary agency to establish a viable list of clients, and any agency that had one thousand clients in 1948 would have been the largest literary agency in the world. Moreover, Hedges claims that these one thousand clients had produced two thousand manuscripts, even though most of those clients were war veterans. This raises the obvious question: when did these veterans write all those works? How did one thousand veterans, who had returned from the war over the past two years, manage to write so much so quickly, and could it all have been good enough to make the cut at a demanding literary agency? Were all of those veterans writing poetry and fiction in their spare time? After all, newly returned from the front, they felt a pressing need to find employment. If we assume that Hedges agreed to represent only the best of the work she received, her claims become even more absurd, since in order to choose the one thousand clients she says she represented, she must have considered the work of thousands more (agencies typically accept a meagre 1 per cent of the submissions they receive).[141] And in order to consider the manuscripts of so many thousands of writers, she would have had to be assisted by a fairly large staff. That large staff would need a large office.

This observation made me wonder about the physical offices of Hedges and Southam. They must have been grand, I thought. But how to verify that assumption? The only way to determine the size of the Hedges and Southam offices in room 333 of the Dominion Square Building was to seek out the blueprints of that building. Fortunately, the original blueprints are housed in the Centre for Canadian Architecture in Montreal. The third-floor plan of the Dominion Square Building shows the offices leased by Hedges and Southam quite clearly.

The blueprint scale is ¼″ = 1 foot. Using this scale, we can calculate that the office of Hedges and Southam was approximately 350 square feet without any furnishings. If we subtract the square footage of space taken by, say, two desks at 20 square feet each, we are down to 310 square feet. Then we need to deduct the space taken by the many filing cabinets required to organize the two thousand manuscripts Hedges says she was handling. A four-drawer filing cabinet would hold about 150 manuscripts. Even if Hedges had jettisoned half of the manuscripts she says she was representing, that would still leave one thousand manuscripts, which would occupy about seven filing cabinets, each filled to the brim. Each cabinet occupies 4.5 square feet; six would occupy 27 square feet. So the available floor space in the office is down to 283 square feet. Add a few chairs and a coat stand and the room becomes even smaller. The bottom line is that Hedges claims to have been handling two thousand manuscripts by one thousand authors out of an office that barely had enough open floor space for two people to move between desks. It sounds impossible. It was.

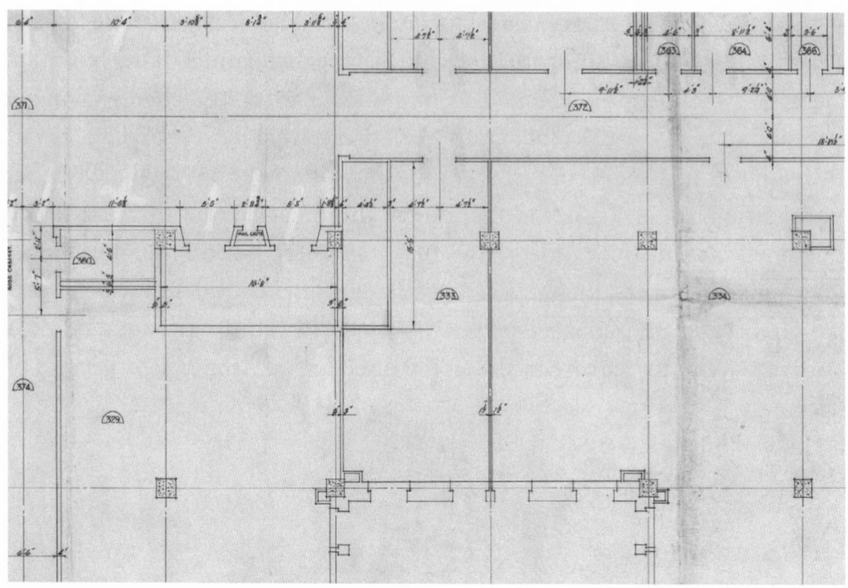

Figure 3.7
Hedges, Southam and de Merian office plans, 1947, Ross & Macdonald, architects. Partition layout of third floor for Dominion Square Building, Montreal (detail), 1929, ink on linen, 95 x 147.7 cm.

The above digression may seem flippant, but it is one of the few instances where Hedges's hyperbolic statements concerning her career can be logically undercut to reveal a particular aspect of her personality: her willingness to promote herself by framing her achievements in larger-than-life terms. This is not a negative comment on Hedges. In fact, it is her penchant for exaggeration, her imaginative forms of self-representation, that set her apart from most other writers of her time. She was in many respects a colourful operator who knew how to leverage her accomplishments to maximize her career. This aspect of her personality has been entirely erased, along with her career in general.

After 1948, the trail goes cold on Hedges's agency. There is no listing for the business in the 1949 Montreal telephone directory. No advertisements for the agency appear that year. And of the thousands of manuscripts Hedges claims to have handled, none can be found. Neither can any correspondence between Hedges and those thousands of authors she claims to have represented. There are no records of any sales. The scant correspondence that does remain suggests that Hedges simply abandoned the project sometime in 1948. Perhaps this had something to do with the changing fortunes of her husband, Geoffrey, who had been named Commissioner of the Quebec Provincial Division of the Canadian Red Cross Society in early 1948. Or perhaps it was the result of her own sense of accomplishment as a result of the Olympic nomination. In any case, she abandoned the agency and went on to write poetry and, for the first time, novels that would find publication in Canada, the United States, and England. In the next chapter, I consider the poetry and fiction that Hedges published between 1949 and 1952, three years that marked a turning point in her career, and in the direction of Canadian writing.

CHAPTER 4

1949–1952

The summer of 1948 marked a tumultuous moment in the history of Canadian culture. On 9 August sixteen members of the Automatistes group of artists in Quebec, including Jean-Paul Riopelle and Paul-Émile Borduas, released Refus Global, an explosive manifesto announcing a revolt against the conservatism of Quebec society and the Catholic Church. The manifesto called for a "resplendent anarchy" that would replace the authority of the church and conservative academic pedagogy with a new political order celebrating abstraction, internationalism, and a wholesale interrogation of the status quo. The sixteen signatories of the document rejected capitalism, history, government, authority, and all of the narratives that had subjugated various forms of artistic freedom and creativity, especially in Quebec.

One can speculate about the extent to which the release of this radical document affected Hedges. Like many established anglophones, she might have embraced the liberal, anti-communist ideology implicit in the document. As Judith Ince explains, francophone liberals denounced the publication, while anglophone liberals tended to endorse it:

> The hostile reception given the Refus Global within Quebec, however, was also a function of a fact uniterated by the liberal francophone press: although the manifesto's vociferous denunciation of communism conformed with a fundamental tenet of liberalism, its attack on other, equally important components of liberalism was the real motivation for liberal condemnation of the manifesto.
>
> While francophone liberals inveighed against the Refus Global as too dogmatically polemical and as an effrontery to universal truths, anglophone liberals lionized it. The state of English Canadian liberalism in 1948 largely explains why it supported this group of French-

> speaking artists. To be a liberal in postwar English Canada signified a repudiation of both the radical left and the reactionary right … The war on the right was to be waged against Duplessis, regarded by anglophone liberals as the incarnation of corrupt conservatism. Significantly, it was the Automatistes' apparent denunciation of the Quebec status quo and Duplessist values which secured their esteem among English Canadian liberals … The Automatistes' antagonism towards the status quo per se responded to another area of liberal thought: anticommunism. To anglophone liberals, hostility towards the status quo symbolized the vitality of Western-style freedom, in contrast to communist regimes where dissent was not tolerated … While hostility towards the left and right was perceived as a manifestation of cultural liberation by anglophone liberals, they simultaneously defended the notion of political contentless art. "Political content" was generally understood as Marxist content.[1]

If liberal anglophones welcomed the challenge to the status quo embodied in Refus Global, their French counterparts had little patience for its broad-based rejection of Quebec values. The release of Refus Global initiated a fierce storm in the French media: "some 100 articles, almost all of them negative, came out immediately after it was launched."[2] Faced with unrelenting criticism in French Canada, Borduas (often seen as the central figure inspiring the group) was forced to resign his teaching position at l'École du Meuble. Dealers refused to accept his paintings. Galleries locked him out. His wife and children left him. In 1953, Borduas fled Quebec and moved to the US and then to France in 1955. The Automatistes drifted apart. Yet the impact of their radical stance, and their embrace of contemporary art forms – including Cubism and Surrealism – made a lasting mark on Quebec and Canadian art and shifted aesthetic values away from conservative forms in writing, painting, sculpture, and dance.

Given the earth-shaking impact of the Automatistes in French Quebec, and the extent of the controversies surrounding them, it is surprising to discover how little mention is made of the movement in the English press at the time. Even today, English coverage of the group and its collectively signed manifesto remains scant. The discrepancy between French and English responses to Refus Global gives new meaning to the concept of two solitudes that Hugh MacLennan captured in his novel of the same title. It was as if a powerful ideological earthquake had shaken Quebec's francophone art world to its core, while on the English side hardly a tremor was felt. In his commentary on Montreal life in the 1940s and 1950s, for example, William Weintraub makes no mention of the Automatistes at all, although he devotes generous space to the many writers and cultures that intermingled in Montreal in those years. Similarly, in his recent history of Canadian literature, *Arrival*, Nick Mount makes no mention of the movement either. What is even more surprising is Hedges's apparent ability to continue her writing in 1949 and the early 1950s as if nothing had changed or as if the movement did not have a profound effect on art and literature in Quebec. In those years, and earlier, she was living down the street from the very building in which the Automatistes had displayed some of their early and highly provocative artwork.[3]

Hedges was not alone in her conservatism or in her distance from experimentalism in art and literature. The novelists and short story writers who surrounded her were fundamentally realists engaged in mimetic pursuits, while the poets in her milieu were drawn more to modernist values than to the anti-hegemonic activities associated with abstract and surrealist art. Even in her family she could see resistance to the Automatiste aesthetic. Her cousin, Patricia Nora (Trudi) Dawes, had married Robert Wakeham Pilot in 1940. Pilot was an accomplished artist, to be sure, but one who had little in common with the likes of Riopelle and Borduas. A few years after the publication of Refus Global, Pilot was named president of the highly conservative Royal Canadian Academy of the Arts. He was primarily a landscape painter whose works were appreciated by Winston Churchill, Queen Elizabeth, and the Duke of Edinburgh. The mere mention of those quintessentially British names reminds one of just how tied Hedges was to the English community in Montreal. There is little evidence of her mingling with French intellectuals or artists, but that was not unusual in Montreal in the early 1950s, when parents often instructed their children never to go east of St Lawrence Boulevard, lest they be swallowed by the devil, who resided only on that side of the city, among the others, *les autres*, the French.

The separation between Hedges's world and the radical universe of the Automatistes was not a separation defined strictly by language: Hedges had been educated in France and Switzerland; she spoke French very well. Nor were these radical artworks being displayed in some far-flung corner of the city. Hedges was living on Sherbooke Street, home to most of the major art galleries at the time, including several that were exhibiting experimental and abstract art. The particular solitude she inhabited had much more to do with ideology, religion, and class consciousness rather than an inherent dislike for radical experimentation in art.

Hedges made no mention of the Automatistes in 1949 or the following year, but she did enter the fray, briefly, in a 1951 letter to the editor of the *Gazette*. The occasion was the display of a statue by Robert Roussil at the Agnes Lefort Gallery, which had opened in 1950 at 1028 Sherbrooke Street West (a few blocks away from Hedges's home at the time). At the request of the city's morality squad, a municipal court had ordered that the statue, called *La Paix*, be removed because Lefort had "violated a city ordinance by exhibiting a nude statue."[4] The statue showed a nude man and woman embracing and holding aloft a human embryo, over which hung a dove of peace. Before it was ultimately removed (by Roussil himself), the statue was vandalized by a city lawyer who believed it was obscene.

In its coverage of the story, the *Gazette* noted that "the display of nude or semi-nude statues in public places without the permission of the chief of police is forbidden under section nine of city by-law No. 1025."[5] The incident said a good deal about the moral climate in Montreal in the early 1950s. While municipal by-laws prevented the display of statues depicting nudity, the city itself was internationally renowned as a hot spot replete with brothels and strip clubs, many of which were controlled by organized crime. In 2015, the Centre d'histoire de Montréal held a special exhibition, called "Scandal! Vice, Crime and Morality in Montreal, 1940–1960," which illustrated the extent to which the city was known as the "Paris of North America."[6] As the exhibition's curatorial commentary makes clear, Montreal

> was one of the last cities on the continent to still have a functioning red-light district during the Second World War. Hundreds of brothels operated openly, a few yards away from the best-known nightclubs. Gambling dens and bookmaking counters proliferated downtown and spread to all four corners of the city, enriching gangs who were also involved in heroin trafficking. The police weren't doing enough to reassure honest citizens until the occurrence of shocking events provoked a major scandal.[7]

The "shocking events" revolved around the 1946 gangland slaying of Harry David, a mob boss who was shot dead in broad daylight in downtown Montreal (right around the corner from Hedges's agency office). The killing prompted citizens to demand a public inquiry into vice in the city. The Caron inquiry (1950–53) was formed in response to this demand. Anyone living in Montreal at the time could not have ignored the promiscuous aspects of city life, nor could they be under any illusion that this was a place where public morality necessarily prevailed. Yet there was the city's morality squad, insisting that a statue of a nude figure be taken down, a statue on display in the midst of an urban landscape that was internationally known for its sexual openness.

Notwithstanding the city's steamy reputation, Roussil could not have been very surprised by the police action. Two years earlier, another one of his statues, *La Famille*, had also been confiscated by police because it depicted nude figures. Part of the public resistance to Roussil's work had to do with his connection to the Automatistes, who were generally perceived to be following amoral practices in their anti-conservative art. In her letter to the editor of 8 March 1951, Hedges applauded Lefort's stand "in refusing to allow the police to remove the figure from her property."[8] Hedges felt that "the figure seems to be lumpy and confused, and somewhat unduly preoccupied with the generative symbols," but she notes that she liked *La Famille*, which she had seen first "in an open field near the sculptor's home in Cartierville, where I had gone expressly, on a rainy night to boot, to see it for myself."[9] She recalls that "I had heard that Mr. Roussil had revolted against the more pedestrian materials, such as plasticine, and was trying to prove his theory that natural materials, such as wood, stone, etc., should be the medium of sculptors with serious intentions."[10] As to the controversy surrounding *La Paix*, Hedges argued that "I do not believe the statue will harm the sensibilities of anyone."[11] She added: "Perhaps if those who feel so deeply about it would bend their talents of reproof, and their watchdog instincts towards the curbing of big-time crime in this city, it would be a more effective use of moralistic energy and outraged citizenship."[12] Hedges made it clear that she was under no illusions about the city's moral profile.

Despite the image of self-sacrifice conveyed in her letter (it was a "rainy night" but Hedges willingly sacrificed herself "to boot" because of her deep commitment to art), it is clear that by this point Hedges's curiosity about Roussil's experimentation and his sculpting media had been genuinely provoked. It would have been difficult for her to avoid seeing Roussil's controversial statue outside the Lefort Gallery, since at that time she was living a few blocks from Lefort's establishment near the other fine art galleries on Sherbrooke. She was a neighbouring witness to the statue scandal.

On one hand, Hedges was exposed to a changing art world that was preoccupied with politics, radicalism, and a more open approach to sexuality. On the other hand, she remained caught up in an English social world that remained profoundly conservative. One aspect of that world was identified with McGill University. Every time Hedges looked out the window of her sixth-floor apartment at 900 Sherbrooke Street West, she was also looking over the McGill campus, a long-standing bastion of Englishness. When she left her apartment building, she entered the English world of downtown Montreal. For Hedges, as for many Montrealers, the city was bicameral. The majority of anglophone and francophone residents experienced the city from very separate perspectives and inhabited very different urban geographies, crossing lines only occasionally for city celebrations, shopping, financial matters, or rare social events.

Hedges invested in artistic traditions and remained interested in the same forms that had attracted her as a younger woman. She lived in the same Golden Square Mile of the city that she had inhabited since 1926. And she was attracted to events that were attached to the past. On 23 November 1949, to celebrate its twentieth anniversary, the Montreal Repertory Theatre performed W. Somerset Maugham's *The Constant Wife* at the Guy Street Playhouse. While Hedges chose to invest herself in the play she had acted in twenty years earlier (in this sense, not much had changed), other theatre venues were embracing an entirely different approach to set and costume design that reflected some of the radical shifts taking place in the art world (from this perspective, everything had changed).

The set for *The Constant Wife* was designed by Hans Berends, who was described as "l'auteur des décors réalistes qui font beaucoup pour créer l'ambiance de l'époque et donne un cadre approprié au sujet."[13] While Berends was attempting to create verisimilitude for English audiences, Alfred Pellan was doing just the opposite in French theatre, and he was doing it earlier. Pellan had returned to Montreal in 1940 at the beginning of the war, after studying art in Paris. In addition to producing Surrealist-influenced abstract paintings, Pellan engaged in stage and costume design. For example, in 1946, he designed the set and program for the French performance of Shakespeare's

Twelfth Night at the Théâtre Gesù. Danielle Léger describes Pellan's impact on the production this way:

> Cette production propose un « véritable poème plastique en mouvement » où « chaque personnage prend l'aspect d'un tableau surréaliste » et où les composantes scénographiques « recréent continuellement la symphonie visuelle ». L'artiste visuel Alfred Pellan (1906–1988) est l'auteur des décors, des costumes et des maquillages de ce spectacle, conférant une ampleur inédite au concept de « tableau vivant » et suscitant le débat autour de la création scénographique.[14]

Léger also describes the program, designed by Pellan:

> Exécutée d'après une gouache sur carton de 1946 intitulée *Le comédien,* la composition symétrique s'inspire des procédés cubistes et surréalistes. La figure stylisée du comédien y apparaît en fond de scène. Les visages qui bordent le plateau évoquent à la fois les pendrillons, ces rideaux étroits donnant accès aux coulisses, et les spectateurs.[15]

Although Hedges gives no indication that she attended French theatre performances, it seems clear that she remained curious about the challenges to convention embodied in the work of many francophone artists. It was almost as if she wanted to experience these new forms privately, as if she saw in them some kind of seductive transgression that she could not openly embrace. She made a private trip to see Roussil's controversial sculpture on a rainy night in order to satisfy her curiosity, or her longing. She wrote about works of art that were under attack for their depiction of the human body, but her letters intellectualized those works, allowing her to distance them from her immediate present. She could only touch so much. Her poetry became a means of embracing in words what she could not physically hold.

Hedges's third book with Ryerson, *Words on a Page*, appeared in 1949. Unlike Hedges's previous work, this was a conventional book with hardbound covers, rather than a chapbook. For this publication, Hedges paid the production costs of $405, which, her book contract states, "represents the actual manufacturing cost of $375 plus 8% tax." In return, Ryerson Press would pay Hedges a return on her subsidy at the rate of 81 cents per copy along with a royalty of 10 per cent of the list price, totalling $1.01 per copy. In order to break even, then, the book would have to sell four hundred copies. The arrangement spoke to the perilous state of the Canadian publishing industry at the end of the decade. Canadian publishing was still dominated by American and British publishing houses, and Canadian literature often took second place to works published in the US or overseas. Even today, any sale of more than five hundred copies of a book of poetry is considered better than respectable. The chances of Hedges breaking even on *Words on a Page* were remote. But because she had the funds to support such a publication, she was able to keep her work in front of the public, restricted as that public might have been.

It is difficult to determine whether the poems included in *Words on a Page* were written in close proximity to their date of publication, but in her acknowledgment to the volume Hedges notes that some of them had previously appeared in her two chapbooks – *The Flower in the Dusk* and *Crisis.* In one sense, then, she saw this book as a way of introducing readers to her work afresh, since the chapbooks had received such limited distribution. But it also signalled that Hedges's own aesthetic had not shifted much, despite the radical changes in the art world that she witnessed during this period.

The book opens with "Onwardness,"[16] which praises the way humans have "strong resolve / Not to be lost, nor wasted, nor destroyed." People want to "Buy survival at the end of time." But the age has led to alienation, to an inward-turning coldness, as she says in "Man Alone": "As we look pleading in our neighbour's face / We see within his unrelenting eyes / His own entrenched reflection, steely cold."[17] Other poems repeat the emphasis on loneliness and human fragility. In different ways, Hedges keeps coming back to the same question: How can humans be saved in the postwar world? Do religious and spiritual values still hold, or is it necessary to embrace a new order and to understand human actions in a new way? The question has implications for the poet as well. In "Withered Asters" (accepted by Earle Birney for publication in *Canadian Poetry* magazine in 1948) Hedges interrogates the poet's role:

Poets once gave us the stars, or pink asters
Saga and song and the whisper of leaves
At day's ending: the poet today is a man

With a flag, and a chip on his shoulder
His sounds like strong drink making froth
In his cup: so we laugh as we read
Or we sigh on a stumbling prayer
Of our own. A man is a man if he makes
His own verse, if hears the cock crow
Unafraid, and can smile at each dawning[18]

Hedges did not believe that poems should carry a political message. She also did not recognize that in one way or another, all poems are political. A poem about the dangers of writing political poetry is a political poem. A poem about a rose is also a political poem. Although Hedges would not explore this irony, her understanding of the ways in which poetry was changing had a direct impact on her sense of self. Often in her poems the speaker is divided between worlds, pulled in two directions at once. She was simultaneously self-assured and doubtful about her own role as a writer, as she confesses in "The Helpless Poet":

Have I the right to make a verse of this?
Man is a spectre, staring at Armistice,
Bending with swollen stomach on his land
The plowshares falling from his nerveless hand
Into the rubbled furrow, made by war[19]

While a number of the poems in *Words on a Page* represent attempts to come to terms with the devastation and identity loss associated with the war (illustrated by works written or published by Hedges between 1946 and 1948), others deal with issues that were of immediate concern in 1949, the year of the book's publication. For example, in "Strike," Hedges attempted to portray the effects of a prolonged labour strike on the household of one of the workers (the *Vancouver Sun* called it a "proletariat poem"),[20] a clear response to the labour unrest she saw around her. Two prominent strikes occurred in 1949: the Montreal teachers' strike (which ran for a week in January) and the bitter asbestos strike (which began early in February of that year). Both strikes were met with strong action by the Duplessis government, which was determined to crush the unions.

Hedges tried to imagine the mind of the striker and the price paid by his family for the labour action. Although Hedges had disavowed political poetry in "Withered Asters," here she was, writing political poetry about current events that were affecting daily life in the province and the city. Hedges imagines a conversation between the striker and his wife:

"Say, Charlie, did you pay
The grocer's bill? I told you to
Last week." His laugh is easy.
"Oh those guys are smart
Out there. If they say picket
Picket it is. They'll never let us starve."
"But Charlie," low, "there's just a hundred left
Only a hundred, say remember
We paid down a wad
On the new radio
And the dinner-set."[21]

That is the conversation indoors. Meanwhile, outside, the city is in chaos. There is a general sense of calamity:

The radio voice is choking out the news.
Ships cancelled! Power cut off!
Panic everywhere, people jamming
Into the trains, going and coming back
With glazing eyes, turned red
From fear, not hate[22]

What is Hedges's response to these events? While she might have had little sympathy for socialism and labour movements in general, she did feel for the families and individuals who were affected by the strike. She thought it was mobilized by hate, a by-product of the war ("Fear squeezes hate out"). Hedges's answer to this hate was to recommend love:

Oh, God, let me try loving now!
Oh, God, before it is too late
Let us try loving![23]

This did not seem like a practical suggestion, given the ferocity and the ramifications of the strikes. As Pierre Trudeau put it, the asbestos strike was "a violent announcement that a new era had begun."[24] He went on to describe his response to the profound changes in Quebec society associated with the strike:

> What I found … was a Quebec I did not know, that of workers exploited by management, denounced by government, clubbed by police, and yet burning with fervent militancy. I was later to describe the strike … as a "turning point in the entire religious, political, social, and economic history of the province of Quebec."[25]

Hedges's recommendation that this kind of militancy and violence could be resolved through love seemed a bit naive, to say the least. The events of the day could not simply be explained as "All violence, all war / Is someone's kiss ungiven," as Hedges suggests in her poem "History of a Kiss."[26] She seems to have read the increase in violent labour confrontations as a symptom of her own sense of loss and betrayal. That sense was often reflected in her more personal poems about love and passion. They are not accomplished poems, but they serve to reveal, sometimes obsessively, the extent to which Hedges struggled with the desire to confess, to say more, to display her innermost feelings about romance, sensuality, sex. Yet she could not do that completely. The love poems show her occupying a position on the edge of passion, ready to plunge in, to surrender to her desires, and then pulling herself back from that precipice so that we are always thinking: Tell us more, there is more.

Of the thirty-eight poems in *Words on a Page*, fifteen are concerned with love and desire. In "Shall We Dance?" the speaker waltzes with a former lover whom she thought was lost to another woman he met when he went overseas to fight in the war. She reasons: "A woman sleeping with another woman's man / In war can be forgiven if she keep / The centre pure."[27] In this case, her lover returns, minus a leg. But they are dancing and she has taken possession of him again. "Nostalgia" finds the speaker dreaming of a younger self "Taut with untried desire,"[28] as if that untried desire still haunts her and drives her on. Hedges includes "Invitation à la Valse," with its fantasy about a mystery lover and her dream of them together, "As though we had kissed warmly / Alone and happy in an empty room."[29] In "The Wave," the speaker likens her erotic fulfillment to the physical touch of the ocean waves ("I am a wave which dies against you" until "my bubbling whiteness spends itself").[30] Hedges sometimes thinks of sex in terms of violent imagery, as in "The Moment," when a fleeting feeling of attraction "is like a blade" that "ravishes in passing."[31] A similar image appears in "The Blade," which figures the speaker's lover with "the blade of passion held between your teeth," the same "blade of passion" that is "feeling for its mark."[32] Another reverie, "Reluctant Awakening," depicts its speaker dreaming of her lover. She is "Blind in the glare / Of Summer's lusty noon."[33] Hedges's romantic associations are typically aligned with the seasons. Spring and summer bring the heat associated with passion. In "Spring Fever," she lures her lover into the woods and is surprised by his or her ardour:

> It was I who proposed that we go
> You appeared to be cold
> How could I then know
> That your love was so bold?[34]

In "Saguenay," her male lover is a painter ("He with his colour and his brush").[35] She wonders how to seduce him with her words ("I with my words ready to drop / In patterns and seductive webs").[36] However, Hedges's poems about passion and desire are not always signed as heterosexual. This makes them more interesting. While clearly she imagines male lovers in many of her poems, others present a more ambiguously gendered lover. *Words on a Page* – the book – is packaged in tributes to Hedges on its front flyleaf. While some of the blurbs focus on Hedges's "fine perception" and "precision of phrase," others point to different aspects of her work. As an excerpt from the *British United Press* review says, "She can vividly lay bare a woman's heart." It is precisely that vividness that seems to attract the reviewer quoted at length on the book's back cover – Elizabeth Douglas in *The Montrealer*. What was it about Hedges's work that prompted Douglas to write at such length? She begins her commentary by claiming that "Of all the radio-speakers on questions of the hour, there is none better informed, more utterly honest and fearless and more patriotic than Doris Hedges," whose voice is "vital," and whose every talk is "impregnated with her passionate desire to help Canada." Douglas seems distracted by her own adjectives: "vital," "impregnated," "passionate." Soon, her narrative turns to Hedges's physical qualities, as if those had some bearing on the quality of her poetry:

> Photographs never capture her personality. Let me attempt to describe her. She looks about thirty-five, but states frankly she is over forty [Hedges was fifty-four years old at the time]. Her classic head is always groomed in the most practical way, which incidentally is most becoming. To an intimate friend the play and mood of her features is fascinating. Her eyes light the entire atmosphere, her colouring glows and she *lives* the idea, when the idea is for general good.

This kind of commentary is quite unusual for back cover copy. But then again, it was written by "an intimate friend" who was obviously attracted to Hedges. There is no hard evidence to suggest that Hedges was involved in any kind of romantic relationships outside her marriage to Geoffrey. On the other hand, he is never mentioned in any of her work, which returns frequently to the depiction of frustrated romance, the desire for another, the dream of living a different life. Hedges did not have to use Douglas's description of her physical appearance on the book cover. She chose to do so because it focused on her apparent youthfulness, on how she was "becoming" in the eyes of others, on the glowing colour of her complexion. In other words, part of the way Hedges chose to sell her book was by linking it to her physical appearance, an early example of her understanding that celebrity and physical attractiveness often went hand in hand.

The strategy employed on the back cover of *Words on a Page* provides insight into one prominent aspect of Hedges's personality: she was a relentless female self-promoter in a man's world. Hedges understood how difficult it was to break in, to gain recognition, to be judged a success. Even after her agency closed in apparent failure, she kept invoking her status as an agent and as a businesswoman in order to gain credibility in the public eye. By the same token, she saw her career as a broadcaster and public speaker as another means of establishing her credibility in a male-dominated system. And when she spoke to various audiences, she seldom missed the opportunity to promote her own achievements.

A good illustration of Hedges's self-promotional methods can be found in a speech she gave toward the end of 1949 to a group of patients at the Ste-Agathe branch of the Royal Edward Institute for Tuberculosis.[37] The talk presents insight into her poetic values. Hedges expresses her regard for the odes of the Greek poet Simonides, whom she read in translation. She mentions that her poem "Loneliness" was called "a modern example of the Classic

Ode" by Sir Andrew Macphail.[38] The concrete social function of the ode in ancient Greek culture spoke to her as a model for poetry's ideal role in modern society.

Then she lightens her talk with a humorous anecdote, describing an incident that happened the day before she was to give a spring lecture to McGill students on the topic of poetry:

> I mentioned this [lecture] by chance to a friend the evening before, and he asked me what my subject would be. When I replied "poetry", he exclaimed, "Poetry! At ten o'clock in the morning. Good God!"
>
> I mention the remark of this nice, perfectly well educated Montrealer, to illustrate what I think is a deplorable attitude towards poetry.[39]

For Hedges, poetry had to be concrete, understandable to the everyday reader. Ornate Romantic or experimental flourishes had no place in her poetics. She also believed that politics had little place in poetry. Hedges did not want to be a poet "with a flag" and she rejected the obscurity of much of the modernist verse that had gained prominence over the past decade. As she explained to her audience, "Poetry, you see, should be clear to the man on the street."[40] She added: "If it isn't, it misses its true function. Obscurity is out of date. What people long for is philosophy, and religion, and the truth, in simple form."[41]

Now Hedges segues into self-promotion. She complains that even though she and her audience "have had access to books all our lives," very few people take advantage of this privilege. She wonders why people will not invest in books and asks, "How can the writer exist if we don't buy his output?"[42] Perhaps this comment was prompted by Hedges's frustration with the sale of her own two chapbooks. She didn't mince words. Book buyers were skinflints: "People who would be ashamed to cadge for anything else they wanted will unhesitatingly pay $2.50 for a meal, or $5.00 for a theatre ticket, will think twice before spending a dollar-fifty on a book which will last them a lifetime."[43] Hedges presses the point by noting that in Great Britain, the average individual "spends about $2.00 a week on drink and tobacco and about four cents on books." She ends her complaint by making an observation that must surely have been the product of her brief experience as a literary agent: "unless you who read, will support Canadian writers by buying their books, the

Canadian writer will continue to be forced to go across the borders of this land in order to make enough money to live by his profession."[44]

One might feel considerable sympathy for the TB patients who had come to hear Hedges speak, only to be accused of being cheap, of not supporting Canadian writers, and of spending fifty times more on liquor and tobacco than they did on books. Their own condition as patients seemed to be untethered to the address. In fact, Hedges was there to ask them to spend money: "I wanted to make this plea for the Canadian writer, because we have very few opportunities to speak about ourselves, and I for one never miss one if I can help it. The younger writers need your help. And you in this hospital can exert a special influence on people to buy and enjoy books."[45] Was Hedges saying that the patients could exert this "special influence" because they were in a position of asking those who came to visit or who felt sorry for them to open up their wallets and invest in literature, especially at that time of year (Hedges noted that "we are now approaching Christmas")? Was she, in this way, actually exploiting the hospital patients to advance her own self-serving cause? The answer appears to be Yes.

The self-advertising continued. Hedges says she is glad to have been asked to speak about poetry because "poetry is not appreciated today, and especially is it not appreciated in this country."[46] Part of the reason for this lack of appreciation, she explains, is that contemporary poetry is too obscure ("I dislike abstract and obscure poetry because I mistrust it"). But Hedges notes that her own poetry offers an alternative that can be trusted because it achieves what so much other poetry doesn't: "*communication* between the poet and those who will read his poem." To this end, she tells her audience that "I propose to read to you some bits and pieces of rhythmic prose and also some verse, which I think will hold your attention, and say something to you."[47]

Before reading a number of her own poems, Hedges takes steps to ensure that her audience understands that she is about to offer them a satisfying alternative to other poetry of the day, as well as an alternative to contemporary fiction, which she pronounces boring: "if you want to read yourself to sleep, you might try some of the so-called modern novels going about, full of nothingness and vapid thoughts and unreal people. You'll sleep all right [*sic*]."[48] The alternative to this soporific modern fiction is clear: the writing of Doris Hedges. From this point on, Hedges engages in several forms of self-promotion. She talks about the lectures she gave to "the Women's Division of our Royal Canadian Air Force," how (unlike so many others) she is a careful reader of newspapers "from day to day and week to week," and how her singular attention to detail established her credibility "in newscasts on the radio."[49]

Hedges recalls the level of detail that informed her 1943 story, "I Put Away Childish Things," which had been published in *Good Housekeeping*. There could be no doubt, in Hedges's mind, that she had achieved massive success with this story because, after it was published, the magazine was "inundated by letters from all over the United States, to be forwarded to me, from people who had lived in Burma and who wanted to correspond with me as they thought I had just returned from the war there."[50] Hedges casts herself as a celebrity besieged by fans of her inimitable realism.

She ends her talk by returning to the subject of poetry. After providing a brief history of poetry (in about ten lines) she reads from her own work as a way of closing the lecture, including the poems "Loneliness," "The Wave," "Glass Houses" ("pirated all over the place" Hedges notes), "Helpless Poet," "Strike," "Poet's Protest," "The Flower in the Dusk," and "Prayer." The audience, upbraided for its stinginess and lack of taste, is finally subjected to Hedges's reading of eight of her poems, which would have occupied the major part of the so-called address. The sanitarium patients certainly got more (or less) than they bargained for.

Hedges used a similar form of self-promotion in a radio talk she delivered on 3 May 1950 entitled "The Poet and the Community."[51] It begins with the same anecdote she used in the TB hospital address, except that in this case the friend she meets who questions her interest in poetry becomes "a class of college students" that she had addressed. This provides a frame for a discussion of the poet's role, which Hedges orients toward the training of young people, particularly those who hope to become writers. Hedges argues that the age has produced a culture of philistines who care little for poetry, a "deplorable attitude towards one of the finest of the arts"[52] that also demonstrates "a lack of appreciation of the kind of brain the poet possesses." She says:

> The insecurity we feel today is not only material. It is also moral and spiritual. God seems to be nowhere. The scientist has taken God's place, and men run about wildly looking for some comfort, and some feeling of order which they cannot find. People are getting more and more frantic in their search for warmth and sunshine at the base of

> their roots. […] I have been asked to read some of my own poetry in this broadcast, so I will read the poem STRIKE, from my last book, WORDS ON A PAGE, because I think it illustrates the confusion of the world.[53]

Hedges reiterates her aesthetic principles, emphasizing clarity of expression in poetry and how its function and purpose are to move her readers. "The poet should bring his verse into the people's lives through the medium of sheer clarity and pleasure."[54] She also claims to abhor art for profit's sake and to hate how "nothing flourishes except those products which can bring in money."[55] She then expresses a deep nostalgia for "simple things" and a disdain for "abstractionism in paintings and obscurantism in poetry," which, she argues, "lead to nowhere" other than "blind alleys of undisciplined self-expression."[56]

Hedges did not offer much solace to those members of her broadcast audience who hoped to become poets: "I do not recommend any young writer who must earn his or her living, to attempt to do so by writing and publishing poetry! Unless these writers are very exceptional indeed, they will starve like the poet Chatterton, in an attic."[57] To put it bluntly, Hedges said, "there is no money in poetry. It is as simple as that. Poetry has prestige value, and very little else today."[58] Clearly, Hedges was preoccupied with the devaluation of poetry in favour of literature that could generate a profit. Prospective authors were living at a time when "nothing flourishes except those products which can bring in money."[59] The negativity did not stop there. Hedges felt that students did not truly enjoy reading poetry. Rather, "poetry is read forcibly by students, written by a few fanatics, and bought hardly at all."[60] Meanwhile, classroom teachers were doing little to remedy the situation because, lacking discernment, they pursued the latest literary fad rather than more demanding poetry. Hedges argued that "it is impossible for young people to make judgements on what is bad, unless they are first fully instructed in what is good."[61] Why has poetry failed to attract an audience? Why are teachers so misguided when they talk about poetry? Why does no one buy it? Hedges proposed this answer:

> The mass of people we call the public, are today under a terrific strain of fear, and are haunted by a sense of insecurity. Poetry, generally speaking, is not down to earth enough to reach the heart of the

> ordinary man. It is fashionable in these days, to laud the novelist and decry the poet. Partly, this is because there is a particular school of poets who deliberately, or through lack of technique, make their poetry ineffective, from a human point of view, by being obscure in meaning. The ordinary man in the street cannot understand that kind of poetry, and who can blame him?[62]

In order to avoid this obscurity, the teacher, like her students, needs to be schooled in good taste because "taste is a matter of training" but "we are gradually but perceptively, dulling our sense of good taste in all things, including art and literature and human relationships."[63] Hedges speaks about how "a poet's idea germinates for a long time" in the poet's mind "before image becomes clear to him."[64] She claims the world's lack of regard for poetry is a terrible omen for the future and reflects the desperate state of the world, although she never offers a reasonable explanation for this occurrence.

Hedges goes on to compare the differing methods employed by novelists and poets. She observes that "the fiction writer takes material into his mind, sieves it through" while "by contrast, the poet very seldom writes directly about what he sees. The idea germinates more slowly."[65] In other words, novels were fundamentally mimetic, the product of a rational winnowing process on the part of the writer, while poetry was metaphoric, transformational, and not necessarily tethered to immediate reality. The same year, Hedges wrote another public address, titled "The Mind of the Poet." It developed a number of the themes explored in the earlier broadcast, particularly the idea that "the mind of the poet is necessary to civilized life" but that civilization "is at a low ebb" because "the poet is not accepted as being as important as the novelist."[66]

Hedges had not yet written a novel, but that would soon change. One of the factors influencing her decision to undertake a novel was no doubt the impact of the Massey Commission hearings in 1949 and 1950 and the release of its influential report in 1951. Hedges's *Dumb Spirit: A Novel of Montreal* appeared the following year. In January of 1953, the YM-YWHA *Beacon* listed *Dumb Spirit* as one of many recent Canadian novels that demonstrated the resurgence of literary culture following the Massey Report. The *Beacon* observed that "at the close of 1952, it is well to take a retrospective glance back over the year and to recall some of the more significant recent Canadian publications which, in encouragingly increasing numbers are justifying the hopes engendered by the Massey report."[67]

As a former literary agent and aspiring novelist, it would have been difficult for Hedges to ignore the events leading up to the creation of the commission, which was established in order to address the state of the arts and culture in Canada following the Second World War. As Paul Litt observes in his study of the origins and operation of the commission, the Liberal government of Louis St Laurent initiated the study in response to a growing sense of cultural nationalism that emerged in the years following the war, and to sustained frustration in the arts community about the absence of supportive government action on its behalf. At a conference in Kingston, Ontario, in June 1941 – "the first national conference of artists in Canadian history"[68] – creators gathered to express concern "about their marginal status in Canadian society"[69] and "to lobby the government for support."[70] Three years later, on 21 June 1944, a collective of artists' groups engaged in a march on Ottawa in order "to win recognition of their importance in the life of the nation."[71] Although Brooke Claxton – then the minister of national defence in Mackenzie King's government – became the chief proponent of establishing a commission that would investigate the status of the arts in Canada in the postwar years, the Commission itself did not become a reality until 1949. As Litt says, "by establishing the Massey Commission the [St Laurent] government implied that it had a more general responsibility in cultural affairs and that it intended to approach this responsibility in a more conscious and coordinated fashion."[72]

Central to the focus of the Massey Commission was the problem of dealing with the incursion of American culture. The subject had first been addressed legislatively in the War Exchange Conservation Act (1940) and, later, by the Foreign Exchange Conservation Act (1947), both of which attempted to manage American cultural influx. But the Massey Commission took a broad approach to the realization that in broadcasting, entertainment, and the arts in general, Canada was dominated by American values and American productions. The idea was to turn the tide in favour of Canadian content and Canadian producers. This shift was catalyzed by the creation of the Canada Council for the Arts in 1957. But the transformation of the cultural landscape took place slowly. So much had to change, especially in publishing. It is worth noting the frequently cited figures in the Massey Report concerning the state of Canadian publishing when the commission was announced in 1949. In the report, the commission provides a table comparing the number of novels and books of poetry published in Canada in 1947 and 1948 to the number in the US and Great Britain (see table 4.1).[73]

As the table indicates, the number of novels published by English Canadian writers had actually decreased significantly over a year. Any novelist who hoped to be published in Canada faced steep resistance, with only fourteen novels published in 1948. The commission articulated a number of the challenges facing Canadian publishers that contributed to this paltry number. It gathered information from across Canada by holding a series of public meetings and by receiving briefs from a wide range of individuals and arts groups. In Montreal, hearings were held from 23 November to 6 December 1949. During those hearings the commission heard from a local critic who summed up the challenges facing Canadian novelists:

> A critic in Montreal has said to us that too often our publishers, through lack of courage or imagination, neglect an opportunity to launch a good Canadian author and thus increase their business. We were reminded that it was an American publisher who undertook to translate and publish in English *Bonheur d'Occasion* by Gabrielle Roy, easily the most successful Canadian book internationally since the war. The Canadian publishers also missed their chance with Edward Meade's novel, *Remember Me.* It was published by a British firm in London and ten thousand copies were sold in a few months in Great Britain alone. We learned that Canadian book sellers ordered only fifteen hundred copies for sale in Canada, and that no Canadian publisher has undertaken to issue a reprint. Canadian publishers are, of course, not alone in this matter; since publishing began the history of literature is marked by similar miscalculations. In Canada, no doubt as in other countries, the publisher may sometimes with justice complain that the writer wants inspiration, while the writer may retort that the publisher lacks acumen.[74]

We have no idea whether Hedges attended the public hearings in Montreal, but we do know that she was in the city during those hearings, since they were scheduled around the same time she addressed the TB patients in

Table 4.1
Book publication statistics from Massey Report, 1951

1947	Fiction	Poetry and drama	General
Britain	1723	352	243
United States	1307	463	224
Canada (English-speaking)	34	40	8
1948			
Britain	1830	423	180
United States	1102	504	295
Canada (English-speaking)	14	35	6

Ste-Agathe. If she was indeed present at any of those commission meetings, it could not have been encouraging. What then did the publication of her first novel in 1952 signify in terms of a changing publication climate in Canada following the release of the commission's report? Although the YM-YWHA bulletin would have us believe that its release encouraged the publication of more Canadian novels in Canada, the fact is that it remained difficult for Canadian writers to find Canadian publishers. Often, as was the case with Hedges, publication venues still had to be found outside Canada. But here the situation could be deceiving. For example, *Dumb Spirit* was published by Arthur Barker, a British publisher. Yet most Canadians understood it to be published by McClelland and Stewart in Toronto since that is how it was advertised. However, no copies can be found of the title bearing the M & S imprint. It appears that in this case, and probably in others, McClelland and Stewart was simply acting as the Canadian distributor for a title published outside the country. The Canadian publishing industry was not yet ready to take many risks on new writers, as the Massey Commission's table makes clear.

What was it that led Hedges to Arthur Barker? It is an intriguing question because it bears on the way Hedges understood her opportunities as a writer in the postwar years. There is not much information on Arthur Barker. He founded his publishing company in 1932. Barker seems to have been mainly interested in thrillers, ghost stories, and tales of the supernatural. This might account for his interest in Hedges's *Dumb Spirit*, which is certainly a kind of ghost story. Perhaps Hedges knew about Barker through her brief stint as a literary agent. Or perhaps she came into contact with him through Noel Langley, whose novel *The Rift in the Lute* (also known as *The Innocent Abroad*) was published by Barker in the same year as Hedges's novel (Barker published only two novels that year). Langley also wrote fantasy fiction and is best remembered as the writer who successfully adapted *The Wizard of Oz* for MGM's film production.

If Hedges knew Langley, it might have been through her role as an agent, but it might also have been through his activities with the Canadian navy, in which he mysteriously enlisted during the war, but that is a long shot. Or it may have been because Barker was willing to accept subsidies from authors seeking publication, although there is no evidence to suggest this was the case. Hedges was not averse to funding her own books: she financed the Ryerson publication of *Words on a Page* and later would help cover the costs of her other novels and books of poetry. Finally, it may have been because Barker saw in *Dumb Spirit* a captivating and original story. Yet the subject matter of the book seems far removed from the kind of exotic titles that attracted Barker, unless Barker considered the city of Montreal and the characters depicted in the novel to be exotic fare in 1952. *Dumb Spirit* did not receive many reviews. But one British reviewer welcomed the novel because of the accuracy of its depiction of Canadian life (the book *is* subtitled "A Novel of Montreal"). The *Evening Standard* called it "an extraordinarily mature first novel … not only are all the characters convincing and well drawn, but the depth of vision shown by the writer is astounding."[75]

Whatever the reasons accounting for Barker's publication of the book, it can certainly be said that it was like no other Canadian novel, before or since. *Dumb Spirit* is a story told mainly by Waldo, a reincarnated dog. Waldo once inhabited the body of John Barton, an aspiring young Montrealer who rose in the ranks to become a foreman at a local truck factory. When the factory workers he is supposed to manage start to embrace communist causes – to "further the cause of brotherhood" according to one worker[76] – it falls to Barton to ensure that the factory will not suffer from any labour disruptions (the novel appeared soon after the two major labour strikes in Montreal in 1949 and two years after Joseph McCarthy began to claim that communists had infiltrated the US State Department).

Despite its response to the political realities of the day, *Dumb Spirit* is also a novel about "spirit." In this sense, it posits the existence of a spiritual world

Figure 4.1
Doris Hedges, 1952

that had little to do with day-to-day events. In exploring the idea of reincarnation through Waldo, Hedges was also conveying aspects of her personal attraction to spiritualism and theosophy,[77] which remained popular in Canada in the postwar years.[78] In her address titled "The Mind of the Poet" Hedges speaks about the poet in theosophical terms, pointing to "consciousness, perception, imagination, the curious flair that poets have for penetrating through the current veil to the future, and a sixth sense, or keen awareness of the Now, the present moment."[79] For her, "it is through his imagination that a poet reaches an affinity with the truth, and transmits the pattern of that truth into an image which can be clearly understood."[80] In conceiving the novel, Hedges seemed to be torn between the desire to appeal to cultural elitists who flirted with theosophy while at the same time attracting a popular audience that might appreciate the gimmicky and offbeat resurrection conceit embodied in the eccentric Waldo.

While a number of Hedges's poems articulate this spiritualist perspective, there is no evidence to indicate that Hedges participated actively in theosophical societies, nor is there any indication that she was reading theosophical works. However, the discourse she employs in discussing the mind of the poet certainly focuses on theosophical watchwords and ideas: penetrating the veil, apprehending a sixth sense, manifesting an awareness of a capitalized "Now," realizing an "affinity with the truth," entering "the present moment" through "consciousness." In creating Waldo as a resurrected being, Hedges encourages us to see the dog as a spiritual vehicle, as a form of consciousness that is capable of apprehending right and wrong and of returning, from another plane in another time, to address his previous and present life. But on a much more basic level, Waldo is obviously created as a humorous device. In this sense, he has two sides. He is both a spiritualized body and a physically present observer in terms of his ability to witness current events.

Because he is slow to deal with the scheming communist factory workers (some of whom he thinks are foreigner infiltrators), Barton is fired from his position. He chooses to enlist in the army and is sent to fight on the African front. There, attempting to save himself from an aerial bombing, he fails to rescue one of his fellow soldiers, a man who once aligned himself with the communists in the Montreal factory. Barton never makes it to safety. He is killed in the attack. When we meet him in the novel, he has come back as Waldo, who thinks like Barton and tries to act like Barton. The only problem is that this version of Barton inhabits the body of a demanding puppy who is quickly becoming a large dog. Perhaps this transformation is not that odd. Or as Waldo puts it, "How do we know all dogs weren't human once?"[81]

Waldo has human impulses and desires associated with his former life. Yet he has not quite understood that he is no longer human and that when he talks the words come out as a whimper, or as a sharp bark. "Bits and pieces of man-memory plagued him."[82] His identity confusion is understandable. After all, Waldo can read. He likes to "swig" rye whiskey (Waldo's term for lapping it up when guests spill it on a carpet). He can remember himself as a young boy, posing for a photograph "with a Victorian chair under one elbow, and a coy expression."[83] And he can critique the way in which Canadian women are treated by men: "They were lousy with women. They knew so little about the fine art of handling them, mentally or physically."[84] He is also a voyeur: "It was entertaining, watching other people making love and all that, and there was a faint excitement in being able to snuggle down under the breasts of a pretty girl without causing a ripple of resentment."[85] Waldo has opinions about Canadians and what he calls "their sex repressions."[86] And he has a strong sense of the risks associated with big business: "Blood pressure. Arthritis. Thrombosis. Apoplexy. Nervous breakdowns. That's what you're getting!"[87]

Waldo is owned by the Minsons, a wealthy Montreal family headed by Curtis Minson, "one of Montreal's most substantial financial men – an investment broker with a reputation for smartness"[88] – and Hilda Minson, a woman preoccupied with her own loneliness, her unfulfilled sexual desires, and her need to gain recognition in Montreal's upper-class social circles, which she has had trouble entering. The cast is rounded out by Paul Sturt, one of Minson's employees, who has been charged with taking care of Waldo, and by Benny Warren, Sturt's girlfriend, who wants nothing more than to marry Paul and settle down. When Benny greets Paul she feels "light, as though she had had an injection of some drug with happiness in it."[89] She describes this as "the goddess feeling."[90]

Paul is the husband she had always dreamed of, a man who believes that "A girl has a right to expect a man to support her. She has the right to a comfortable home and enough money to keep it nicely. She should have a quiet calm life in which to bring up her children and make a home for her husband."[91] (Waldo opines that Paul has "the damndest old-fashioned ideas about women.")[92] These characters interact with other members of the Montreal business community in a way that allows Hedges to sketch out class distinctions. There are labourers, socialites, disaffected housekeepers, and two teenage boys who ultimately end up shooting Waldo when they try to break into the Minson house. By sacrificing himself for his owners at the end of the story, Waldo figuratively repays his debt to the man he abandoned in Africa, who no doubt has also come back to earth in another form.

As this summary might suggest, the novel is thin on plot. Hedges's main interest is not in the central story, but in using that story to focus on a number of social and political issues that were current in the postwar years. At heart, Hedges was a social commentator; she believed that intellectuals should be involved in the issues of the day. She felt that as a woman she had to demonstrate her knowledge of those issues in order to be accepted as an intellectual. To this end, she used the novel to explore issues of wealth disparity, the threat of communism, concerns about a possible American nuclear attack on the Soviet Union in the early years of the Cold War, the repression of women and female sexuality, and the tensions between English and French Canada.

Waldo may be a dog, but when it comes to appreciating women he has retained many of his human qualities. He thinks of the pretty ones Curtis has affairs with as "damned attractive and hot too."[93] He remembers, almost as if it were yesterday, his love of Effie, his former girlfriend. But he cannot always remember whether she is canine or human:

> Effie! Or some other girl. Oh no! Waldo's mind was suddenly in dreadful confusion. Female faces and forms whirled about before his eyes, women with dogs' tails, and flat black hairy chests. He could see backsides and breasts, but these were topped by long pink tongues and panting breath.[94]

Effie's problem, according to Waldo, was that she "had had her physical desires and worldly ambitions badly mixed." We learn that "Never, for one instant, had Waldo felt that he would have to marry her."[95] The comment may seem trivial in the context of Waldo's doggyness, but it is one of the ways Hedges allows the novel to become a critique of male–female relations. When Waldo shifts his focus to his immediate surroundings he focuses on Hilda, who "wore her usual baffled expression, flat with the unexpressed disappointment which had been her daily companion since the moment she stepped into bed with Curtis for the first time after their wedding twenty-five years ago."[96]

Waldo understands that Hilda's actual pet – her "daily companion" – is disappointment, and that disappointment is directly related to her sex life, as if Hedges were using the novel to express the same kind of unfulfilled sexuality she expressed in a number of her poems. Waldo is not only her replacement "companion"; he is also a surrogate child. As Hilda tells him: "Darling Waldo, you shouldn't growl at mummie, you know. It isn't nice."[97] Waldo may be childlike, but he retains his former adult human interest in sex. In fact, he is able to enter Hilda's mind and to witness her thoughts about her own sexual longings, or, as Waldo puts it, "Being a dog gave you a new viewpoint from which to survey human nature."[98] Waldo's "new viewpoint" allows him to judge Curtis Minson's fidelity ("I'll bet the old boy horses round with someone")[99] and Hilda's sexual frustrations ("She looks as though she hadn't had it for months, years probably").[100] In his mind, he sees Hilda surrounded by a "cage": "it waved around her, veil-like yet he knew it was stronger than any veil. He knew it would prevent anyone approaching her, getting really close."[101] And then he sees the physical demonstration of her inner pain as she thinks about her husband and what has become of her life:

> Her face crinkled up in an awful way and she suddenly burst into tears. She put her hands up over her face and rocked back and forth. Words poured from her in a dreadful sobbing whisper that sizzled on Waldo's sensitive nerves like cold water on a hot iron. "Lonely, I'm so lonely. Lonely. Lonely. I hate him! D'you hear me? I *hate* him. And he hates me."[102]

Hilda reflects that while she might once have tried to resist this loneliness, she has now abandoned herself to it and has withdrawn into a world of masturbatory self-fulfillment:

> Perhaps there had been resistance in her once, but not now. She just sat there accepting her lot, making no effort whatever to change it into what she wanted. All she would do would be to fill her special void with secondary things, tarts stolen with delicious effrontery

> from her own ice-box in the servants' absence, surreptitious buying of a box of chocolates, and eating them after lunch in her room when no one was looking, and what else did she do in her room when she was alone? Waldo remembered what a doctor had once told him, "Eighty per cent of married women do not know what an orgasm is, sixty per cent never achieve one. Masturbation is practised by fifty per cent of married women today."[103]

For a dog, Waldo is pretty good with sex statistics. It is almost as if he is quoting from a study on female sexuality he might have read in passing or while he is licking up spilled whisky from an office carpet and then getting drunk while fantasizing about women's sex lives. Waldo's obsession with sex data certainly suggest that Hedges was up on her reading when it came to that topic. Although Alfred Kinsey had not yet published his groundbreaking book on female sexuality (1953), his *Sexual Behaviour in the Human Male* (1948) popularized the statistical approach to human sexuality. At the same time, the Cold War forced a reconsideration of female sexual mores and the role of women within marriage and the home. Michelle Sibley points out that sexual activity in the 1940s and 1950s was heavily influenced by sex manuals and women's magazines that promoted a double-sided view of female sexuality:

> Beginning in the 1940s, and continuing throughout the 1950s, there was a shift from the advice women's magazines offered readers in the prewar period, provided by experienced homemakers and credentialed experts such as university professors, to that provided by representatives of various "bureaus" and "institutes" in fields such as psychology, sociology, nutrition and child care. The authors of these manuals, considered influential and important experts by society, insisted those females who stepped outside of marriage for pleasure were not only abnormal, they were sexually deviant. As a result, the manuals became incredibly influential in defining female sexual practices from 1950 to 1960.
>
> However, at the same time the Cold War society encouraged female sexuality only within the constraints of marriage, it also distributed messages which embraced overt female sexuality outside of the family. Female sexuality's place in popular culture – including

> film, TV and literature – reflected a powerful new chord in postwar American life: the changing attitudes about sex and a steadily more candid view of sexuality. While the experts were encouraging a version of female sexuality that was discrete [*sic*], popular culture was displaying female sexuality in more open ways than ever, through icons like Marilyn Monroe and successful novels such as Vladimir Nabokov's *Lolita*.[104]

Hedges completed *Dumb Spirit* during this period. This might account for her portrayal of Hilda Minson (through Waldo's eyes) as a person who could explain her own sexual frustrations in statistical terms, but it also presents her as someone who understands herself as a person whose fundamental sexuality has been denied. Although it would be risky, of course, to make a direct parallel between Hilda's sexual frustrations and Hedges's conception of her marriage, it is noteworthy that Hilda says she has been disappointed ever since she "stepped into bed with Curtis" for the first time after their wedding, "twenty-five years ago." If *Dumb Spirit* was sent to the publisher in 1951, "twenty-five years ago" would have been 1926, and that is the year that Doris married Geoffrey Paget Hedges. Leaving aside this chronological parallel, it is also worth noting that Hedges, like Hilda Minson, was married to a man who was deeply involved in business with bankers and industrialists. After all, Geoffrey Hedges was a member of the Hedges tobacco clan, had directed the company's Canadian operations, and had also worked as a stockbroker on the New York and Montreal stock exchanges. His place in the world of high finance could only have been accentuated through his marriage to Doris, a member of the eminent Dawes family. The high-society values displayed in *Dumb Spirit*, then, were not at all foreign to the author. Equally familiar was the landscape inhabited by the Minsons – downtown Montreal, the Ritz-Carlton Hotel, and the Golden Square Mile – the same landscape inhabited by Doris and Geoffrey. Waldo, it seems, shares a number of his owners' fears when it comes to business. Even when he is approached by a stranger in an office elevator, Waldo perceives an immediate threat: "Potential Communist," he thinks.[105]

These points of tangency between the novel and Hedges's daily life encourage the reader to see the story as a commentary on many of the issues that Hedges broached in her public addresses and letters to the editor. She was trying to understand the demands made by the labour movement. In

Dumb Spirit, Benny Warren becomes the well-to-do character who sorts out those demands:

> As for all this lying propaganda about her own kind of people, that was all poppycock, and had to be stopped. Benny's eyes turned from green to grey as she thought about it. These books written by people who did not know what they were talking about, books describing what the writers called "society," in Montreal and elsewhere, jabbing at a group of people because they had more – well – more elegance and better manners than the rest. Jabbing at the men of big business in a snarling way which was ineffectual because it was done so ineptly. Benny had read some of these books, so popular with the masses of people. The aura of wealth and ease and calm acceptance of the possession of more beauty than some others, all this seemed to turn hell loose in the minds of those who saw it. But why shout and rave about socialism and its principles, when what they really wanted, if they were honest enough to admit it, was the same sort of life themselves! The innate hypocrisy of it was so tiresome.[106]

Benny doesn't stop there. She defends those living in wealthy Westmount ("Westmount wasn't at all as it was being painted by the writers who were being read by so many people all over the country").[107] Why should those people not have a "good life," Benny wonders, "with niceness and give-and-take in it, and holidays in the country, and music and the theatre, and people with soft voices and trained minds and a deep, if somewhat narrow, ideal of right and wrong."[108] These ideals are consistent with Hedges's own. She believed that those who were wealthy and educated were meant to lead and to create ethical standards for those less fortunate, those who were ostensibly not smart enough to understand the difference between right and wrong.

Through Benny, Hedges comments on some of the popular Montreal writers who were being read "by so many people" at the time. One senses envy. She is referring, of course, to novelists such as Hugh MacLennan, Gabrielle Roy, and Gwethalyn Graham, each of whom critiqued the wealthy English residents of the city and offered sympathy for those who had been denied cultural and financial agency. One senses the magnitude of the political tensions swirling around Hedges in the postwar years. Some of these had to do with attacks on wealth and intellectual elitism. Others had to do with the shifting but ambiguous status of women. And still others were focused on the identity of French and English Canadians.

Maurice Duplessis, re-elected in 1944, had little patience with the federal government. His affiliation was with the Catholic Church and with those forces bent on crushing the province's unions. Hedges might have sympathized with those anti-union sentiments, but what would have been harder for her to accept was the gradual incursion of a rising French Canadian middle class into the sphere of business. That was a domain that had always been dominated by the English. Yet Hedges was also a Canadian nationalist and she understood that French Canadians had sacrificed themselves for Canada during the war. She sought a means of bridging the gap between her English sense of entitlement and her realization that patriotism inevitably meant that such entitlement had to be shared.

In the novel, Hedges represents the French Canadian perspective through the character of Armand Ligne, who is the son of a Quebec lumber industry magnate. After his father's death, Armand finds a surrogate father in Hanson Buck, a partner in the expanding lumber company. Armand has fought in the war and returned to find the business that was once controlled by his father now in English hands. He struggles to quell his resentment and to accept Buck's attempts to include him in business decisions. Through her depiction of Armand, Hedges inserts an editorial perspective that might be more appropriate to a political opinion piece than a novel:

> Before the war he had been too young to take much interest in what might turn out to be his future work. His education had been like that of most of his French Canadian compatriots, in a Roman Catholic Seminary where he had learned more about classical culture and religion than about business or the history of the world and his country, especially the political history. He had been taught that the English were aggressors, that the Protestants were infidels, and that the world was a remotely evil place where young French-Canadians must rustle their way without material benefit from outside pressures which affected them in a geographical sense. The closeness of the United States and the thousand ramifications of that influence on Canadian business and life in general, he had been told, were vaguely

> destructive to the Catholic tradition; and the partnership in the British Commonwealth he had learned to mistrust with the fierceness born of biased history teaching.[109]

What would have been the alternative to this kind of education? What would remedy the misperception (surely in Hedges's eyes) that the Commonwealth was a mistake or that the English had systematically oppressed the French, not only in Quebec but throughout the world? Hedges suggests, through Hanson Buck, that Armand's Catholic education has hampered his ability to succeed: "The boy had talents but, in Hanson's opinion, they had not been exploited in the right way. He should have gone to McGill and taken a professional course of some kind, probably chemical engineering."[110]

The arrogance of Hanson's viewpoint was in fact central to the problem. Historically, anglophones assumed that their institutions provided the road to success while French Canadian institutions and the values they supported could only lead to isolation, insecurity, and failure. Given this kind of polarizing consciousness, it was difficult to see how the distance separating the two solitudes could ever be bridged. Hedges accentuates this distance by focusing on the one-time relationship between Armand and Benny. He had courted her before the war, but after the war he had

> withdrawn from his courtship of Benny because it seemed too hopeless, and because of pride, and fear too, fear of tackling a problem so old and so entangled in the life of the country. Why, only the other day, on November eleventh, the Remembrance Day parade had separated, the Protestants to hold a service in their own church to honour the dead, the Catholics to kneel separately in their cathedral for the same purpose. Yet the dead had been buddies and had given their lives for Canada, not for French Canada, or English Canada. Whose fault was it?[111]

Through the severed relationship between Benny and Armand, Hedges struggles to understand the fundamental severance at the heart of Canada: "Both of them felt not only a personal sorrow and loss, but something deeper and more painful, a dark schism at the base of life, a lack and a waste, something gone wrong that should have been better planned."[112] Benny realizes that "I shouldn't be thinking of French-Canadians as 'they.' It's so important to come closer. But how?"[113] The novel offers little in the way of an answer to this question, other than to suggest that human and paternal generosity might heal the divide. Perhaps Armand will learn to trust the quasi–father figure of Hanson Buck. But even that configuration implies that the relationship between the English and the French is patriarchal and hegemonic. The French must behave like grateful children when dealing with their compassionate English elders. They can own part of the property, but only if they play by the rules established by the existing owner. Armand's conflicted business relationship with Hanson parallels the relationship between the French and the English in the larger enterprise called Canada.

Ever the self-advertiser, Hedges travelled to Toronto to promote the novel after its publication. A brief notice in the *Gazette* for 8 May 1952 records that "Hedges is in Toronto at the invitation of her Canadian publishers, McClelland & Stewart. On her program are several radio interviews, lunch with the Toronto Branch of the Canadian Women's Press Club, a press conference and a meeting with the Canadian Authors Association."[114] Despite this exposure, *Dumb Spirit* does not seem to have attracted much of an audience. The novel received scattered reviews, none of which were particularly enthusiastic. But this lukewarm response did not stop Hedges from moving ahead with her poetry and fiction. In fact, she seems to have become even more determined to pursue her career as a writer. Over the next two decades Hedges published two more novels and three books of poetry, the last of which appeared one year before she died in 1972. Hedges seldom gave up.

CHAPTER 5

1953–1956

On 29 October 1952, a short notice in the Montreal *Gazette* announced that "Mr. and Mrs. Geoffrey Hedges are spending three weeks at the Ritz-Carlton, prior to taking up their residence at 9 Redpath Place."[1] This was the large home they would inhabit for the rest of their lives. Although a description of the property could not be located for 1952, an earlier description of the house when it was rented indicates that it was quite a grand place for two people:

> No. 9 Redpath Place, in the most exclusive residential district of Montreal, containing large living room, dining room, kitchen, pantry, reception hall and cloak room. Five bedrooms, three bathrooms, laundry, two store rooms. Heat, hot water and janitor service included in rent.[2]

While the Hedges were settling into their new lodgings, Doris was also celebrating the publication of *Dumb Spirit*. Despite the scant attention paid to the novel, Hedges's literary activity was recognized by the *Gazette* in a column devoted to those writers for whom 1952 had been "a splendid year."[3] The paper noted that *Dumb Spirit* "added to" Hedges's "already established reputation" as a poet.[4] Meanwhile, Hedges was working on her second novel, *Elixir,* published in England by Arthur Barker in 1954. This was her second book with Barker, who was interested in fantasy fiction. Barker sold the novel's Canadian rights to McClelland and Stewart, which had recently come under the direction of Jack McClelland, who was focused on expanding his list of Canadian writers. The company was clearly invested in Hedges's work, as were Montreal bookstores. On 13 February 1954, the *Gazette* carried three advertisements for the title on the same page: one for Burton's books, a second for Eaton's, and a third from the publisher itself. This kind of triple exposure for a new novel was rare, especially in 1954. A month later, Morgan's Department Store placed another ad in the *Gazette*. Local booksellers were banking on this author and her new novel.

Hedges had always written about the world she knew best – one associated with the Golden Square Mile in Montreal, a downtown area that was home to many of the country's wealthiest industrialists. As Harriet Hill noted in her review of *Dumb Spirit*, Curtis Minson, the novel's well-to-do central character, "devotes the only satisfying part of his life to business," while his wife, Hilda, is "caged in wealth" and "deprived by her wealth of the household tasks with which she could cope."[5] In this way, Hill argues, Hedges manages to approach "the 'mores' of the class about whom she writes with irony."[6]

But is it really irony? Or does Hedges actually assume that the only way one can succeed or form a distinct identity is by acquiring wealth? In coarser terms, one might ask: Did Hedges's view of Canadian identity include those who were not part of the business or professional elite? Hedges wanted to see herself as part of a broad artistic community. She wanted to support those (particularly children) who were disadvantaged or the victims of crime. She believed that her volunteer work on behalf of Canadian war brides or her promotion of youth centres took her out of her comfort zone, proved that she could contribute beyond the confines of her class. Yet for Hedges, wealth was both a privilege and a prison. Again and again we see her expressing frustration about the limitations imposed by wealth and privilege – the same limitations that provided her with a refuge from the working-class issues that she ostensibly wanted to address.

Hedges's writing about improving the condition of underprivileged people often appeared in the pages of the Junior League publications, which were supported through advertising directed toward Montreal's elite – ads for stylish hats, expensive jewellery and annual fur storage at Holt Renfrew ("Do not wait until you discover that *first* moth … Hasten Your Furs to H.R.'s Cold Storage Vaults … NOW!").[7] Readers of the *Junior League News* were lured by advertising for fine linen and handkerchiefs, Shetland wool sweaters, custom-made lampshades, and the ever-popular Sunday evening buffet at the Ritz. The magazine ran the same banner at the bottom of every page: "patronize our advertisers – remember they patronize us." One of the prominent advertisers in the Junior League magazine was the Benson and Hedges tobacco company, managed in Montreal by Geoffrey Hedges. At the end of the war, in a column next to advertising for custom-made lampshades and fur storage in Holt Renfrew's refrigerated vault, Hedges observed that "if no one, they say, has amassed a fortune out of this war, why is it that furriers and jewelers cannot supply enough of the finest mink skins and diamonds to customers in a buying spree which is the largest in the history of Canadian commerce?"[8]

The idea of shopping as a form of patronage would have appealed to Hedges, with its suggestion of regal hierarchies and benevolence provided by those associated with power and money. The Junior League held its monthly meetings at the Ritz-Carlton Hotel, which also housed the League's business office. Since Hedges actually lived at the Ritz for several years, it would have been very convenient for her to attend these meetings or to become involved in the day-to-day affairs of this upscale benevolent association. From her quarters in the Ritz, or (later) her house on Redpath Place, Hedges wrote essays and lectures about the need for teen centres that would offer social alternatives to wayward and delinquent youth. She talked about soldiers and frustrated workers protesting in the streets. She promoted a vision of democracy that involved voters from every class. But she spent little time in the streets, political demonstrations left her feeling anxious, and she had little patience for those who were poorly read in philosophy, history, or literature. Yet these were the very people she claimed to depict in her novels, which she billed as explorations of contemporary Canadian life.

The dust jacket of *Elixir* makes Hedges's aims crystal clear. The story is described as "a novel of contemporary Canadian life," written by an author who possesses a unique skill set: "perhaps because of a cosmopolitan experience and much travel," the dust jacket says, the author "is able to study her Canadian scene from the outside looking in, a rare quality in writings from the new world." The inside cover flap goes on to note that the wealthy hero of the novel – Michael Dorkin – is meant to surprise readers because they "do not know the modern Canadian, as he is to-day, how he feels and behaves." The jacket copy also reveals Hedges's sense of superiority as a woman who has travelled, providing her with exposure to European experiences that elevate her in relation to her readers, most of whom would not have enjoyed the privilege of travelling overseas. Hedges sees herself occupying the role of elite observer – one who views her subjects "from the outside looking in," as if the characters she writes about are subjects in a lab experiment, diminutive new-world beings whose pedestrian habits are observed from the author's superior, "cosmopolitan" vantage point.

Because *Elixir* was published in England, the cover copy may also represent an attempt to position Hedges's work as an original examination of those odd colonials – Canadians – whose habits and lifestyle remained unfamiliar to the British reading public. In this sense, Canadians are implicitly cast as exotic others: little is known about them, yet somehow they exist and they thrive in their "new world" ethos. However, the exotic creatures in Hedges's literary laboratory bear little resemblance to what they are supposed to depict – "the modern Canadian." In fact, Hedges demonstrates again that for her, the "modern Canadian" is a wealthy person attached to a wealthy family living in Montreal or its upscale suburbs. In other words, Hedges's fiction does not reflect the life of working-class or even middle-class Canadians. The "modern" Canadian is a person who inhabits Hedges's rarefied milieu.

While Hedges might have imagined herself as the author of a realistic novel depicting everyday life in Montreal, the storyline quickly undermines any sense of verisimilitude. The plot is summed up in a *Winnipeg Free Press* review by "R.M.C.," who notes that "first of all, you've got to have a kindly feeling toward witch's brew and mysterious potions."[9] That's because the story centres on the figure of Michael Dorkin, a wealthy industrialist and chemist who has made his fortune by inventing special paints. Michael has just turned fifty. He believes that now is the time "to have some fun with what one had, and he had plenty, a solid business, a fine family, good health."[10] Michael has already succeeded in inventing one very successful paint – a "luminous" variety that has dramatically increased the revenue of his company and prompted a purchase offer from an American firm (a proud Canadian, he turns down the foreign suitor). Now he hopes to go one step further by creating the formula for "a new paint that would be absorbent of odours, and act as a deodorant on the wall or furniture it adorned."[11] All he had to do was to find the "elusive element" that would complete the formula.

Soon after his birthday, Michael does indeed discover that rare element – it's called "pneudomidine" – and, after returning home one day, the whole paint formula comes to him in an epiphany. He runs into the house and up to his private "experiment room" where he quickly concocts the magic solution he has been dreaming about – the solution that will finally allow him to formulate the deodorizing paint. But in his excitement, Michael mistakenly drinks the clear liquid in the glass containing this chemical concoction instead of a nearby glass of water. Soon, in a Canadian echo of *The Picture of Dorian Gray*, the chemical begins to affect Michael. His hair turns from grey to black, his posture improves, his feet begin to dance on their own, and he feels young and virile again. He has inadvertently invented and ingested the elixir of eternal youth.

Michael's family is used to his little experiments. The last one, which caused a small explosion, happened when he tried to create the luminous paint. But this time, Michael does not emerge from his experiment room. What was he doing up there? His wife, Lucy, becomes concerned. And her concern is amplified by the fact that her two teenage children – Jane and Robin – are both in the house. To make matters worse, Jane has been joined by her friend Karen Hipps, and Robin is expecting one of his friends to arrive soon. The potential for family embarrassment looms large. Encouraged by Emily, the live-in maid, Lucy decides to see what Michael is up to. When she discovers him in his room, he is staring at his image in a mirror, "roaring with mirth." To Lucy, "he sounded like a faun, like one of those wild creatures that run about in the woods, drinking from horns."[12] For Hedges, the faun figure is always associated with youth and sexuality, as she illustrated in her 1957 account of dancing with Nijinsky in Paris when she was still a teenager.

If Hedges truly meant to depict Michael as "the modern Canadian as he is to-day" (according to the novel's dust jacket), her British readers – not to mention her Canadian audience – might have been somewhat alarmed to discover that Michael's transformation is presented as something that could happen to any aspiring Canadian, at any time. But it turns out that Michael's resurging youthfulness is more myth than modern, particularly in the problems it presents to his family. Or, as the *Winnipeg Free Press* reviewer put it, "His family were naturally perplexed: What to do with Dad? That was the question. His wife rather liked this dashing Apollo – at first. But as time passed she decided he was a bit too much of an Apollo."[13] The Dorian Gray conceit about eternal youth and sexuality reflects Hedges's interest in fantasy and science fiction. The publisher of *Elixir* – Arthur Barker – had already released Hedges's *Dumb Spirit*, with its emphasis on spiritualism and reincarnation. While the publisher might have accepted Hedges's work because it appealed to his own interest in fantasy literature, the level of fantasy she achieved did not always impress book reviewers. A case in point is Claude

Bissell's response to the novel in his *University of Toronto Quarterly* review, where he writes that "Mrs. Hedges persistently digs away at the vein of crude fantasy that she unwisely uncovered in her first novel, *Dumb Spirit*."[14]

In *Elixir,* Michael Dorkin's situation allows Hedges to explore many of the subjects she returns to in her fiction: the longing for youth, the representation of sexuality, class consciousness, and the nature of Canadian identity. Her depiction of Michael's return to an earlier, sexualized self is tied to a kind of animality, as if youth and desire were always savage, always attached to something unregulated and wild. Robin notices this "appalling transformation":[15] "there was something strange about his father, something more strange than the effect of the stuff his father had drunk. Michael looked positively wolfish, like the cat that ate the canary."[16]

Michael's sense of self-satisfaction is tied to his revived sexual energy. If Lucy thinks of him as a "faun" or as a "wild creature," that is no doubt because the faun figure is a potent symbol of fertility who is half-human and half-animal, often represented as a man with a goat's horns, ears, and legs. When Michael looks in the mirror, he sees "that half-Michael, half-someone-else,"[17] as if he had morphed into a mythical satyr whose feet dance to a sexual rhythm that defies human control. Michael "fiddled with his feet, noticing that they were moving in dance steps" on their own. "Well, what of it," he thinks. "He had always loved to dance, and it had been one of his repressions, carefully concealed, that Lucy never seemed to want to go out dancing."[18] Yet Lucy is prepared to accept the new Michael, even with his animal impulses. She tries to comfort him: "'Oh, Michael darling, please don't feel badly about it. We shall just have to get used to it. That's all.'"[19]

Easier said than done. As it turns out, Lucy has been sexually traumatized, not because of any direct sexual assault, but because of medical issues that have made her sexually unresponsive. She "nearly died having Jane."[20] But even before that emergency, Lucy had suffered from internal problems that allowed her to rationalize her fading interest in sex:

> After all, Lucy wasn't a young woman any more and she thought it was high time they calmed down and behaved like married people with grown children. She had little things wrong with her, things that she had been neglecting since the children were born; there had been a mild threat from the family doctor that she had better go into hospital for a while and, as he called it, "get patched up." But Lucy had

> always made excuses against going into hospital. She hated them. Now, however, she felt ill some of the time, and Michael didn't seem to care about being gentle.
>
> I guess I'm just not that kind of woman, she said to herself. In fact, once and timidly, she had said this to Michael; but he had looked at her with his new face, with those eyes that had always gone up a trifle at the corners, but which she hadn't noticed before. He had said, without sympathy, "All women are that sort of woman, and the sooner they act that way the better society will be."[21]

In these words, Michael gives voice to a troubling dynamic in Hedges's writing. Her female characters often express sexual desire, but that desire tends to be suppressed by their perception that men don't understand female sexuality. Or, like Michael, they tend to stereotype women as whores who refuse to recognize themselves in that role. Part of the fantasy at play in *Elixir* is the dream of finding a man who does not possess this monolithic conception of women. Perhaps, in his transformed identity, Michael will come to recognize her as an individual. Ironically, Lucy does not attach this dream of Michael to something he might become, but to something he might have been in an earlier and more animalistic form, as if his offensive attitudes were the product of the culture he inhabits, a culture that needs to be undone. But of course, this dream of a cultural devolution comes into conflict with Lucy's conception of herself as a contemporary woman. In this conception, she understands herself to be a sexual object and she begins to feel that she must play the role of such an object in order to retain her status, both as woman and as Michael's wife. What Lucy ultimately understands is that her husband wants her to act like a whore.

The temptation to play this objectified role is only furthered by Michael's newfound youth, which goes hand in hand with his rampant lasciviousness, even when teenagers are involved. So he leers after Jane's friend, Karen: He "studied Karen's luscious figure and full lips" while "his eyes poured over Karen in a liquid sort of way, and although his lips did not move they looked redder than Michael's mouth had been, and once or twice he ran his tongue over his lips in an animal way."[22] When he is not being depicted as an ogling rake, Michael is portrayed as a romantic seducer who is almost too hot to hold. When it comes time to help Karen carry her suitcase to the guest room, Michael opts out:

> He merely made a courteous gesture with his hand in a vague way and came on down the stairs. He did not offer to help with the suitcases. He was looking at Jane with an amused smile. As he passed Lucy, he put his hand briefly on her arm and pressed it. If the old Michael had done this it would have said, well, you handle it dear, I'll stand by. But now it felt like Robert Taylor in a sultry desert movie, making love to someone he shouldn't. The touch went right through Lucy in a hot, unaccustomed twittering of the nerves.[23]

The reference to the Robert Taylor movie is revealing. Michael must have been thinking of *Westward the Women*, the 1951 film (directed by William A. Wellman) about a scheme hatched by Roy Whitman (played by John McIntire) to send marriageable women to California in search of future husbands. The idea is that once they reach Whitman's Valley, the "husband-hungry" women will marry the men who are waiting for them and put down roots. Whitman hires Buck Wyatt (Robert Taylor) to lead the wagon train of 200 mail-order brides. The year is 1851. Most of the women who survive the harrowing journey do pair up with the men, after proving their toughness and resourcefulness during their challenging trek across the country. The "sultry" romance in the desert that Michael recalls takes place between Taylor and his co-star, Denise Darcel. *Westward the Women* was first screened in Montreal on 7 March 1952, around the time that Hedges was writing *Elixir*. It must have made an impression on her.

Hedges plays on Michael's newfound energy by framing him as someone who imagines himself leading hundreds of women across the desert. He will be the macho hero whose voyage west becomes a tale of mastery and seduction. Part of the fantasy involves the idea that all these young women will be under his control. In the advertisement, Denise Darcel (eventually seduced by Taylor) is pictured sitting at his feet. But of course, Hedges is also imagining this pilgrimage through the desert, filled as it is with images of male control and domination, as a symbolic journey. Lucy, too, imagines the hot touch of Robert Taylor and herself as his "twittering" desert bride. She thinks of the film, and then she thinks of her husband's recovered prowess:

> This new amorousness of his had excited Lucy at first. She had felt wonderful and cherished and glamorous. But that had passed, and quickly, into a sense of being trapped into being someone she knew

> she wasn't, playing a part she felt she did badly. The velvet slacks, for instance; Lucy stopped fiddling with her hair and sat back with her eyes closed, remembering.
>
> She had been sitting on the chesterfield after dinner two days ago, in the slacks and her "nice" blouse, and Michael had come over and sat down on the edge of the chesterfield and had started being "that way." He had pushed Lucy down on her back and had started what she had always thought of as "mauling" her about. There was a gleam in his eyes, and he had been quite rough and determined.[24]

Here, and at many points in Hedges's work, sexuality is equated with male violence. No wonder Lucy avoids Michael's advances, especially from his reinvigorated self, which leaves Lucy frightened about being raped. As he moves toward her soon after his transformation, Lucy "recoiled, cringing, against the door."[25] This is not surprising. After all, he had approached her "like a panther."[26] Soon after, he tries to seduce Karen, in what is one of the more disturbing scenes in the novel. It depicts a sexual assault:

> Michael stared down into Karen's eyes contemplatively. The look lasted for a long time. He knew she could not look away and it gave him a pleasant and titillating sense of power, a godlike feeling. He prolonged it. And then he put the glass decanter down and took Karen into his arms in one quick panther-like movement. He put his mouth down on to hers, hard, and kept it there.
>
> Karen went limp in his arms. Michael could not tell if she was giving in or had merely gone into a sort of swoon. In any case, there was no response from her lips. Michael's breath came faster and his body vibrated. He held Karen brutally to him, trying to force some feeling from her. Her head went back a little, and she moved her limbs under his. He could not tell whether she was trying to get away from him or beginning to yield.
>
> There was a small sound from the door. It had swung open, and Jane stood there, swaying with the door. Her eyes were blazing with some odd emotion. Michael's arms came away from Karen and his lips from her mouth. She staggered and had to hold on to the arm of a chair in order not to fall. She was very pale, and sweat had come on her upper lip.[27]

When Jane discovers her father forcing himself upon her friend, she struggles for understanding and feels betrayed: "'So this is what you do, when my back's turned. This rotten – '".[28] Is their relationship incestual? One might think that Michael would be panicked by Jane's discovery, that he might be filled with shame. But just the opposite happens: "He thought, well, that was too bad, but she had to learn about life one of these days," and even while he is thinking this, "he wasn't sure which girl he was referring to, his own daughter, or Karen."[29] He convinces himself that the assault can be explained as an innocent paternal gesture: "After all, here were two children, immature kids, it might have been a fatherly embrace he had been giving Karen."[30] He thinks he can just write off the event with a few paternal words: "'Jane, when you're older, you'll understand about this better. Karen's an attractive girl, and I thought it would be fun to see if she was old enough to be kissed, that's all. Now be a good girl and calm down, will you?'"[31]

In Hedges's work, heterosexual sex is often sex by assault. In this case, the relationship between Michael, Jane, and Karen is complicated by the fact that (previously unbeknownst to Michael and Lucy) the two young women are also involved in their own lesbian relationship. Jane feels betrayed by her father, and by her female lover as well. Michael is shocked to discover that the two young women are sexual partners. He feels that "here was something he did not understand, something not quite right."[32] Without a moment of self-reflection, Michael is quick to register his revulsion at the very idea that his daughter might be sexually involved with another woman. He "stared at them, disgust sweeping him. Something must be done about this, and at once; but what?"[33] His answer to the question seems ludicrous: "He must see Lucy!"[34] But why? To tell his wife that he has just forced himself on his daughter's friend? Michael senses that he must get Jane away, "somewhere, anywhere."[35] Meanwhile, Lucy has also witnessed her daughter's attraction to Karen, and has heard her "speaking in that grown-up, passionate voice" she seems to reserve for her friend.[36] In fact, Lucy's suspicions about the two young women had been triggered earlier, when – what a coincidence! – she had been trying on a dress at a store and heard Jane and Karen whispering together in the next cubicle: "there was an intensity of emotion in one of the voices that made Lucy uncomfortable, as though something desperate might come out of the conversation."[37] Lucy tries to ignore her realization that the voice she hears is her daughter's, but in fact she envies the women's intimacy.

When Jane emerges from the fitting room it is clear she has been having sex with Karen: "Her face was flushed and shiny, and there were untidy wisps of hair hanging down under the brim of her hat; but she was full of life, a new and frightening sort of life that Lucy had never thought her capable of."[38] She realizes that "Jane had never given her own mother one-tenth as much affection."[39] Spurred on by jealousy, she tells herself that

> she would have to do something right away about that horrible Hipps girl. But what? She had heard – but Lucy wasn't even going to think about such nasty things. She had given a few worried thoughts to the newspaper reports about children taking to drugs, but she had banished that at once. Her children would never do such ghastly unnatural things.[40]

From Lucy's perspective, being a lesbian or a drug addict amounted to much the same thing. Both would inevitably result in social ostracization and potential legal trouble.

While sexual assault is something Michael expects his daughter to understand when she is older, lesbian love is treated with revulsion. He believes that Jane's attraction to Karen reflects his failure as a parent. But perhaps it was not the result of parental failure. Perhaps, he thinks, "these things happened in the best of families."[41] What Jane was going through with Karen was just a "juvenile tizzy,"[42] Michael reasons, although what he is really thinking about is "the terrible thing that was happening to Jane."[43] How will Michael and Lucy deal with this lesbian problem? Michael tries to comfort Lucy by explaining that "Jane's just a child. She'll get over it; and trotting her around Europe will be the best cure in the world"[44] for what Michael obviously perceives as a disease. Lucy blames the relationship on herself: "'Oh, Michael, I've been such a failure as a mother,' Lucy said in her little lost voice."[45] She wants "to fling herself down on the floor at Jane's feet and ask for forgiveness."[46] Michael is revolted by her "defeatism." After all, the solution to Jane's lesbianism was simple: "This needed firmness, discipline, a kind but stiff return to parental authority, that was all."[47] Later, Lucy agrees, arguing that "'We've got Jane back from a sort of Hell, and it's up to us to put her on the right path now, a young path, something fun and gay and like a young girl.

She's just been sick, that's all.'"[48] For Michael and Lucy, the "right path" means removing Jane from her sordid relationship with Karen. This they might accomplish by taking her to Europe for the summer, "and if that doesn't do it, fix her up over there at some finishing-school, or whatever they call them these days, until she gets over it."[49] One thing they agree on is this: "you aren't going to see that girl again"[50] they tell Jane. This pronouncement devastates her:

> Staring at Jane's back, Lucy felt like an executioner. Jane's shoulders started to move, her body to heave, and sobs tore out of her into the silence of the room like live things, hitting at Lucy and hitting and hitting. Lucy got up from the chair and went across swiftly to her daughter. For a moment she stood there listening to the unyouthful sobbing, and then she put her arms tight around Jane, and turned her around to face her.
>
> It was awful, what she saw in Jane's face. It was real pain and darkness, not at all young or uncertain. She had to go through it sooner or later, Lucy thought, her heart breaking for Jane; either one way or the other, we all have to go through it. Her arms tightened around Jane, and suddenly Jane went limp, and her face went down heavily on Lucy's breast.[51]

When Lucy says that "we all have to go through it," is she expressing sympathy for Jane because she too has experienced the pain of being cut off from a female lover, or is she saying that all love ends in loss? Does she identify with Jane's sense of injustice because she has been subjected to the same kind of injustice? Her attempt to comfort Jane may simply be the result of her desire to provide solace. But in offering her sympathy Lucy finds herself in an intimate physical embrace with her daughter which may point to their sexual solidarity. Is this a mother comforting her daughter, or is it a love scene?

> "Oh, darling, darling," Lucy whispered. She drew Jane down on the bed, which was nearest to them, and held Jane close in her arms. It was the first time she had ever done this, she realized. Jane's childish pains and illnesses and sorrows had meant few tears and little

> repining and no call on Lucy's tenderness. This was different. Jane was all abandoned and helpless on Lucy's breast, and Lucy's love rose to meet it. As she held her daughter to her, she felt Jane's arms clinging to her, and that also was the first time in either of their lives. They were flesh of each other's flesh, close, and intimate, and right.[52]

Michael's son Robin seems to be aware of the sexual transgressions in his family, partly because "there's a lot of chitter-chatter going around" in his social circle about the Dorkins, "and I'm not sure it isn't well founded," he says.[53] While he and Michael are playing golf, Robin tries to provide some advice from his youthful perspective, cautioning his father that an overseas trip or a European boarding school might not cure Jane's "sickness" because, as he sees it, the condition needed to be treated as a form of mental illness: "That sort of thing – you know – a kid doesn't get over it, as you seem to think, so easily. Sometimes it needs a stronger cure, a psychiatrist, something like that."[54] Besides, Robin argues, Jane is already "not a child" who can be moulded to fit her parents' idea of what is normal: "Gals like Jane are mature, jelled mostly, by seventeen. It takes more than a trip abroad to unjell them."[55] Robin is quite serious in asserting that Jane's "condition" is the result of her upbringing. Does he mean that Lucy's own lesbianism influenced her daughter's sexual orientation? And does he mean that Michael neglected to intervene? His father seems shocked by this suggestion:

> Michael said lightly, "You blame us then?" He stopped and started walking up on to the green. "You actually blame us for this thing Jane has let herself in for?"
>
> "Well, who else is to blame?" Robin's voice was more than unfriendly now; it sounded hostile. He had stiffened, and his eyes were hard, and blue, and accusing.[56]

The scene, along with the depiction of Jane's love for Karen, exploits many of the tropes associated with homosexuality in the 1950s. Hedges's characters make it clear that they see homosexual love as an aberration, "a sort of sickness,"[57] "a mess,"[58] the wrong path, "a sort of Hell," a "juvenile tizzy,"[59] a "terrible thing,"[60] "something dreadful,"[61] a form of misbehaviour, the result of a lack of parental love, an expression of freakishness.

Michael returns home, shattered by Robin's accusations. Yet even in the midst of his panic, even during a conversation in which Michael and Lucy discuss their resolve to cure Jane of her so-called illness, Michael sets about assaulting Lucy a second time, right in front of Jane:

> Lucy felt that he was trying to be the old Michael, impelled by the urgency of the problem, but that the thing itself was not touching him very deeply. There was suddenly, in Lucy, a great desire and a great need to bring him back to her. She went to him swiftly and kissed him. She started to say something about Jane, to get him out of the room and allow Jane to pull herself together, but Michael's eyes had gone dark. He was smiling now and suddenly alive. He kissed Lucy back, with persistence, holding her lips under his. Lucy cried out, in protest, and pulled herself away almost in horror. She stood in the doorway, shaking, looking from Michael to Jane and back again, her cheeks drained of colour and her heart in turmoil.[62]

Reflecting on this assault, Lucy tries to come to terms with her situation:

> Life is like this, she thought, it's a mass of horrible things, and impulses, and acts, just under the surface. We don't really know anyone else at all, not with any certainty. The loneliness of life was in Lucy. This was the first time she had felt it as a truth. As she looked from her husband to her daughter, she straightened and a new strength stiffened her. She had fallen down badly. She had not been a good wife or a good mother. She had gone along, smugly and happily, like a skiff on the surface of deep waters, never looking down into them, or making sure that she knew the ropes, not thinking of storms.[63]

Lucy's guilt is palpable, as is her sense that Jane's relationship with Karen has no place in the kind of upper-class milieu she inhabits. Passages such as these reinforce the sense that Hedges also occupied a conservative milieu, one she both transmitted and transgressed. In many respects, her attitude toward homosexuality reflected those of her social class, but they were also a response to Cold War values and to the "Lavender Scare" that affected homosexuals during the 1950s. As Jessica Toops observes:

> The Cold War era of the 1950s is often connected with the "Red Scare" and the idea that the spread of communism must be stopped no matter the cost. People remember the persecution that those who were suspected of being affiliated with the Communist Party faced. What is often forgotten within textbooks is something that many refer to as the "Lavender Scare," which was the fear that homosexuals had infiltrated the government and that they were spreading their influence throughout the United States. Persecution of female homosexuals was pervasive during this time. The Lavender Scare had detrimental effects on lesbians, such as the loss of jobs, military status, social status, and isolation from society.[64]

Toops notes that "being suspected of being a homosexual during this era was just as serious as being suspected of being a Communist, as it was believed that homosexuality was equally as dangerous as Communism."[65] During the McCarthy era,

> persecution of lesbians in government agencies, entertainment, and especially the military was common and often harsh, but it is important to note that these were not the only areas touched. The workforce was heavily hit by the impact of both the Red Scare and the Lavender Scare. The "loyalty security investigations" … often led to homosexuals being fired. This was made possible by a 1953 executive order by President Eisenhower that listed "sexual perversion" as grounds for firing.[66]

This attitude toward homosexuality was not limited to the United States. John Belshaw and Tracy Penny Light describe its impact in Canada:

> During the Cold War, the Canadian military and RCMP worked assiduously to root out from their ranks, and from higher levels of the civil service, anyone thought to be homosexual or otherwise sexually "deviant." Security officials exposed subjects to homo-erotic images and used a device that measured pupil dilation to determine whether the subject was aroused. The so-called fruit machine was bad science, and it damaged (and destroyed) careers, as did Cold

> War-era interrogations of suspected security risks associated with homosexual orientation.[67]

Given the widespread condemnation of homosexuality and the dangers of being outed, it is not surprising that Michael and Lucy Dorkin are so worried about their daughter's attraction to Karen. In many ways, they have adopted the homophobic values that surround them. They inhabit a world that is notable for its sexual stereotyping and objectification. While homosexuality is depicted as dangerous, as a kind of insanity, heterosexual relations don't seem to be much safer. Hedges presents women through the eyes of her male characters as sex toys and flirts. When they are not the subject of "mauling" they are portrayed through a series of stereotypical and degrading clichés. The wife of Michael's business partner (Monk Cardle) is depicted as "a stupid, pretty woman, with no discipline at all, and no taste."[68] Monk thinks of her as "a damn pretty woman, not very smart but full of life."[69] Michael's view of women does not rise much above his partner's. For him, women are marked by their subservience. When he thinks about seducing Karen, he complains that the methods of seduction are a "lot of nonsense, manners, waiting about for women, bowing and scraping, the Saints, all that rot. Women like to be taken hold of and made to toe the mark."[70] Perhaps this is why he has found it so difficult to find an office secretary he approves of, and why the novel is punctuated by a series of women who try to assume the role, like Lydia Harkness. When she is in Michael's office, he finds that "the pull of Lydia's seductiveness gave him a mad desire to sweep her over to the couch in the corner, and ravish her there and then. No other proof of his maleness would do."[71]

This attitude toward women is intergenerational. If anything, Michael's son expresses his conception of women in terms that are even cruder than his father's. At a party attended by the whole family, Robin sees a woman and describes her as "a cute little piece" to his own mother.[72] When Robin discovers that Karen works as a ghostwriter, he thinks: "imagine a gal with such curves having intellect!"[73] And when his father is introduced to Karen for the first time, Robin is there. From his perspective,

> she looked like a silly, bewildered child without any self-possession whatever. Just a dumb cluck, Robin thought, not for the first time.

> He was the only one in the family who had known that Jane was that sort of dumb, from the beginning. Even when she came home, triumphant, with prizes and chairmanships from the school, Robin remained unimpressed; a dumb bunny, bound to get herself into trouble one day, he summed Jane up, affectionately but clearly.[74]

Robin has little patience for his sister's interests and less in the way of sibling affection. When it comes to women, he thinks of himself in disciplinary terms. Jane has stepped out of line in her relationship with Karen and he "wanted to slap her."[75] But he also understands that Karen wields power because she appeals to his father's newfound lust.

Despite the misogynistic gaze of Hedges's male characters, she has trouble ultimately condemning them or allowing them the self-consciousness that might encourage a change in perspective. Instead, she sees the repeated patterns of lasciviousness and female objectification as a product of Michael's age reversal. In other words, men will be men, and young men will especially be young men who have not yet grown out of their sexist obsessions. At the end of the novel, the potion wears off, and Michael is at least smart enough to realize that drinking another glass of pneudomidine will not solve his family problems, which have in fact been brought on by his return to youth. His grey hair returns. Michael and Robin now think of Lucy "with love."[76] The family unit has returned. All is forgiven. The "old Mike" is back, "with the wrinkles around the eyes, and the nice smile that made you love him."[77]

It is difficult to understand Hedges's conception of sexuality in this work. She allows Lucy to forgive Michael for his sexual aggression and even for his assault on a teenage woman who is intimately involved with his own daughter. Perhaps she was attempting to create a kind of romantic potboiler that was addressed to female readers she imagined were restless under the pressures of conventional domesticity. Hedges also understood that a revolution had taken place in how female sexuality was being represented in fiction published after the war. As Natasha Frost points out, a burgeoning market for pulp novels had transformed the literary marketplace. Novels depicting lesbian relationships and other sexual orientations found a wide audience:

> A publishing revolution in the 1940s had put millions of inexpensive paperbacks in the pockets of soldiers – a democratic way to entertain

troops that transformed the way people thought about paperback books. Pulp fiction was the end result. The books offered as many racy subgenres as there were sexual proclivities, all marketed to the men who had now come back from the war. They were cheap and disposable, designed to be read and tossed out. Yet the most successful among them sold in the hundreds of thousands or even the millions – and many of these were lesbian pulps.

Tereska Torrès' 1950 novel, *Women's Barracks*, is often cited as the first example in the genre, and the one that launched hundreds more. Inspired by her own experiences of the war, the novel tells the tales of torrid affairs between butch officer types and their femme subordinates. It sold some 2.5 million copies, and was the 244th best-selling novel in the United States before 1975, despite being banned for obscenity in multiple states.[78]

Hedges may have introduced a lesbian motif to her fiction in order to appeal to this new market. She was fifty-eight years old when *Elixir* appeared. It was her second novel. She had written two Ryerson chapbooks along with a book of poetry, published several short stories and two novels, and started a literary agency. She had money. She had friends in high places. Yet still she was generally ignored. Soon after *Elixir* was published, in early 1954, Hedges wondered, in an interview with a *Gazette* reporter, "why we are so slow to appreciate our own products and our own talents."[79] The reporter interviewed Hedges "at her home on Redpath Place." She must have been accompanied by a *Gazette* photographer, since the account of this meeting with Hedges appears along with a photo of the author, credited to "Gazette Photo Services."

In the interview, she does not describe herself or the condition of the writer in Canada in particularly uplifting terms. She complains that "I don't see any sign of appreciation at all much of the time."[80] It bothers her that "Montreal has not produced more women of national and international calibre."[81] Hedges seems to be comforting herself when she remarks that "a writer shouldn't allow herself to be discouraged by one or two or three rejections."[82] But it would appear that she was indeed discouraged by the reception of her work and the trajectory of her career. Later that year, in October, Hedges was addressing a new poetry group organized by the Canadian Authors

Association. She told her listeners – most of them aspiring poets – that "if a poet wants money, heaven help him!" She went on to suggest that a hopeful writer or poet should pose these questions: "Do I want money from my work? Do I want success? Do I want to do good work and let the rewards go hang?"[83]

Apparently, Hedges was willing to heed her own advice to "let the rewards go hang" when it came to her own poetry, since she published *The Dream Is Certain* with Christopher Publishing House in Boston in 1954, the same year that *Elixir* appeared. How Hedges found her publishers remains a mystery. Like her British publisher – Arthur Barker – Christopher Publishing House was relatively obscure. It is difficult to get a detailed sense of the range of Christopher House publications; there is a list of their titles at Bibliopolis.com.[84] Hedges's poetry book would stand in the company of such diverse titles as *Is There a Santa Claus?*; *Afterworld Effects: A Psychic Manuscript*; *The Wampanoag Indian Federation of the Algonquin Nation*; *Rhymes of Puppy Love*; *Longhorns Bring Culture*; *Theosophists Reunite!*; *A Vampire and Other Stories*; *The Philosophy of Ignorance*; and *The Constitution and Religious Education*, to name but a few.

One possible thread that united Arthur Barker and Christopher Publishing was their interest in books about spiritualism, religion, resurrection, and concepts of the afterlife. *The Dream Is Certain* is a long narrative poem that addresses these concepts. The copy I purchased included a small card in an envelope addressed to "Dr. Nicholls" in Hedges's handwriting. The card says, "To Dr. J.V.V. Nicholls, Merry Christmas from a new patient." Nicholls was a highly respected Montreal ophthalmologist who was named chief of ophthalmology for the RCAF at the beginning of the Second World War. After the war, he worked at the Royal Victoria Hospital. Dr Nicholls's scientific contributions covered many areas, including macular edema in association with cataract extraction,[85] a fact which makes one wonder whether, in 1954, Hedges suffered from an eye condition that might have affected her writing or perception.

The title of the book derives from Daniel 2, Verse 45. Hedges quotes the verse in the epigraph:

> Forasmuch as thou sawest that the stone was cut out of the mountain without hands, and that it brake in pieces the iron, the brass, the clay, the silver, and the gold; the great God hath made known to the king

> what shall come to pass hereafter: and the dream is certain and the interpretation thereof sure.[86]

In this verse, the statues made of iron, brass, clay, silver, and gold are crushed by a boulder cut from a mountain by the invisible hand of God, a sign that God's will takes precedence over the desires of earthly kings and that His divine kingdom will never be destroyed. The title poem introduces the central character in this narrative poem: Regen, whose name derives from the word "Regeneration," which can be seen in a torn tract that covers her infant body. It "lay askew / On a bloody pavement" where a street urchin finds her on "H-Bomb day."[87] So "Regen came / On the heels of a storm."[88] God looks down upon the devastation wrought by the bomb; he sighs at "man's apathy in the face of death." But one could see that apathy coming, even before the figurative explosion, because "The tempo of the world" was "sluggish and inert"[89] and "Man's will" seemed "shaken and gripped / By as fine a fear as ever."[90] Why did this happen? How did humans take this disastrous turn? Hedges proposes an answer:

> Perhaps the course of history
> Would have been different
> If men had turned to God
> In the nineteen-fifties.[91]

The state of the world in this "Age of Confusion" is "A grisly monument to putrefaction," the result of people abandoning their faith. Instead of following the rule of God, Hedges writes, "The smartsters found a useful drug" called "Oblivion,"[92] a mental creation that allowed them to deny reality and to reject God's saving grace. The foundling called Regen could rescue these unbelievers, but only if they fully accepted the idea of regeneration associated with her name. Clearly, Regen has been given by God; she is a homunculus who bears the code of salvation. As her urchin rescuer looks down upon the child and touches her "in wonder," the atmosphere "Was suddenly clean, and a light / Came within him."[93] Meanwhile, in heaven, the angel responsible for human forms on earth – Hedges calls her "Clotho," after the mythological figure who was responsible for deciding when humans would be born and die – looks down in shock on this unexpected creation:

"Give me my chart," said Clotho, "quick!
There's been a birth down there."
Then Clotho stopped, bewildered.
Clotho said, "but wait, this thing is strange:
I have no model, nothing to guide me here:
This maiden Regen is an unknown kind."[94]

As Regen matures, she must confront human mortality. She clutches a rosebud in her fist, and when she releases it the rose is "Fading already" and Regen "wept in sorrow." But the urchin reassures her and conveys his love. It becomes "a happy time" for them.[95] Hedges distinguishes Regen's attitude toward death from that held by poets, all of whom "have watched the leaves falling / In Autumn and seen sadness in it."[96] But for Regen, the falling leaf was a symbol of "life flowing onward"; she was not affected by the urchin's worldly concerns because her spirit was "strung between the earth / And highest heaven."[97]

In the second part of the poem, humans awaken to the fact that they have survived the bomb. They think, "We must be supermen!"[98] Filled with a sense of their own salvation, people forget to take any lessons away from the violence they have witnessed. Instead, their greed returns. They dig for gold. So does the urchin who rescued Regen. But under her influence, he tosses aside the gold nuggets he has unearthed. Regen feels drawn to the man who would abandon these mortal treasures. Under her influence, he has been made pure. She tells him: "Your eyes are beautiful and clean."[99] They are in love, participating in "earth's fresh burgeoning, / And of God's plan."[100] Meanwhile, those who had not cast away their gold remained moribund, "robot men" who ignored "the goading flail of destiny."[101] They had no future. They faced a "yawning space."[102] If they let the gold go, if they could abandon their greed, the renewed world associated with Regen might still draw them in. But giving up the gold makes them hungry. The urchin sees their hunger; he sees their pain. He understands that he is caught in an allegory of failed salvation. Perhaps it is too late. He envies Regen's optimism about human fate, an optimism based on faith:

"This faith so deep in you, this faith in man,
This faith in God-in-man, this faith in God,
Where did this come from?"[103]

Regen tells her urchin-lover that she will go up to a mountaintop to pray. But before she makes the journey, she encounters a neighbour who is still searching for nuggets beneath the earth. He has no faith in God. In fact, he chastises Regen for her own faith: "you must be mad / Indeed to trust your hopes to Him."[104] When Regen responds that she will go to the mountaintop "to pray for you / And for all men" it becomes clear that she is a Christ figure who will make the ascent with her disciples in mind. She wants no company on her voyage. She must be alone, and although "crowds began to file / Towards the hilltop in a mute despair,"[105] her followers understand that "hope was abroad / Again, burning in Regen's footsteps as she went."[106] They see that "the earth was given to man to tend, / To use, to nurture and enjoy eternally."[107]

Regen reaches the mountaintop, only to discover that "All man was here / Upon the mountain top."[108] Salvation would be difficult to achieve in such crowded quarters. But who are these men? Why is this sacred mount so crowded? The people here, it turns out, are not real believers. They have not made an authentic pilgrimage in search of God. Instead, they are newspaper hacks and photographers who have rushed to the mountain because their job is to "Smell out a story / Even before it happens."[109] Their desire for that story is just another form of digging relentlessly for gold. These people with "Noses for news" think it's all a show:

Wonder if they know
Who this God is
This God who'll speak
If we pray
Hurry hurry hurry
God hasn't spoken yet
Plenty of time
Squeeze in here
For a coupla nuggets
No room to kneel[110]

The fake believers think God will speak, even if the audience is filled with doubt about his power: "God'll talk anyhow / He'll dam well hafta."[111] But God remains silent. The world goes cold. Yet even in the face of this warning the masses believe God will change his mind. They implore him to "Get going God":

Start the world rolling
Make the birds sing
And the fields
And oh yes
Plenty of nuggets[112]

No lessons have been learned. The sky turns dark. "The air was as sickly as death."[113] All around, "men died as they stood."[114] At the foot of the mountain, the urchin waits for Regen, praying with the flowers, "For they loved Regen's beauty."[115] A symbol of continuing fertility, she carries the child fathered by the urchin. But, since this is an allegory about the loss of faith in a modern world consumed by greed, her child must be archetypal, the eternal product of the union of two people who still have faith. It is "the world's child." It represents "nature / Agathistic, undefeatable."[116] The child embodies the agathistic idea that all things tend toward the natural good, if only that goodness can be released. Its embryonic body, carried by Regen, stands as a physical reminder of the need to reconcile the belief in a benevolent god with the existence of evil in the world. For a moment, near the end of the narrative, human good emerges in a member of the crowd. Regen has fainted, and a man steps forward to cover her with his cloak. Regen's hands "went out in majesty / Of grateful gesture, joy, acceptance."[117] She slips into the crowd and makes a swift descent. Now "Her face was bright as sunlight" and "as she came / A scented breeze lifted the flower petals."[118] The sun begins to shine. But no sooner have the people surrounding her felt this warmth than they begin to suspect this radical transformation. Why has the world gone golden? Why this warmth from the sun? Why this greenery, "spread upon the hills"?[119] Hedges does not allow her story to end on a note of redemption. Instead, the people who have witnessed the transformation wrought by Regen begin to think of it as a show put on by a charlatan:

Men felt in haste for nuggets hidden within
Their garments, laughed, said, "Christ!
What suckers are we all to let a showman
Take us for a ride like this."[120]

In these words, the crowd casts Regen as a fake Christ, a showman, a "clever guy with smart invention"[121] who is just trying to sell his listeners a bill of goods. She is rejected. Christ is rejected. Regen and Christ merge:

The crowd dispersed, recalcitrant, still sunk
In unchanged arrogance, not heeding as she cried
"At least this man you call a tramp was good,
An honest man, a gentleman, and kind.
His core, his heart, is pure"[122]

Her words are lost in the air. The crowd returns "blindly once again to earth / To find more nuggets and to artless winnowing."[123] The end of the poem finds Regen and the urchin, together again, waiting for "Another chance, a thousand chances" to make the world right again, just as God begins, once again, His endless wait."[124]

The Dream Is Certain makes it clear that Hedges was a committed Christian who believed that the modern world she inhabited had lost its way. It's not surprising that in order to find a publisher for her work Hedges had to align herself with a small company in Boston that favoured the kind of Christian symbolism and faith celebrated through the figure of Regen. Yet Hedges's message seems quaint for its age. It was almost as if Hedges imagined the book as existing in another era. Or perhaps she herself wanted desperately to exist in another age. The book seems out of place. After all, *The Dream Is Certain* was published the same year that Elvis Presley cut his first record, McCarthyism reached its peak, and the World Series was broadcast on TV in colour. Poetry was also in transition. Hedges's *The Dream Is Certain* would have to stand next to crucial works published that year, including Louise Bogan's *Collected Poems*, W.H. Auden's *The Shield of Achilles*, Wallace Stevens's *Collected Poems*, Philip Larkin's *The Less Deceived*, and William Carlos Williams's *The Desert Music and other Poems*. In Canada, Hedges's work would face such titles as P.K. Page's *The Metal and the Flower*, F.R. Scott's *Events and Signals*, and A.J.M. Smith's *A Sort of Ecstasy*, to name just a few important collections released in 1954. In this crowded field, Hedges's *The Dream Is Certain* went largely unnoticed. Ever the self-promoter, Hedges was not pleased about that.

Hedges's dissatisfaction with the reception of her work had become apparent even before *Elixir* and *The Dream Is Certain* were released in 1954. Early in 1953 she had written to William Arthur Deacon, the book editor for the *Globe and Mail*, to complain that her two Ryerson chapbooks had not been reviewed in the paper.[125] She noted that along with her chapbooks, she had also sent Deacon "a poem dedicated to yourself, and written in my own fair hand."[126] She wonders indignantly: "Didn't you get these?"[127] Then she proposes a meeting with Deacon on 3 February. This letter appears to have gone unanswered. The next year, Hedges wrote to Deacon again, this time to encourage him to review *The Dream Is Certain*, her new book of poetry which had appeared in 1954. Hedges enclosed a photo along with her letter, "in case you might like to use it."[128] Deacon again declined to answer. Irritated by Deacon's silence, Hedges wrote to Oakley Dalgleish, the editor-in-chief of the *Globe and Mail*, to complain that Deacon had not responded to her letter and still had not reviewed her books, even though "I also sent my new photograph" and a copy of the title.[129] What more could Deacon want? Hedges was blunt about her complaint: "It is irritating to a Canadian writer to be ignored in his own newspapers, so I am bothering you about this matter, although I hate to do it."[130]

It took Deacon almost three weeks, but finally he responded in a long letter to Hedges. He was not pleased about what he refers to as "your two complaints about me to Mr. Dalgleish."[131] Deacon notes that because he did not have a secretary he was forced to type letters himself when necessary, "and, when doing so, neglect the work which is my main responsibility here and for which everything else must wait or be left permanently undone."[132] He pointed out that "30,000 new books are published annually" and that "we review a maximum of 500 or one in 60."[133] In choosing which books to review, Deacon writes, "we must use our own judgement" on what kind of material the paper's customers "want to read about."[134] He also argues that "if, as you say, I have already reviewed all your previous books, then certainly you have had more than your share of attention."[135] Deacon closes by noting that it is not unusual for books of poetry to go unreviewed, mainly because "very few people have interest in this type of literature" and that while "fifty years ago poetry found a good market in Canada" the same could not be said for 1954, since "the kind of poetry being written has lost the ear of the public."[136]

Deacon was right. Canadian poets had not found a wide reading public, and the audience for novels and short stories remained small as well, a situation that led to the organization of a crucial conference of writers that took place at Queen's University in 1955. Although conveniently referred to as the "The Kingston Conference," the actual title of the gathering was "The Writer, His Media, and the Public." More than one hundred writers, editors, literary critics, librarians, and publishers came together to discuss the challenges facing both the publishing industry and individual creators. It followed the release of the Massey Report in 1951. Perhaps the most important document in Canadian cultural history, the Massey Report was particularly notable for its identification of problems facing Canadian writers and for its recommendation that an arm's-length body be established to support Canadian creators. This recommendation led to the founding of the Canada Council for the Arts in 1957.

The participants in the Kingston Conference had absorbed the findings and recommendations of the Massey Report, but none of its recommendations had been implemented by 1955. The conferees focused on an important set of questions, as outlined by F.R. Scott in a short article that summarized the origins and purpose of the event.[137] Scott wondered whether, "despite all the barriers erected by race, religion, language, and geography," it was still possible to identify a literary community in Canada, just as it was possible to identify such literary communities in other countries:

> Have Canadian writers such a sense of community? Do they mostly know one another and work together in the same informal way, or are they isolated and cut off from themselves and from the public? What problems do they face in such a country as this, in the days of mass communication and rapid economic expansion? Have they adequate opportunities for the publication of their work? Is their concern with "the book," in any form other than a paper-back perhaps outmoded?[138]

Scott observed that in response to these questions, the conference explored what he called "the literary assembly line" – the process that brought together the writer, the publisher, and the consumers of creative writing – namely literary critics, general readers, students, and librarians. As Scott put it, the Kingston event "was not so much a writers' conference as a conference on writing and its dissemination."[139] It was generally agreed by the conference participants that, in Canada, "the writer was suffering from neglect, and that steps should be taken to make the public more aware of the good writing that was available."[140] To this end, the conference participants produced a list of seven recommendations to increase the profile of Canadian writers and the sales of their work: (1) to introduce more courses on Canadian literature into public school curricula; (2) to increase the coverage of Canadian literature at colleges and universities; (3) to urge provincial governments to increase support for Canadian writing; (4) to keep significant works by Canadian writers in print; (5) to establish fellowships and scholarships for those dedicated to the study of Canadian literature; (6) to introduce a cash prize component to the Governor General's Awards for writing; and (7) to encourage the government to increase its purchase of Canadian books for distribution abroad.

Many of these recommendations were addressed through the founding of the Canada Council two years after the conference. But in 1955, as the conference proceedings make clear, there was a prevailing sense of frustration shared by many Canadian writers. While Hedges was not listed as one of the conference attendees, she could not have missed the fact that it was happening, nor could she have missed the rather negative view of Canadian writing that emerged during the event, which was widely covered by the Canadian media and attended by a number of Montreal writers including Leonard Cohen, Louis Dudek, Irving Layton, F.R. Scott, and Miriam Waddington. Had Hedges attended the conference, she might finally have been able to meet William Arthur Deacon, who had resisted Hedges's attempts to see him in Toronto a year earlier and who had dampened her spirits concerning the promotion and reception of her work. Perhaps it was Deacon's letter, and the disappointing view of the value of poetry it conveyed, along with the subsequent conference findings, that prompted Hedges to turn away from writing poetry. She did not publish another poetry collection until *For This I Live*, in 1963. But this did not mean she would give up on promoting her career or making her opinions known in local newspapers.

In March 1956, a letter from Hedges to the editor of the *Gazette* appeared, commenting upon the Autherine Lucy affair, which involved the first African American woman to attend the University of Alabama.[141] Lucy applied to enter the university and was accepted in 1952. However, after the university administration learned that she was black, her admission was rescinded. In 1955 the NAACP obtained a court order forcing the university to re-admit Lucy in 1956, making her the first African American to be admitted to a white public school or university in the state. However, when she arrived on campus for her first classes, riots broke out and the car that protected her as she moved between buildings was pelted with rocks by an angry mob. She could not complete her studies. Lucy returned to court and with the aid of the

NAACP she secured a contempt of court charge against the university and its upper administration. Although re-admitted, Lucy was eventually expelled from the university on the basis of a technicality. The conflict highlighted the racial divisions that characterized the American South. In Montreal, members of the McGill Student Council protested against Lucy's treatment. Hedges took note of their protest and felt the need to weigh in. The students put forward a resolution that would authorize the Students' Executive Council "to write and encourage Miss Lucy in her stand" and to say that "if she is forced to leave her struggle, that a scholarship from student funds would be provided for her if she wishes to study at McGill."[142] The motion was defeated. Hedges supported those who had voted against the resolution because "it is easy to be carried away by a general emotional appeal, and youth is especially responsive to a sentimental pull."[143] She went on to argue that "the University of Alabama has already asked us to 'mind our own business,' with which I completely agree. What do we know about a problem which is peculiarly American, and one which is intimately and inextricably woven into American history?"[144]

By saying that the Student Council should "bend its brains and brawn to Canadian problems and stop dangerous meddling in the affairs of others,"[145] Hedges was also saying that Canadians should turn a blind eye to racism, as if the fact that such racism existed in another country was none of their concern. In making this judgement, Hedges aligned herself with the bigoted attitudes of the Alabama administrators and students, rather than with those who were trying to promote human rights. This is an odd stance, given the fact that during the 1950s considerable attention was being directed toward civil rights legislation in Canada.[146] The debates surrounding that legislation brought issues of discrimination onto the national stage. Hedges may have wanted the students to avoid controversies particular to the US, but she did not seem to be particularly concerned about racism in Canada, an issue that had existed throughout Canada's history and was very much present in Canada in 1956. As Maureen Kihika observes:

> during the sixteenth to the end of the eighteenth century, at the time of their first historical migration to Canada for instance, Blacks in places such as Quebec and Nova Scotia were limited to working as soldiers, general labourers, spies, entertainers, and domestic workers.

> Following this, in the period between [the] nineteenth to the mid-twentieth century, when the second significant wave of Blacks entered Canada through the Underground Railroad, increased reports on exploitation and prejudice experienced by Blacks persisted, despite the perception that these fugitives were entering the "promised land." In this period, many Canadian counties and cities such as Winnipeg made it illegal for Black people to run for office, sit in juries, purchase land or own business licenses. While immigration policy reforms during the third wave of Black migration to Canada, beginning from the mid-1960s to the present, are considered more tolerant through their facilitation of larger numbers of racialized immigrants, Blacks in Canada continue to be marginalized in terms of job opportunities, income, and occupational status.[147]

Hedges's squabble with the McGill Student Council over the Lucy affair was one expression of the frustration she was experiencing with her career in the mid-1950s. Her public profile had been devalued. She had been reproved by Deacon in her attempts to get more coverage of her poetry. Her recent titles had not sold well. There were few reviews. She could see that the kind of poetry and fiction being written by others was dramatically different from her own. If only in domestic terms, Hedges had to compete with several increasingly prominent Canadian poets – including Louis Dudek, F.R. Scott, A.J.M. Smith, Dorothy Livesay, Raymond Souster, Irving Layton, Leonard Cohen, and P.K. Page.

While a number of these writers had literary agents, Hedges had to represent her own work, a humiliating circumstance for the woman who had started Canada's first literary agency. Nevertheless, Hedges found some modest success. An article in the *Gazette* for March 1956 indicated that a new story would be appearing in the *Canadian Home Journal*;[148] a second clipping, in early 1957, indicated that another would soon appear in *Maclean's*.[149] Hedges was still able to place her fiction in these popular magazines, and she was still able to attract a radio audience. Her poem "The Red Cross in War and Peace" was read on CBC's "Bob's Scrapbook," which was broadcast coast to coast.[150]

Hedges was consistently preoccupied with her reputation as a writer. But she was also interested in travel and was fortunate enough to be able to afford European vacations. In early April 1956 she left Canada for a two-month sojourn in Spain. When she returned at the end of May, it was to the happy news that her two new stories would be published in early 1957. The *Gazette* also announced that she was working on her next novel, which would be published the same year.[151] Hedges must have felt renewed after her two-month trip; she no doubt relished the idea of being back in the public eye.

CHAPTER 6
1957–1972

The story Hedges published in *Canadian Home Journal* was called "Masquerade." Focused on a wealthy woman who leaves Canada for a European vacation in search of renewal after the death of her husband, the title points to the existential issue its central character must confront during her soul-searching journey. Elizabeth Dubry has lost her sense of identity. She has enough money to buy the most expensive designer outfits and to fly to Europe in first-class comfort in a sleeper berth, an extraordinary privilege at the time.[1] Yet she understands that she has been living in the masquerade of a loveless marriage. Her pretty outfits are only costumes meant to disguise her inner sense of loneliness and her anxieties about advancing middle age. "I'm forty-five she thought, let's face it!"[2]

Although she is surrounded by "two stalwarts" at her upscale home in Toronto's Rosedale district, the servants don't do much to offset Elizabeth's loneliness. The death of her husband reminds her that "she had had to fight feeling lonely and unneeded."[3] She realizes that "I never really loved John. I tried, but I didn't really love him."[4] Just when Elizabeth feels that she has found the perfect hideaway – a small hotel near a beach in Brittany – she encounters a "tall, and handsome, and citified" man who is also staying at the hotel. He is, according to Elizabeth, the "sophisticated type."[5] Soon she discovers that he is Paul Avers, the famous clothing designer whose very creation she happens to be wearing the day she first meets him. Paul strikes Elizabeth as eminently attractive. He arouses her long-lost sense of passion:

> Through the dark glasses, she could see that he was very handsome, with a finely shaped face and dark blue eyes, very intense. He had well-shaped hands, tanned. His shoulders melted nicely into his arms, not bulging. He had no hair on his chest. It was simply a fine

> expanse of unblemished skin, also tanned. It was his mouth that she looked away from, the mouth of a male man, a passionate male, a very alluring mouth. Elizabeth recognized strength and sensitiveness and humour. The old thing in Elizabeth fought like a tiger. Why not?[6]

One wonders about the expectations of Hedges's audience, mainly women who read the *Canadian Home Journal* in search of practical advice, but also for romantic stories set in exotic places that could only be experienced via the printed page. Predictably, by the end of the story (it all happens in four pages) the couple has fallen in love. Elizabeth has met her romantic destiny, a real "male man" who is also a "passionate male." There is a lot of "unblemished" male maleness here. That, it turns out, is what Elizabeth discovers she has been looking for. The couple will no doubt live happily ever after.

While the story offers a fairy-tale ending, its presentation in the magazine is surrounded by advertising and marginalia that remind the reader of the incessant presence of reality, including advertisements for Mum's Deodorant, Wizard Oven Cleaner, Dr. Scholl's callous treatment, baby cold medicine, an article on teenage acne, Sani-Flush toilet bowl cleaner, Lavoris mouthwash and gargle, a better brand of false teeth, a free book on rectal and colonic disorders, special chocolates that help people lose weight, and a promotional article by the Religious Information Bureau of the Knights of Columbus that begins with a warning: "You Hear Strange Things about Catholics." Any reader might have left these pages feeling a cornucopia of emotions.

One set of emotions that Hedges never openly articulated concerned her actual husband, Geoffrey, whom she married in 1926. Although Geoffrey had worked as a stockbroker and tobacco company manager, he was seldom seen in public. Most of his appearances were at formal engagements – fundraising events, philanthropic gatherings, formal teas or banquets. He travelled often with Doris to the United States, the Caribbean, and Europe. But one still gets the sense that Geoffrey was reclusive. Unlike Doris, he did not seek the public eye, even after he took on the position of Quebec Division Commissioner for the Canadian Red Cross Society in 1948. Of course, one needs to be cautious about making connections between the subject of Hedges's poetry and fiction and her home life, but it is also true that so much of that writing is preoccupied with women who are lonely and who imagine having tight-knit families, exceptional children, passionate love affairs.

If "Masquerade" is read as a trope, it can be seen as expressing symbolic grief over the death of an imagined husband or the death of sexual desire. Perhaps this is one reason why Hedges found herself writing more about the sensual experiences of her youth or about fantasized lovers who could revive what she called "the old thing" that "fought like a tiger" to reassert itself. That "tiger" was very much present in her *Maclean's* piece, titled "A Tango and a Feast with the Faun." Hedges described it as a "story," even though it was more of a brief memoir about her encounter with Nijinsky as a young woman in Paris in 1911, when she was fifteen years old. That memoir has already been discussed. It is worth returning to it briefly, in order to situate it in the year it was published in *Maclean's* – 1957. Doris was sixty-one. The recollection of Hedges's teenage dance with Nijinsky in Paris is a record of sensuality remembered, almost fifty years after the fact. It is also a deep expression of loss and of longing for an exoticism the narrator has been unable to find ever since. Hedges seems to be dreaming of a relationship that would never materialize. The more she thought about that kind of change, the more she seemed driven to remember a time when she was young, free of marriage, able to explore the sensual side of her nature that marriage had bottled up. It is hard to ignore the fact that so much of Hedges's writing focuses on dysfunctional families, strained marriages, frustrated sexuality, and dreams of imagined lovers.

Hedges's next novel continued to explore deficiencies in family relationships. *Robin* was published in 1957, the same year that Geoffrey retired. It's a coming-of-age story about teenage Robin Blount and his well-to-do Montreal family. Robin seems to be clairvoyant. He possesses the ability to see danger before it happens and to rescue people who might be in harm's way. He is also capable of remembering some kind of traumatic event he witnessed as an infant, an event that has continued to haunt him right up to the time we meet him as an accomplished student and athlete at the age of fifteen. What we discover over the course of the story is that Robin's deceased mother, Emily, was in fact not his birth mother. Rowena, his biological mother, abandoned Robin so that Emily could claim she had a child with John Blount, her husband of many years (the same situation applies to Robin's sister Mandy, whose birth mother is also not Emily). Emily wants to pretend the child is hers, to make it "as though I had really had one."[7] John, Robin's actual father, has kept the truth from his son. Yet burned into Robin's mind is an image he retains from his christening, which was attended by Emily and an unknown woman who turns out to be Ruth Hander, the nurse who witnessed Robin's birth and attended to him as a young child. Ever since his birth, Robin struck people as somewhat strange: "The baby had an uncanny expression in its eyes, and it had taken John Blount a year or two to get to love it."[8]

To secure her silence about Robin's illegitimacy, John paid off Ruth at the time of Robin's birth. Now, fifteen years later, Ruth has run into medical problems that are complicated by her poverty and alcoholism. She is also alienated from her own son, Lennie, a violent young man who has turned to drink and crime. When Ruth sees a newspaper story celebrating one of Robin's many athletic triumphs, her envy of his comfortable life leads to a risky decision: she will blackmail John Blount by threatening to reveal the true story of Robin's birth, which she has recorded in a diary. Lennie promises to reveal Robin's true identity if he is not paid $4,000 to remain silent. In the meantime, however, Robin has discovered his true mother, who has rented a cottage near a beach in Maine in order to observe her son while he is there on vacation with his family. Eventually the truth comes out. Robin meets Rowena and understands that the mystery he has felt about his life is actually about his repressed sense that his biological mother has abandoned him. Meanwhile, Lennie shows up to collect the payoff from Robin. He stabs Robin and leaves him for dead. But Robin is rescued and eventually recovers. He becomes the family hero.

By the end of the story, with the riddle of his birth solved, Robin is able to enter into his own marriage with Hermes, a young woman who is the daughter of a woman his father is dating. Hedges links Robin to this modern quasi-goddess whose name narcissistically reminds him of his own interests: commerce, sport, travel, and the ability to bridge the boundaries between real and imagined worlds. She reflects him. The more contemporary usage of the name Hermes also ties Robin's future wife to the famous French clothing designer. Marriage is equated with fashion. The novel ends in anticipation of their happy future: "Inside their eyes was a dream of a place of quietness, a place of laughter, a place of love. And work to do, above all, exciting work to do, and the world their oyster. If there was an answer to the distress in the world, these two would find it."[9] Robin's sister, Mandy, shares this view of Robin's potential. She tells her brother he might think about becoming a diplomat, because "You're popular, and suave, and distinguished looking. You've got a brain, and you can talk the hind legs off a donkey."[10] A happy ending for Robin and his bride-to-be is all but guaranteed:

> Robin thought, it seems impossible, it's just like a dream. But Hermes' hand in his, the scent she wore, her hair at his shoulder, and the green, dauntless, adoring eyes she turned on him, filled him with elation and belief. *It was real.* It must be real. Oh, yes, as real as tomorrow and the day after, and all the fights and successes and victories ahead. Here was something, at last, worth fighting for, something so suddenly precious that Robin's whole being vibrated with the urge to meld himself into life and be part of it.[11]

Hedges's novel went practically unnoticed. A small advertisement appeared in the *Gazette* soon after the book's publication. It promoted *Robin* as "the story of Canadian Youth striking out for themselves in a world of higher values."[12] It was "a book of the near future," according to the ad.[13] Hedges had always been a strong supporter of Canadian values. She may have imagined *Robin* as a kind of predictive novel about Canada's potential, which would be linked to the happiness and potential of Robin and Hermes. But Hedges does not make a strong case for the younger generation as the embodiment of Canada's future. Instead, she seems focused on the connection between personal wealth and national destiny. Hermes has led a life of privilege. She expresses no particular commitment to the nation and not much in the way of concern for political or social ideals. Robin also lacks a social conscience. His central ambition is to become an engineer so that he can make money investing in new mining projects in the Canadian West.

While the novel does not succeed in portraying Hermes and Robin as convincing examples of a future generation of Canadians, it does convey Hedges's interest in the changing status of Canada in the 1950s. She was drawn into the emerging narrative of national pride that followed the Second World War. Hedges was impressed by Canada's increasing role in NATO after it entered the alliance in 1949, the same year that Newfoundland joined Canada, making it the second-largest country in the world. She also recognized other historic events that marked Canada's distinctiveness: the establishment in 1949 of the Supreme Court of Canada as the final court of appeal (rather than Britain's Privy Council); Canada's role in the 1950–53 Korean War, to which it committed 26,000 soldiers; and the release of the Massey Commission Report in 1951, with its focus on expanding and improving the status of the arts in Canada. *Robin* was published in 1957, the same year the Canada Council was founded.

Hedges had been predicting the future glory of business in Canada for many years. In *Elixir*, which appeared three years before *Robin*, she described the Canadian businessman as a person who "sees everything, he can turn his head like lightning, and he's a damn smart operator in his plodding way."[14] Later, in *Elixir*, we witness a conversation between Jack Hilliard and Michael Dorkin. The narrator tells us that "they were both thinking how grand a thing it was to be Canadian, with the building of the country a trust in their hands, an exciting trust, with rainbows in the future of it."[15]

In Hedges's view, Canada's "rainbow" potential was tied to the development of its natural resources. Those resources offered extraordinary business opportunities to entrepreneurs who were prepared to invest in them. As a person accustomed to equating financial and personal success, Hedges linked her pride in Canada with the financial possibilities offered by the country's resource-based industries. During the war, Canada had delivered steel and aluminum to the Allies. After 1945, new mines were opened for iron ore, potash, copper, zinc, and uranium, launching Canada's mining industry into "its greatest period of expansion."[16] Hedges had grown up in a family known for its acumen in turning those resources into capital. Her grandfather, James Pawley Dawes, played a major role in the management of the Dominion Bridge Company; he understood the political machinations that allowed steel to be turned into money. Dawes was also associated with Montreal's Allan family, which had extensive holdings in Canada's railway industry.

The building of train lines in Canada was directly linked to the discovery of mining resources. For example, mining magnate Jules Timmins developed iron ore mining in the Ungava region of Quebec, starting in 1941. In order to access the mineral, he had to expand the transportation infrastructure, a project that led him to collaborate with six American companies to construct the 400-kilometre Quebec and North Shore Labrador Railway between 1951 and 1954. It created thousands of jobs and massive income for Timmins and his partners. The project attracted international attention and served to underline the relationship between Canadian natural resource development and untold wealth. Given her family's own historic connection with the steel industry and railways, Hedges would have shared in the widespread assumption that Canada's coming of age had a great deal to do with mining and engineering.

Hedges had been unable to find a conventional publisher for *Robin*, which indicates the extent to which her star had fallen. While Canadian writers were experimenting with new forms in works such as Ethel Wilson's *Swamp Angel* (1954), Earle Birney's *Down the Long Table* (1955), or Mavis Gallant's *The Other Paris* (1956), Hedges was writing conventional fiction that seemed to come from an earlier age. In failing to interest a commercial publisher, Hedges was driven to embrace vanity publishing, which meant that she would pay for the production of her novel and would be responsible for promoting the book as well. In fact, she may be the first Canadian writer to have established an association with Vantage Publishing, one of the early American vanity presses. Although vanity publishing had been available in the US since 1920, when Gordon Dorrance founded Dorrance Publishing, the largest American vanity press was Vantage, which began publishing author-subsidized works in 1949.[17] Vanity publishers provided an alternative to the royalty model of traditional publishing. By allowing any author with sufficient financial means to publish his or her book, vanity presses issued what were usually substandard works that could not meet the expectations of mainstream publishers. As Howard Sullivan observes,

> the very use of the term vanity publishing implies contempt for the book produced and a judgment on the author and publisher – on the former because he has chosen an unorthodox way of attempting to achieve a recognition his talent does not merit, and on the latter because he has pandered to another's weakness for his own profit.[18]

Given her choice to invest in the publication of her novel with Vantage, it is unlikely that Hedges received any editorial feedback on her work, a factor that may account for some of the wild leaps of logic and many of the continuity errors that appear throughout the novel. Timothy Laquintano notes that vanity publishers were criticized "for producing low-quality books and failing to act as gatekeepers."[19] As a result, "aspiring authors were warned that publishing with a vanity press could be a career-killer, and commentary in articles and trade journals suggested publishers and librarians were exasperated with the quality of the books that rolled from vanity presses and the treatment of authors who used them."[20] The same could be said of book reviewers, who had little respect for vanity publications. One of the earliest examples of a self-publishing failure was Henry Harrison's first novel, which was described by the *Salt Lake City Telegram* as "the worst book ever published."[21]

Robin may not be the second-worst book ever published, but it leaves much to be desired. It is based on the premise that an infant could remember the few people who attended his christening and then remain haunted by those figures until the discovery of his birth mother sixteen years later. Hedges's range in describing characters is particularly limited in this work. Emotion is often reflected in characters' faces, as in, "Color came into John Blount's face, an angry color," but soon "his face cleared of anger and the flush faded."[22] Sometimes the similes seem particularly forced. When Robin spends any time with his aunt Elaine, "he always felt sort of squeezed, like an orange after the juice has been pressed out."[23]

While the novel is weak in terms of characterization, it is revealing in terms of the way it describes family life. To what extent do the family relationships pictured in the novel mirror those in Hedges's life? In this context, how much can we read into Hedges's description of John Blount's former relationship with his deceased wife? It is a relationship built on domination and female subservience:

> He had loved his wife, because she had been the only person in his life who had belonged to him completely, loved him inordinately, and been utterly obedient not only to his desire for her, but also to the life he ordained for her. She had no life of her own when he married her, and she was therefore able to fit into his with soft complacency. Not that Emily had not had a firm little character. John Blount would not have been able to stand living with an unintelligent or weak woman, but Emily had been, when he first met her, like a photographic plate, waiting for someone to make an impression on it. It had been thrilling and exciting, and also heady, even to him, to find the perfect mate – a reflection of himself.[24]

John Blount is looking for his own image. The marriage is his mirror. Hedges seems to understand the position of a woman who is forced to subjugate herself in marriage, who is expected to reflect her husband's whims and values at the expense of her own. She also seems quite comfortable in presenting characters whose qualities are based on the wealthy people who had surrounded her all her life. For example, Linnie LooGuaj, John Blount's sister, "had lived high, wide, and handsome, and she took some pride in the fact that it had all been done with finesse, discretion and artistry, hurting no one, and leaving no stink behind that she could think of."[25] At one point, Linnie is fantasizing about her next trip:

> Where shall I go this time, she thought, her mind, with its vast experience of travel, suddenly roaming in every direction, making a series of small and enticing pictures. The deep blue of an undulating and gentle sea, behind the curving line of a beach that smelled of coral and coquinas. Waving branches of oleander, blazing fields of tulips. The exciting slope of a great mountain side dotted and friezed and redolent with jonquils and hyacinths. Small, chic beaches, with cabanas and umbrellas and careless people with gorgeous bodies, and the smell of gin. The relief of luxury after a war. The booming forties. These tiny, clear pictures filled Linnie LooGuaj's eyes with dreaming, so that they looked wider and bluer and more intense than ever.[26]

Like Hedges, Linnie lives at the Ritz, where her main frustration is "never getting parcels, or telegrams, or phone messages."[27] This is not a woman who has much sympathy for socialists or those who are not as privileged as she. Her brother, John, seems similar. When Linnie tells him she has invited some new neighbours to join them, John declares that "they sound ghastly" and adds, "Social creditors are usually ghastly."[28] He's the kind of man who quotes Kipling in the "pronounced British accent" he had acquired at Oxford,[29] an accent he retained until he discovered that "it lost him customers; besides, it was phoney, not Canadian."[30] Robin's birth mother, Rowena, comes from the same class. She thinks of her life in terms of the reading she has done. From Goethe she learns that "we are shaped and fashioned by what we love."[31] Rabelais teaches her to "*Fais ce que voudras.*"[32] And Oscar Wilde convinces her that "life itself is the first, the greatest, of the arts."[33]

The novel's central characters serve to reinforce the liberating power of money and the equation between money, education, and social class. From this perspective, a poor person must necessarily be an uneducated person who is often caricatured or subjected to ridicule. While Hedges's wealthy family members drink champagne that's brought to them by their servants, people like Ruth Hander are depicted as drunks who pass out on the kitchen floor, or as illiterate foreigners who have not learned how to speak proper English. One of Lennie's friends is Mat Kluk, whose heavy accent is associated with his criminal activities, or as he says to Lennie when they are robbing a house: "I zink I hear somezink."[34] When Lennie asks Mat if he is carrying a gun, Mat's response is clear: "Zertainly not, ve only got knives."[35] But Lennie, born in Canada, also reveals his lack of education. His blackmail letter to Robin testifies to his poor schooling: "By this time you must of got the dough. (4,000). Put it in small bills in an onvelop and leave it under the TV set at the house at St. August when you leave, and leave the front door on the latch. No tricks or I'll send my old ladies diary to a noospaper."[36]

Hedges treats this kind of semi-literacy with disdain. Her criminals are always poor. She doesn't seem to believe that working-class people or those who have not attended upper-class schools will be able to partake in the massive opportunities offered by a booming Canadian economy. The benefits of such an economy, in her view, will flow mainly to those who already have money and power. The most consistent theme in this inconsistent novel relates to the depiction of Canada as a dynamic young nation with massive potential. Robin is the physical embodiment of this national potential, as is Hermes. During a dinner party, one of Linnie's friends, Mrs. Felter, even goes so far as to assert that "a woman can learn as well as a man"[37] and that women might eventually participate in the future of the nation, if only they would "emancipate" themselves by erasing their femininity and by behaving "sensibly," like the men around them:

> "Women in Canada haven't even begun to emancipate themselves," Mrs. Felter said, as they pushed their chairs back and started to leave the room. "To me, it's just plain silly. I always had an exaggerated conception of big business. My father never took my mother into his confidence, and when I tried to make him tell me, he thought me queer and had me packed off to a finishing school in France."
>
> She laughed, a little gruffly, remembering her ignorance, and its disappearance in the world of machinery into which her husband has taken her at their marriage.
>
> "I don't say it's easy," she said, "but a woman, if she keeps her head, and realizes that men will forget she's a woman if she behaves sensibly, can compete in the market as well as any man. After all, this is 1958 and not the dark ages."[38]

Canada's potential is expressed in several ways. When Robin goes on a walk in the forest, he puts his hand on a boulder and can feel it vibrating.

What kind of message is this vibrating rock sending to Robin, its human medium? It was "a rumble like big machinery, down in the earth. It was quite loud and demanding. It said, 'power, power, power.'" Over and over, so clearly that Robin said aloud, 'Well, so what? Everyone knows Canada's full of it, 'way down there.'"[39] A little later, Robin comes back to the idea that "'Canada's getting pretty darn big and powerful.' He thought of the eerie vibrations in his hand, the trembling like an eagerness which he had felt in the big rock. 'Maybe we ought to get to know Canada first,' he said."[40] In these words, Robin gives voice to Hedges's belief that Canadians did not know their own country and, as a result, could not appreciate its potential. She wanted to convey its distinctiveness to her readers and to convince them that they could get the education and training they needed in Canada, rather than in Britain. Robin wonders, "What *was* he going to do? How *was* he going to use himself?"[41] At first, these questions make Robin feel like an outcast:

> There simply did not seem to be a place for a person like himself, not in business, not in the professions either, not in a remote and studious one-track scientific career, not in society. There must be something, he cried inwardly, there must be, there must be; or must I make something for myself? But how?[42]

Robin comes to understand that his first task is to obtain a university education, but it would have to be a Canadian education, at a Canadian school. This is why he chooses to attend McGill University:

> Robin had decided against Oxford after all, and was going to McGill in the autumn. I'd like to go over there later, he thought vaguely, but for the time being, there seemed enough to learn in Canada, right here at home. Everything was going on in Canada, which in 1959 was booming with prosperous delving and sparkling with power.
>
> In the West, in the North, the world's most important power developments were no longer developments but accomplished fact. In the East, the population had trebled, and housing was one of the greatest problems. Canada was teeming with outsiders: men and women with technical knowledge and know-how, men and women who followed the prosperity of the pioneers, men and women who came to Canada "just to see." It was no longer possible to feel that

> Canada was still a remote country, with a few dour and hardy folk doing all the work and taking all the profit, and saying as little about it as possible. No, in 1959, Canada's face was definitely lifted, to the sun of material wealth.[43]

The passage sounds like an expression of the kind of materialism that appeared in Ayn Rand's work. Hedges might well have been a Rand disciple. Rand's *Atlas Shrugged* appeared the same year as *Robin*, yet her ideas about materialism had been apparent ever since the publication of *The Fountainhead* in 1943. In *Atlas Shrugged*, she imagined what would happen in a world in which intellectuals and idealized industrialists went on strike, withholding their special talents from the public. For Rand, power came from the "rational selfishness" of those who had succeeded in business and the creative arts. She disdained socialism because she felt that it encouraged unproductive people to subsist on the wealth and creativity of others. Like Rand in *Atlas Shrugged*, Hedges focused on the railroad industry and examined the implications of nuclear technology and the atomic bomb. She presents Robin as the kind of Randian individual who will become a mining magnate with a superior education. After obtaining an undergraduate degree in engineering from McGill, Robin planned to "go to England," where he would take "a special course at Oxford. He would then be equipped to dig into Canada's riches in an educated way, a civilized way, and not like the greedy methods that so many were using."[44]

In her attempt to reconcile the educational advantages offered by Canada with the more traditional academic perks to be found at Oxford, Hedges often lapses into critical commentary on the state of the arts in Canada at the end of the 1950s. One can see her struggling with the tension between her sense of national pride and her recognition that pursuing the arts in Canada could be a lonely affair:

> So many books had been written, hurriedly, and at the last moment, about Canada, that the Canadian writers felt disgruntled and angry with themselves that they had not thought of writing sensible books about Canada long ago. People in other lands no longer demanded stories about Indians and the wilderness of the woods as symbolic of Canadian literature. Together with the trade brochures and the immensity of the promotional agencies and their output, a small,

> shy shoot of literature was only now beginning to put its head out of the morass of money and self-importance. Canada's theatre, always strong and flourishing, boomed now with musical shows and smart living-dining-room comedies with a slightly decadent flavor. It was the decadent flavor that people demanded and that brought them into their twenty-five dollar seats in the new theatres.
>
> Painting had long ago become a matter of abstraction, and music, always snobbish, wavered between demand and genius, so that only a few "amateurs" continued quietly to compose and to work at it, without audiences or desire for audiences. Small, closely guarded groups of musicians, poets, and painters, still existed, holding together by the sheer weight of loneliness and the desperate need for fuel for their brave service to the arts.[45]

One could read the above passage in self-reflexive terms, as an expression of Hedges's own sense of loneliness and isolation as a Canadian writer, and of her need for social recognition, the "fuel" that would energize her lonely pursuit of art. But one also gets the sense that for her, Canada was the country of the future, despite this isolation. Its potential could be realized by Canadians who understood its material value. Robin dwells on this point in what sounds like a tribute to Ayn Rand:

> Sometimes he thought he would like to represent his country in some way, diplomatically perhaps; but that had passed. What was a country anyhow? And Canada was being perfectly represented now by the men and women she sent across the narrowed world, people with clear-cut and materialistic ideals, and without inhibitions about values which hampered their thinking, and actions.[46]

Hedges was determined to distinguish between a post-colonial Canada that could manage its own development and the persistent view that it remained a minor outpost of the British Empire, a wilderness populated by savages who roamed an inhospitable landscape dominated by snow and ice. When Robin's sister, Mandy, meets an Englishman who takes a romantic interest in her, his attitude toward Canada reinforces this perception of the country:

> Then Mandy met a young Englishman who still felt that "the colonies" presented better opportunities for such as he, and who was planning to go to Canada, in search of his fortune, which he intended to hew out of deep beds of ice and in the defensive face of hordes of Indians, Eskimos, and other uncouth folk.
>
> When Mandy, rather tartly, reminded him that Canada was no longer a "colony," and that although Eskimos and Indians were respected citizens of Canada, they were not likely to be romantically menacing, the young man merely said, "Oh, I say, I do apologize," and went right on with his theme, unchanged.[47]

Hedges seemed to be unaware of the unwavering prejudice that characterized Canada's stigmatization of Indigenous peoples, despite the widely reported use of residential schools as tools of assimilation and repression. As Erin Hanson notes,

> Residential schools systematically undermined Aboriginal culture across Canada and disrupted families for generations, severing the ties through which Aboriginal culture is taught and sustained, and contributing to a general loss of language and culture. Because they were removed from their families, many students grew up without experiencing a nurturing family life and without the knowledge and skills to raise their own families. The devastating effects of the residential schools are far-reaching and continue to have significant impact on Aboriginal communities. Because the government's and the churches' intent was to eradicate all aspects of Aboriginal culture in these young people and interrupt its transmission from one generation to the next, the residential school system is commonly considered a form of cultural genocide.[48]

Indigenous peoples, like immigrants, did not have the right to vote and encountered frequent discrimination and overt racism in housing and employment. They were also still subjected to the punitive terms of the Indian Act and the Gradual Civilization Act. Mandy's assertion that these Indigenous peoples were "respected citizens of Canada" could not have been further from the truth. In fact, Hedges was writing *Robin* at exactly the same time as the

"Sixties Scoop" practice of separating Indigenous children from their families for adoption by white families was initiated. Despite its name, the "Sixties Scoop" began in 1951.[49] Given Hedges's preoccupation with the relationship between parents and their children, it is unlikely that she would have been unaware of the adoption program.

Although *Robin* often sounds like it was written to promote upper-class, white Canadian values, there is an eccentric side to the novel that reveals Hedges's often amusing preoccupation with fantasy, science fiction, and spiritualism, another preoccupation she shared with Ayn Rand. She had already written about a man who is resurrected as a dog and about another who reverses the aging process by drinking a magical potion. In *Robin*, she punctuates the narrative with odd incursions into science fiction, as if she is tentatively experimenting with a new form but does not trust her command of that form enough to apply it to an entire novel. Sometimes, these sci-fi digressions come out of the blue, so to speak. In one instance, we find Robin absorbed in an article on atomic bombs. It was

> a summary by a very competent reporter, of atomic progress during the past four years, from 1954–1958. The world had hung between life and death for so long that people had begun to forget the peril, to forget the danger of nervous fingers on the triggers of death-dealing instruments which now were available to more persons than the mind liked to contemplate. There were, it was said, atom bombs small enough to be carried in a pocket, and lethal enough to destroy London. There were germ bombs powerful enough to sicken and kill all populations. There were invisible rays bottled up in plastic containers, which could, it was said, render inert all energy for miles around them. The sun was still pleasant for suntanning, and as an amorphous glint on nature, but as an object of veneration and respect or even fear, the sun had taken a back seat to the very real white-hot radiation which at thousands of miles could cause disease, insanity, and a horrible crawling sort of dying.[50]

Here, Hedges shows herself to be eminently aware of the threats posed by nuclear armaments after Hiroshima and Nagasaki. As early as 1946, she had delivered a radio address on the risks and benefits of atomic energy. Her talk took place on 29 June, two days before the beginning of the US Navy's "Operation Crossroads," which was designed to study the effects of a nuclear explosion on American warships by detonating two bombs near test ships brought to Bikini Atoll in the summer of 1946. The first bomb, nicknamed "Able," was detonated on 1 July 1946. The second, "Baker," was activated on 25 July 1946. The project generated a lot of controversy. Critics argued that the explosions would cause needless environmental damage and would pose risks to the Bikini islanders and military personnel. The navy also wanted to examine the effects of a nuclear explosion on animals. To this end, it transported 200 pigs, 60 guinea pigs, 204 goats, 5,000 rats, and 200 mice to the test site; they were placed in cages above and below decks on the target ships.[51] The explosions left hundreds of men exposed to radioactive contamination. (The experiment also had fashion consequences: it spawned the bikini bathing suit phenomenon.)[52]

In her address, Hedges argued that "human character and good citizenship must ensure that atomic energy is used to serve mankind and outlaw its use as an instrument of war."[53] She believed that too many people deferred to scientists, rather than thinking through the issues, and that this kind of deference was risky because it placed too much power in the hands of science. At the same time, Hedges clearly understood the potential benefits of nuclear energy. It would have been difficult for her to miss the debates about nuclear power, which seemed to dominate the media every day. Two years before *Robin* appeared, news agencies reported on a meeting of thirteen nations that gathered in New York to discuss "atomic energy progress." Magazines published conceptual images of vast atomic power plants and of cities run on nuclear energy. At the same time, the media reported on a string of tests designed to enhance the potency of nuclear weapons.[54] It was the age of "duck and cover." But it was also an age of optimism concerning the peaceful use of nuclear fuel. As a Montrealer, Hedges would have known that the first nuclear reactor in Canada was to be established as a joint British-Canadian endeavour called the Montreal Laboratory, set up in 1942 under the auspices of the National Research Council of Canada. It was called the National Research Experimental Reactor (NRX) and was designed to be the most powerful research reactor in the world. The project was moved to Chalk River, Ontario, in 1946.

In 1952, Atomic Energy of Canada Limited was established by the government to promote the peaceful use of nuclear energy. Perhaps more safeguards should have been put in place by then: that year, there was a loss of coolant in the NRX reactor at Chalk River, resulting in a meltdown of the core and a hydrogen explosion. Radioactive water – 4,500 tons of it – was discovered in the cellar of the power plant. It was dumped in ditches near the Ottawa River, contaminating the area with radioactive material and requiring a massive clean-up effort.[55] This did not deter the construction of other nuclear power plants. Starting in the mid-1950s, Canada planned to construct twenty-five nuclear reactors over thirty-five years. By the time *Robin* was published, in 1957, there were two heavy-water reactors operating in Chalk River, with another two set to open that year.[56] Robin refers to a similar operation in the novel, when, while watching a TV show, he hears "the president of a large Canadian power Corporation in the West" discussing how

> "This year, weather permitting, we hope to produce enough power to start the World Power Corporation on its way. This project has been some time in the making, but we are now ready to go ahead with it. The work on the great plant is almost completed, and very soon the world will feel the impact of the progress man has made in dynamics and in the use of atomic power for peaceful purposes."
>
> Robin sat in his bare feet, thinking, inflamed with the speech and its implications. The world had been waiting for this, the largest power project ever conceived. Robin had not been aware that it was so close to reality. To him, the thing had seemed a little nebulous, if exciting. What was going to be done with all this power? Robin thought, he said, "peaceful purposes," but did he mean it? And then he smiled, remembering the words "weather permitting." God had certainly taken His world down several pegs in that way, of late.[57]

Despite his reference to divine intervention, Robin still worries about the effects of a radiation leak, which could affect thousands of people. He also realizes that there are other forms of mass destruction, including germ bombs and invisible rays. "The H-Points were the latest invention of destructive power. They were rumored to be as light as an aspirin pill and about as easy to dissolve. When detonated, however, their silent and grisly work would wipe out millions of square miles in an hour."[58] Robin's interest in the future of humanity does not stop with his fear of these instruments of mass destruction. Hedges allows Robin to imagine the effects of climate change, which was certainly a rare interest in 1957. At first, he envisions the ways in which humans will be able to monitor and control such change:

> it was difficult to imagine sun-worshippers in these days, and even more difficult to think of nature as something to be reckoned with. Even storms had been controlled in certain areas, and drought was in the process of total cure. Drought areas like Texas and the Sahara had been conquered by new methods and newer chemical application and the magnificent discoveries of man's inventive genius.[59]

Then he tells us more about the effects of climate change:

> The weather had been increasingly erratic and strange all over the world. Men of great knowledge had tried, and were still trying to find reasons for it. Men had no sooner begun to conquer disease then this other difficulty arose. Weather. Plain common-or-garden cold and wind and snow and hail and rain, coming in all directions, and at all times, and in places where such conditions had never happened before. Montreal, in fact, had become a foggy, damp place, and chilly in summer instead of in winter. The tourist business had fallen off badly, and even the new traffic tunnels and parkways around the city had not served to attract visitors. The new helicopter airport had brought a crowd at first, of curious people, but the accidents caused by collision between selfish helicopterists who wanted too much of the air, had caused the heli-port to fail. Now it was being reconditioned in a hush-hush atmosphere, for something that, rumor had it, was a landing for the space ships which the scientists insisted were already hovering in the outer reaches with friendly desires towards man.
>
> Weather permitting! You mean, God permitting, Robin thought.[60]

Robin understands that human inventions might control the weather, so long as "we don't let them blow up in our faces."[61] But ultimately, human fate is in the hands of God. When Robin begins to speculate about the future, his mind starts to get the better of him. His ears start to vibrate with "a strange sound," as though "millions and millions of humming, living things were battling to get out of a ball of atmosphere."[62] As he begins to speculate on the source of this buzzing, he is driven to consider that some foreign power had implanted a "devilish machine" in his brain, or perhaps it was not devilish but "something grand and magnificent like those new planes, better and even faster than the jets, which could get you to Europe or Asia in a matter of a few hours."[63] A few pages later, Robin's imagination takes him further. In a dream, he encounters a strange man emerging from what is clearly a space ship. Robin, feeling proprietorial as a resident of Earth, demands that the alien explain his presence. The alien responds, "I did not intend to come down here. Something went wrong in my – space ship. Something magnetic I did not expect in this exact locality. I must refuel before I take off again."[64]

Robin speculates that perhaps the space ship's trajectory had been disrupted by "the new iron deposits we've just found in the Laurentians."[65] For Hedges, as for Robin, it is important for the alien to appreciate the galactic power of Canada's newly discovered mineral wealth. Finally, the alien explains a bit more about his origins:

> "I am from the planet Corfus. We are not seen by the Earth yet; we have been in existence much longer than the Earth and have lived in harmony with you, unknown to you since the time Earth was formed; but now there are elements, both human and scientific, on Earth, which threaten to disrupt the cosmos entirely. They are caused by incorrect thought and mistakes in the direction of science. We are very much disturbed by this and wish to assist you to rectify the situation before it is out of hand."[66]

Robin is impressed: "You speak good English," he says, smiling. But this is not surprising, the alien answers: "We were forced to learn English in order to communicate," and "we have your books, you know. We have long ago made studies of your cultures."[67] (For Hedges, the one language learned by the aliens must of necessity be English.) Robin worries that "the people on Corfus did not think very highly of culture here below."[68] But soon he is comforted by the visitor from space, who says, "We are looking for the right people to take the lead in helping us to review your values in order to prevent further damage. If your objectives of destruction and hatred continue, Earth will disintegrate, and that would disturb the entire cosmos. We cannot afford to let this occur."[69] Like Hedges, Robin seeks assurance that this destruction will be avoided. He wants to believe that there is a beneficent god who will ensure that the world stays on track. But perhaps the visitor from Corfus has more bad news. Perhaps he has discovered that God no longer exists. "Do you believe in God?" Robin asks, nervous about the implications of the alien's answer. He is reassured: "Yes, we do believe in God," the man tells him, and "we have good reason for this."[70]

It is odd to see conversations about religious belief between an earthling and a space alien in a Canadian novel set in 1957 and equally odd to see discussions about the nature of God tied to observations about atomic weapons and climate change. Both Robin and the space alien give voice to one of Hedges's most sustained beliefs – that God is present in the world, that His presence must be constantly affirmed, and that faith in the world He created is always necessary, particularly at a time when so many norms are being shattered or put in doubt.

While Hedges's concerns about the future of Canada drew her into a strange mix of motifs and ideas, she undoubtedly enjoyed some of the more light-hearted depictions of Canadian identity that emerged around the time *Robin* was published. In the same year, *My Fur Lady*, a satire of Canadians' preoccupation with national identity, opened to rave reviews. It was taken on the road by McGill's Red and White Revue and sold out to audiences across the country. It holds the record for the longest run of any original Canadian theatre production.[71] Doris and Geoffrey Hedges were ardent supporters of Canadian theatre and would not have missed this popular production, which was staged at McGill's Moyse Hall, the same venue where they had performed in *The Constant Wife* many years earlier.

The final months of 1957 in Montreal were frigid. They left Hedges celebrating the coming of spring, which was the subject of a poem she published in *Canadian Poetry* magazine in early 1958:

Spring

But as daylight hours lengthen out
We greet the tiny buds as they appear.
The winter seems a thing to smile about;
Summer is beckoning and spring is here.[72]

Figure 6.1
My Fur Lady program, 1957

By June of 1959, Hedges returned to the pages of the Montreal *Gazette*. In a letter to the editor published on 23 June she complained about an article by June Callwood concerning the treatment Queen Elizabeth II had received during her lengthy tour of Canada, which took place from 18 June to 1 August of that year. Hedges objected to Callwood's assertion that the Queen and the Duke of Edinburgh "will be welcomed – and even cheered if someone in the crowd is confident enough to start it off," but Callwood felt that this was unlikely to happen because the Queen "will be met by uninhibited curiosity, but inhibited enthusiasm."[73] Hedges understood that Callwood was pointing to hostility directed toward the royal couple. This antipathy, Hedges believed, reflected "a combination of indifference, annoyance, and resentment about a monarchy symbolizing the apron strings that Canadians long ago discarded."[74] She felt that the placement of such an article "in an English newspaper" made her "more than angry. It is an outrage."[75] She added that "the glory of Queen Elizabeth" was tied to her ability to promote human understanding and the peaceful co-operation of nations under her rule. "We, as Canadians, should be grateful to any symbol of unity and friendship in such an enlightened community of nations as is expressed in the Commonwealth."[76]

The letter served to underline the extent to which Hedges remained partial to British tradition and heritage. This was not a difficult position to hold in Montreal in 1959. The separatist movement that would soon call Canadian federalism into question had not yet become a public phenomenon; many anglophones in the city proudly declared their allegiance to both queen and country. It was one thing for Quebec nationalists to call this allegiance into question, but quite another for an English journalist writing in an English paper to undercut the loyalty of those who still believed in the importance of the monarchy.

A year later, in 1960, Jean Lesage would be elected premier of Quebec, heralding a new era in Quebec politics. Although Lesage was a member of the provincial Liberal Party, his nationalist policies soon diverged from traditional Liberal principles and laid the groundwork for the Quiet Revolution, which promised to make French Quebecers "Maîtres chez nous." Lesage's nationalism paved the way for the establishment of the Parti Québécois under the leadership of René Lévesque in 1968. For someone like Hedges, who believed so strongly in British values and the power of the monarchy, the decade before her death in 1972 must have been tumultuous. She was witnessing the disintegration of what she and her family had always held dear. Lesage's stance challenged her past, her family's sense of tradition, and her ideas about the future of the country.

The rise of Quebec nationalism in the 1960s was influenced by forces beyond Canada's borders. In *The Empire Within: Postcolonial Thought and Political Activism in Sixties Montreal*, Sean Mills traces some of the profound shifts in global politics that took place during the decade. Quoting Frederick Cooper, Mills notes that the shift away from imperialism began after the Second World War, a period during which "the aura of normality attached to empire for millennia began to give way."[77] By the 1960s, an era of "global decolonization" had empowered ideas of nationalism influenced by "Third World theory." Mills maintains that

> no North American city was as profoundly affected by Third World theory as Montreal. Beginning in the late 1950s and early 1960s, dissident writers in Montreal adapted the ideas of Frantz Fanon, Aimé Césaire, Jacques Berque, Albert Memmi, and others, to develop a movement proposing that Quebec join with the nations of the Third World in forming, in Bennita Parry's words, "different social imaginaries and alternative rationalities."[78]

Mills observes that although Montreal was considered to be "a major centre of North American industrialization and capitalist expansion," local activists "drew on anti-colonial theory to imagine Quebec as a colony and Montreal as a colonial city."[79] This view was not shared by the city's wealthy anglophones. Although two-thirds of the population was French, "in the city's wealthiest neighbourhoods, the commercial establishments of the downtown core, and the halls of the most prestigious financial, cultural, and educational institutions, English prevailed."[80]

Theories of decolonization in Quebec were always complicated by the meaning of the term "decolonization" and by several competing ideas of nationhood that came into play during the decade. While Quebec nationalists might argue that they were a colonized people, others pointed out that "from an Aboriginal perspective, French Canadians were far from being colonized subjects."[81] As Khan-Tineta Horn observed at the hearings of the Royal Commission on Bilingualism and Biculturalism in 1965, French Canadians might well be defined as "the first invading race."[82] However, this thinking would not have been shared by Hedges, who remained largely cloistered in the wealthy anglophone areas of a city that was expanding dramatically and attracting immigrants who were altering the very texture of the place she had known as a child. Yet in some respects, Hedges was insulated from these changes. She did not frequent the small cafes or university gatherings where new ideas about Quebec nationalism were being debated and declaimed. Despite the evidence of a radical shift in Quebec political ideology, the shift toward nationalist politics had yet to affect the daily lives of wealthy anglophones.

As if to illustrate how removed Hedges was from the heated political environment that was developing around her, she learned that "Prayer," one of her poems from *Words on a Page* (originally published in 1949), had been selected for inclusion in *The Golden Year*, a new anthology published by the Poetry Society of America. The collection was designed to celebrate the society's fiftieth anniversary in 1960.[83] In doing so, it looked back to work that had been published a decade earlier, like Hedges's poem, which asked God for inspiration and for the strength to focus on both nature and "the heavens":

O God of Goodness, Forwardness, and Fulness
Let not my feet stray from the path of nature
Nor my heart and soul from contemplation of the heavens.
Keep thou my mind alive and ever searching
And my eyes open to the glow of beauty.
Help my strength that it may flow outward
And return from conflict unvanquished and undimmed.
God of all strength, keep me strong.
God of light, terrify me not by fear of ultimate futility
But let me hope one day to gaze unblinded at the sun
And sing my song of joy in perfect purity. Amen.[84]

The *Gazette* described this as "an outstanding literary honour,"[85] and perhaps it was, but it conveyed no sense of its author as a person influenced by the changes taking place in the culture around her, nor did it demonstrate any shift in Hedges's style or form, which had remained relatively consistent throughout her career. By way of contrast, Leonard Cohen had published his groundbreaking *Let Us Compare Mythologies* four years earlier, while Margaret Atwood published twenty new poems in 1960 alone. Irving Layton had authored thirteen books of poetry by the same date. Both in her writing and in her social sphere, Hedges seemed to be caught in a time warp. She was reluctant to embrace change. Yet at the same time, as a person who was involved in the daily news and in the political currents of her time, it would have been impossible for her to turn a blind eye to the shifting status quo. Life was how it had always been and how it had never been.

Hedges did not publish another work until 1963, when her new collection of poetry titled *For This I Live* was published by Exposition Press. What kinds of activities was she involved in during this three-year publication gap? The short answer is that she and Geoffrey were travelling and enjoying themselves. A review of the *Gazette*'s personals page between 1960 and 1963 reveals the extent to which they found themselves out of Canada. A diary format is a useful way of summarizing this activity:

22 January 1960: The Hedges leave for Jamaica, where they will spend six weeks at the Jamaica Inn.[86] They return 8 March.[87]

14 May 1960: The Hedges sail on the *Homeric* to spend two months in Europe.[88] They return on 15 July following stays in England and Italy.[89]

27 February 1961: The Hedges return from Scottsdale, Arizona, where they have spent a month.[90]

5 September 1961: The Hedges return to Montreal following a trip to Switzerland and England.[91]

5 March 1962: The Hedges return to Montreal after a month's stay at Yeaman's Hall in Charleston, South Carolina.[92]

7 June 1962: The Hedges fly to England for a five-week trip.[93]

12 September 1962: The Hedges return to Montreal following stays in St Andrews, New Brunswick, and Mountain View House in Whitefield, New Hampshire.[94]

14 March 1963: The Hedges return to Montreal after spending a month at the Coral Beach Club in Bermuda.[95]

19 July 1963: The Hedges return to Montreal, having spent five weeks in England.[96]

Between January 1960 and July 1963 the couple logged nine substantial trips, and these are only the more extended voyages noted in the personals section; there were undoubtedly many more local excursions. This kind of travel activity apparently did not leave Hedges much time for writing. It was also the kind of activity that was reserved for the wealthy. The Hedges stayed at luxurious lodges and hotels with private facilities and golf courses.

Now that Geoffrey had retired, there was more time for the couple to indulge in their passion for travel. But Doris was also determined to keep her name in print. However, she was unable to find a conventional publisher for her next poetry collection and so once again turned to a vanity publisher. Exposition Press was a large self-publishing venture with offices on Park Avenue in New York. The company had been founded by Edward Uhlan in 1936. By 1963 it had become a major publishing house. As Timothy Laquintano notes, Uhlan insisted on calling Exposition a "subsidy publishing" company rather than a "vanity" press because "he considered himself honest and he thought there was a genuine need for the work he did."[97] As Laquintano observes, "Uhlan said that he dealt with the 99 percent of books that were rejected by publishers, although he professed to have standards and claimed to have rejected as many books as he had published."[98]

Uhlan maintained this perspective even though, by the end of the Second World War, "the royalty system was so dominant few people other than subsidy press owners were advocating publishing models that would require an author's own capital investment."[99] Although Hedges had access to a royalty publishing system that was booming by the 1960s, she was still forced to turn to an American subsidy outfit. Clearly, she had been unable to find a conventional publisher and there were no vanity presses in Canada at the time. Uhlan himself had mixed feelings about publishing poetry. In his memoir, *The Rogue of Publishers' Row,* he writes that "when one goes fishing for poets, one comes up with some extraordinary catches. I was astonished to discover how many uneducated aspirants to the arts had music in their souls. Some of this music, to be sure, sounded like the death rattle of an alley cat being skinned alive, but still it was music of a sort."[100] Uhlan also pointed out that, on average, it cost an author about $12 per page to publish with Exposition. *For This I Live,* with its eighty pages, would have cost Hedges about $960 to produce, before charges for cover design and any advertising related to the book. This would be roughly equivalent to $8,000 in 2020.[101] Few authors would have been able to raise that kind of money in 1963, just as few authors would be able to raise the equivalent amount today. In other words, whether it was called vanity publishing or subsidy publishing, the process was available mainly to those authors who were comparatively well off. Given her own financial standing, the costs associated with the publication of her book would have posed little difficulty for Hedges, who was used to travelling to exclusive resorts or flying to Europe in the first-class sleeper compartment.

The dust jacket flaps on *For This I Live* provide what is called Hedges's "credo":

> I believe that the only person who should run one's life is oneself, and that the responsibility for one's action lies in one's own hands. Blaming the other guy, or circumstances, or God, is weakness. The challenge of life is here, to be met singlehanded by each one of us in a lonely but spiritually stimulating world.

This sounds like an odd mixture of religious spiritualism and existential resolution. The book flap also directs the reader to the idea that the poetry is "a sturdy affirmation of everyman's accountability" rather than "the offerings of a dewy-eyed ivory tower inhabitant." The description sounds defensive. It was as if Hedges anticipated the criticism that might be directed at her: that the poetry was the product of a privileged elitist rather than a genuine "everyman" whose words were relevant to the period in which they were written. To what extent does the poetry live up to this credo? To what extent does it show a shift in Hedges's poetic stance?

The book is divided into four sections: "Philosophy," "Love," "Nature," and "Satire." In the first section – "Philosophy" – Hedges speaks in the first person about her poetic aims:

> I toss my poems into the air
> Hoping that my gift
> May be caught up
> Into resistance
> To that strange and nebulous
> Phenomenon of the present age,
> Spirit clashing
> Against spirit,
> Robot against robot,
> Reason against love.[102]

Hedges expresses many of the concerns that preoccupied her in the years leading up to the collection: the threats posed by automation – specifically robotics – and the danger posed by nuclear weapons. This is not so much philosophy as a protest against the nature of the age, one that expresses frustration with all that has turned against matters of the spirit and human choice. The protest also explains why Hedges was so reluctant to embrace modernist poetry: for her, it was aligned with the dehumanization she saw around her, as if new poetic modes were themselves robotic and a product of the nuclear age. Tradition would act as a bulwark against this kind of dehumanization, and that meant writing poetry that refused to embrace shifting poetic values.

Again and again in the collection, Hedges contemplates the relevance and power of poetic language in her time. In "Rusty Words" she says, "we have need / Of difficult and troubling words / That will not shake weakly / In their sentences, like men / Crying in unbelief to God."[103] In "Noble Balance," she complains that poets and philosophers have turned away from the forces that would allow them to transcend the pettiness of their immediate time and place – the forces of religion and "the lucid breath / of priests"[104] and of love, which conquers "helplessness," "anger," "wasted causes," "exhaustion," "frustration," "shamefaced ignominy," and "rage."[105] She contemplates the power of writing, when "The pencil and the paper meet / hesitantly, crushing thought between"[106] and her own role as a writer who finds that "The road is painful" because there are so few signs indicating which direction the writer should take, even when such direction is provided by "learned values," without which "there is no knowledge."[107] True, one could step off the established path and follow a new and promising direction ("the fields are greener / to right and left"), but in the end, she concludes that it is better to stick with the known route, "plodding, believing, caring," because ultimately it is the known road that provides wisdom, or "truth there / written in sunlight."[108]

Hedges often offers direct confessions about her state of mind. In "Contentment" she says that "My strongest feelings and my dearest hopes / Are locked within me," and that she believed they "Could never fail to bring me joy" but now "I am less fulfilled and less ambitious."[109] In "Shyness" the speaker expresses her fear of others and "the knife of meeting" those around her who remain "strangers to me." She wonders: "Are they terrified of me / As I of them?" She knows that in acting like "One granite mass uncarved" she has shut them out and contributed to her own loneliness. "What a fool I feel, and drop my guard / Before the friendly battery of eyes."[110] In some of the poems, Hedges presents herself through a thinly disguised persona as a voice of reason and intelligence. In others, she is more insecure about her position and her knowledge. She feels that part of her is rooted in her relation to the earth as if she were an animal, while another side of her is aligned with God. Her challenge is to understand how "I / Am animal and man is God, yet we are brothers / In this earthly partnership."[111]

One gets the sense that this persona – who speaks very directly to us as the poet behind each poem – is not a happy person, at least not in the "Philosophy" section of *For This I Live*. In "Mood," she describes what she does "To run depression off," a depression which has left her feeling "Like a cobweb full of dead flies."[112] She searches for "truth" in nature. In "The Light Heart" she speaks of how "the sorrowing / dark and mysterious thinking / spread through the universe / and men grew weary" of their lives "until all the earth / was encompassed" in "the evil vortex / of human apathy."[113] In "Cry from the Heart" she laments the passing of her youth and wants to return to it: "Give me a bud now, / Oh, give me a green bud / While the Spring is young!"[114] But the problem is that time is passing:

If there were time to laugh
And time to savour it
Flowers and stars
In the heart
Sunset glow
Would cheer us.[115]

The poems in this section of *For This I Live* are not so much concerned with "Philosophy" as they are with the speaker's state of mind and with the self-portrait they present – that of a speaker who is inward-turning, shy, worried about her present, and convinced that the natural world and God will offer her two forms of sustenance, if only the mechanization of humanity and the modern denial of His power could be undone.

Perhaps the next section of the book – "Love" – will offer a more redemptive kind of solace. The section opens with a poem titled "My Dear." It is addressed to the speaker's lover. Hedges so often uses her poems as confessional vehicles that it seems warranted to assume that the persona here articulates sentiments held by the author herself. She feels that love demands a certain consistency that is reflected in her aesthetic. These are not experimental poems that break with tradition; rather, they are traditional in form and expression because "What words are there / Except the old ones, / Laden and golden with the loves / And heart-beats of the ages?"[116] If these love poems were written to Geoffrey, in order "To say what no words can,"[117] then Hedges must have felt ambivalent about the continuing power of her thirty-seven-year-old marriage. Here is the oddly titled "I Am a Slave":

> How beautiful your eyes are, and how hard;
> They are twin rocks, warm in a sunset glow;
> They draw me to you helplessly.
> How beautiful your hands are, and how hard;
> They melt my flesh, caress my beating heart;
> They let me go so carelessly.
> How beautiful your mouth is, and how hard;
> Your lips ravage me, your smile is adamant,
> Seductive as the perfume of a rose.
> How beautiful your voice is, and how hard;
> I drown in its dark river, listening.
> And hearing nothing but my doom.
> How beautiful your love is, and how hard;
> I am a slave that dies against you, willingly,
> Leaving no mark against the shore.[118]

The poem is sexually suggestive. Is it an affirmation of her continuing attraction to Geoffrey? Is Doris his "slave"? Or does the poem express her desire for another lover, for whom she is also a slave? And does she feel that this relationship, if discovered, would spell "nothing but my doom" for a narrator who "dies" against her lover but leaves no trace through which their relationship might be found? The questions raise others about Hedges's private life. If she did in fact have a mysterious lover who ravishes her, who was that man? Or was it a man? Why would Hedges publish a poem in 1963 that revealed an adulterous affair if Geoffrey did not know about it? Or perhaps these poems were a series of confessions about a secret lover, a kind of coming out? She does admit, in "I Am a Lover," that in the past "I hid my heart; I had contempt / For those who loved" but now, rejuvenated, "I put my love / Upon my sleeve

/ Not caring if they see / I wear it there."[119] She advises her readers to "Give love away" just as she has.[120]

Other poems in the "Love" section of the book record passionate dreams and encounters. In "Gentle Meeting" the speaker instructs her lover to "not weep / Or look behind, but leave your touch / Deep in my heart."[121] In "Set Free" the speaker tells her lover that "You are no conjured dream / No idol that my mind evolves, / No glittering illusion."[122] In "World without End" she says, "My heart is strong" and "It flies to rest / Where it is happiest, / Against your own."[123] She ends this section with the poem called "Warning," in which she advises her mysterious lover to "Ask little things of me." She promises that "I will be yours, my dear, forever and a day."[124] My own copy of *For This I Live* bears an inscription in Hedges's own hand: "To Margaret with love." It is almost as if she wrote the collection for a specific person, with a specific relationship in mind. Who was Margaret?

In the "Nature" section of *For This I Live* Hedges praises a clutch of bluebells as a "portent of life's strength."[125] She feels a fraternity with the birds she hears and imagines them celebrating the advent of spring. The release from winter prompts her to warn herself against the "eternal restlessness" she associates with the season ("April is wise; better let April go"). She thanks flowers in a vase for their "mystic loveliness" and the poetic inspiration they deliver: "when I looked at you, / I saw life's mysteries anew."[126] The natural world provides the music that delivers her. "What better music / Can anyone desire?" she asks.[127]

These romantic outpourings are seldom interrupted by any sense of anxiety; nature is always welcome. But occasionally, some of the longing that characterizes much of Hedges's work breaks through the idealized landscapes, as it does in "I Am a Mother," in which she imagines watching her son Johnny (oddly called "man of mine"). He is waving at her from a distance, happy about the sand castles he has built near a "slow-retiring wave" in the "shore-sand."[128] Fantasized children. Fantasized relationships. Hedges's poetry often provided her with a means of escape from what she depicted as a troubling existence. Toward the end of the "Nature" section she interrupts her meditations on the power of nature with the account of an illicit relationship that has been discovered. In "Double Requiem," addressed to the wife of her lover, she mourns the end of her adulterous affair and likens it to the end of a war:

And you, my enemy, have you hatred
In your heart? Do you desire
My death? My suffering? For me,
I have nothing at all of this
And, knowing it, wonder if you, as I,
Go stumbling on the road of war
With lagging feet. There lie the green
Of fields, the golden sky, the dusk,
Tarnished for you, and for me too;
The smoking ruin of our lives
Betrays earth's fairness; oh, my enemy,
Wife of his, sister, mother, do you feel
Hatred? Love is a hidden flame
Waiting to warm our hands; seek
With your woman's grasp, pierce
With your woman's wit this tangle
That our feet are deep in. Stand
As you must behind your man, yet keep
Him pure of hate, untouched by evil.[129]

It sounds like a prayer for forgiveness. Hedges appeals to the betrayed wife not to abandon her husband, not to allow him to hate. It is a remarkable admission of adultery from the speaker of the poem. Hedges seldom employed narrators who did not speak for her own condition at any given time. She was also partial to reflecting upon her own poetry in terms of its marketability, as if certain poetic techniques could be employed to guarantee sales and success. In "Cry to the Gods" we see the businesswoman in Hedges emerging once again. She provides would-be writers with this advice:

You must have difficult essentials
Such as ability to sell your product
Because if you're bad at that
You can be a Rodin or a Bach
Or even a cancer-killer
And still lose out, and die unsold.
It all boils down to salesmanship –
And a good product, of course.[130]

The last section of *For This I Live* – "Satire" – takes on some of the annoyances of daily life. But the poems are hardly satirical. The garbage cans outside are being moved around. They make too much noise ("Silent Trash Can"). The speaker imagines herself as a paper boy "trudging up / the imposing steps of the richer houses" to make his delivery, and puzzling about the headlines, which he cannot understand. He wonders who has the time to read these papers; he wonders "why / there are so many papers full of words."[131] That is hardly satire. It is more like a commentary on the gap separating the literate beings who live in these expensive houses from those who simply climb the steps and cannot read. For Hedges, it is the people in those houses who deal with the world while the paper boy can only ask "who reads it all, who studies it, / who has the time to feel deep down inside / enough to understand, to fix things up."[132] Yet in "The Great Why," Hedges ponders whether even those wealthy readers can solve the problems of the day without resorting to thoughts about God: "so many wide thinkers / Return to their God when they feel a misgiving."[133] In Hedges's poetry, this kind of contemplation is frequently interrupted by her focus on the quotidian: she looks at her mailing list of friends and realizes how many have died ("Mailing List"); she watches the woman on her neighbour's rooftop and wonders whether she is eating a chicken sandwich ("I Am a Roof-Bird"); she reflects upon the amorality of Montreal and its "sex crimes" ("Civic Pride"). At the same time, she returns frequently to her preoccupation with imagined children ("Betrayal") and love affairs that are figured as a form of captivity:

Have you ever been in bed with a man
You love in full trust,
All your womanhood enslaved
And yet victorious in deep breath
Of lushest living?[134]

Hedges ends the volume on a self-reflective note that reminds readers of her social status, a status she was never able to forget in anything she wrote. She wonders:

Has any woman written a poem
about mink before?
Mink is a symbol

of false security,
false glamour,
false picture in the eyes
of empty-minded society.[135]

If Hedges wondered why her poetry did not attract a wider readership, perhaps it was because she wrote for those who, like herself, were owners of mink (as she says, "I have worn mink"). Or perhaps it was because she considered those who had not worn mink to be members of "empty-minded society," people who could not be expected to appreciate the finer things in life, be they poems or furs. She leaves the book complaining about the status of poetry in her age, a complaint that centres not so much on its formal qualities as on its subject matter:

Poets once gave us the stars, or pink asters,
Songs, or a saga, the whispering leaves
Of the trees at day's ending; the poet
Today is a man with a flag, and a chip
On his shoulder, his sounds like strong drink
Making froth in his cup …[136]

For This I Live generated very few reviews; none voiced praise. On the contrary, some reviewers were very direct about their reservations. Marcus Van Steen's review in the Ottawa *Citizen* is a case in point:

> In these 61 poems, Mrs. Hedges makes her poetry clear, and her philosophy simple. Her verse is so easy to understand that there is never any doubt that she has very little to say, and says it with an unoriginality that is numbing.
>
> This is a book for those who feel safe only with the tried and true old copy-book maxims about Love and Motherhood and Friendly Earth, dished up in lines as bland as blanc-mange, and as tasteless.[137]

Hedges would have taken reviews like this to heart, enough to make her question the validity of her writing altogether. She would not publish another book of poetry for eight years. During that period, Doris and Geoffrey continued to visit family in England and to frequent some of their favourite vacation retreats. Over six years, from February 1963 to March 1969, they returned to the exclusive Coral Beach Club in Bermuda five times. During the same period, they visited England twice. They also found time to return to a resort in St Andrews, New Brunswick. Despite her history of contributing to the Montreal *Gazette*, she is absent from the newspaper's pages during the same six-year period. At some level, Hedges had decided to remove herself from public view. Her enthusiasm for writing was waning.

She did publish three poems that may help to explain the source of her silence. In 1967, "Tempo" appeared in *Canadian Poetry*, and the following year, "Loan of Life" was published in the same magazine. Her last published poem was "Alias for Love" in the *Gazette* for April 1969. As its title indicates, "Tempo" is about the passing of time. The poet observes that "With age, laughter sinks deeper / Into the heart than youth permits." For her, the "sudden smile" of her lover is "precious as a memory / Of golden friendship rooted in rhythm."[138] In "Loan of Life," the speaker contemplates the absence of true ownership of her material goods because, in the end, "It's all a loan / from God." Her duty in life, she reveals, has been "to discover / what God meant."[139] While these poems dwell on age and mortality, "Alias for Love" focuses on another topic that deeply affected Hedges throughout her career: the implications of advances in science and technology. The poem is a response to news of the first heart transplant, which took place in December of 1967:

> The heart is now a mobile mechanism
> Moved by surgeons' hands from chest to chest
> In a matter of minutes;
> Must we now make love
> With another man's heart?[140]

Hedges included "Tempo," "Loan of Life," and "Alias for Love" in her final poetry collection, *Inside Out*, published in 1971. Before looking at that collection in more detail, it is worth considering the extent to which Hedges had removed herself from so many of the profound changes swirling around her during the 1960s. Her response to these changes was often to assert the predominance of the past over the present, to valorize remembrance over immediate observation, to warn about the evils of technology, or to critique those who had abandoned conventional religion in their search for new forms of ritual and belief.

Yet how reactionary could one remain in the midst of the multiple revolutions that defined the 1960s, both in Canada and elsewhere? Hedges often wrote about dancing, but she had nothing to say about Chubby Checker and the twist. One would never know, from reading her work, that this was the decade that introduced the Beatles, the Beach Boys, Jimi Hendrix, the Doors, the Rolling Stones, Bob Dylan, and so many others. The most popular song in 1960 was Percy Faith's "Theme from 'A Summer Place.'" By the end of the decade Hendrix had recorded hits such as "Purple Haze" and "Crosstown Traffic" while the Stones had released no fewer than ten albums. The number-one song in 1968 was The Archies' "Sugar Sugar," followed closely by the Fifth Dimension's "Aquarius" and "Let the Sun Shine In." The last two were songs from the Broadway musical *Hair* (1968), which was itself associated with a revolution in ideas about sexuality, style, race, community, and the nature of human love. *Hair*, subtitled *An American Tribal Love-Rock Musical*, is about a Vietnam War draftee who is introduced to the counterculture by a group of hippies who enjoy smoking marijuana and taking LSD. Even if she ignored the musical or had never listed to the Beatles' "Sgt. Pepper's Lonely Hearts Club Band" (1967), Hedges seldom mentions the radical politics that emerged in the massive protest movements against the war in Vietnam, many of which were inspired by anti-imperialist, Marxist-Leninist ideologies. Those protests would have challenged her imperialist values to the core. Yet Hedges seemed to be caught in stasis while all around her the world was being feverishly transformed.

If *Hair* seemed removed from the conservative lifestyle Hedges embraced in her Montreal home, so did the profound shift in art and literature that dominated this decade. Writers began to experiment with postmodern forms; John Barth's famous manifesto, "The Literature of Exhaustion," appeared in 1967. Hedges was writing "Loan of Life" and "Alias for Love" at the same time as Pynchon, Barthelme, and Coover were reconfiguring the contemporary novel. Meanwhile, the Beat poets – along with those associated with the Black Mountain, San Francisco, and New York schools of poetry – were transforming the very conception of verse.

If these shifts – often associated with American literature and art – were not enough to alter Hedges's perspective, there were also new challenges to mainstream poetic practices that were appearing much closer to home during the 1960s. Here one thinks of early poems by Michael Ondaatje, bpNichol's Coach House Press publications and the work of other concrete poets, sound poets like the Four Horsemen, the writers associated with TISH, and the poets connected with the *New Wave Canada* anthology published by Contact Press in 1966. Even closer to home there was Leonard Cohen, who had published *Flowers for Hitler* in 1964 and *Beautiful Losers* in 1966. Hedges turned a blind eye to the radical epistemologies embodied in these works.

If she resisted the experimental art produced in the 1960s, Hedges also seemed to be publicly unmoved by many of the political and ideological shifts that were taking place around her. She was an ardent Canadian nationalist but she never entered into the debate surrounding the creation of a new Canadian flag, which was finally flown in December 1964. And how could she have remained silent on all of the celebrations connected with Canada's Centennial in 1967, or on the relentless hype that accompanied Montreal's Expo 67 World's Fair, an event that transformed the very conception of her own city? By the end of the decade, on colour TV, she could have watched the first landing of a man on the moon in July 1969. Or she could have seen hippies ripping up the social order as they danced and partied at Woodstock in August of the same year. And by October 1970, she could have witnessed something truly frightening – soldiers occupying the streets of Montreal after Pierre Elliott Trudeau invoked the War Measures Act to counter FLQ terrorism in Quebec.

It was against the backdrop of these momentous events that Hedges published *Inside Out* in 1971. Like *For This I Live*, the small book was a vanity project. Hedges had it produced at her own expense in England by Abbey Press, which was not a publisher but a printing company. My copy of the book contains a note in Hedges's hand to an unnamed recipient. It says, "This collection of poetry is my latest. It is published in England, but not available in Canadian book-stores. It is a gift from me to you. Let me know if you would like another copy." The note, and the circumstances of the book's publication, reveal a good deal about the status of Hedges's career in 1971. Obviously, she could not find a conventional publisher for her book in Canada or the United States; for this reason, the book could not be distributed in North America. Hedges turned to an established British printer for the project, a curious decision, since she would have known how unlikely it would be for

Figure 6.2
Doris Hedges, 1968

a privately printed book published outside North America to reach her native market.[141] But it may well be that, at this point, Hedges had abandoned the idea of achieving any kind of prominence as a poet in Canada. The publication of *Inside Out* seems more like a symbolic gesture intended to collect some of Hedges's older poems, along with several new ones. Out of the thirty-one poems in the volume, seven were reprinted from previous works, and of those seven, four – dating back to Hedges's early Ryerson chapbooks in 1946 and 1947 – were reprinted for the third time. The book was advertised by Montreal's Ogilvy's department store in 1971. The photo used for the advertisement showed a picture of Hedges that was dated 1952.

Precisely because it recycles previous poems, *Inside Out* illustrates what beliefs remained constant for Hedges during her entire career. She thought of poetry as a form of self-exploration that often became self-critique. In "Beehives and Bums" we meet a narrator who finds herself at a beach club with couples who just "yack and yack and yack." The women, "bikini-like," are "Just bums in a beehive, expensive too"; they "watch / For envious glances from the men." Everyone is "liquor encrusted." They have forgotten "the tropic paradise we've bought."[142] For Hedges, ignoring the natural world is a cardinal sin. She reflects upon the decadence that surrounds her and realizes that "Some of us know exactly what we are, and where; / I'm one of them: I'm caught, and so are they."[143] A version of the same theme appears in "Background Music," in which the narrator reflects upon the way television soundtracks are muddled and unconvincing; they cannot duplicate the "sounds of trees whispering / In the wind, of seas muttering on the sand."[144] Instead, television divorces its viewers from nature: "We sit in front of the T.V. giant / Helpless and furious."[145] In "Insult to the Trees" the speaker finds herself "On a forest path, where "one strolls / in ecstasy, holding the silence / close to one's heart in gratitude," but then the silence is broken by the sound of a transistor radio that is "bellowing a song / of love betrayed, a whining plaint / filling your sacred peace."[146]

Hedges's skepticism about technology even extended to personal computers. While microcomputers did not enter the consumer marketplace until the later 1970s, the term "personal computer" and "pocket computer" appeared as early as 1962.[147] There were several early models of small computers that Hedges might have been aware of by 1971, including Simon (1950), the IBM 610 (1957), and the Datapoint 2200 (1970). The poem "It's Yours" is about how "this toy that faces you is dangerous" because "it's useful and efficient / But not God." Hedges concludes that one should "laugh in your computer's face" and "turn away to search / For life, and love, and new machines."[148]

That conclusion seems to be a contradiction. Why search for "new machines" when those very machines tempt people to believe they are godlike? Hedges recognized the contradiction and struggled for a resolution that she was ultimately unable to find. This was really a struggle between affirming traditional beliefs over current ones, between the solidity of a ritualized past and the uncertainty of a technologized present. In "Today, Wake Up!" she speaks about "Heroic yesterdays" and how they have been supplanted by "the robot we ourselves have built." She argues that "until we take truth into our hands" we will "die / In nothingness." Her conclusion is that "if we can see / No lesson in the past" there will be "no hope tomorrow."[149]

While Hedges returned frequently to the value of the past, and while she always celebrated the historical myths and traditions that had influenced her conception of human identity, she also stressed the importance of living in the moment. "Precious Moment," as the title implies, implores the reader to "catch a beat of time / Before it disappears." To seize the moment is a form of "living, / Creating, being."[150] The poem "Relinquishment" makes a similar point. In order to experience authentic love, one must revel in life: "He, who has loved / Has twisted life / Between his hands / And wrung it dry."[151] In "Movement," Hedges writes that "Movement is conscious living / The backward step is death."[152] Yet in other poems, like "The When," she seems unclear about what to value more – the present or the past:

> We belong to the Now
> We belong to the Then
> Which means the most?
> How do we judge it?[153]

If "the Now" seems knowable and real, it is also fleeting and illusory because "The present moment as we grasp it / Waves us goodbye and points / To its successor hopefully." This happens "Even before we turn the Is to Was."[154]

Despite her preoccupation with the relation between the present and the past, Hedges found it hard to resist editorializing about some of the social changes she witnessed in the late 1960s. For example, "Do It Alone" is addressed to teenagers who are protesting against the war in Vietnam. Hedges has little patience with their activities. For her, they are only sidestepping life:

> Kids, don't give up on life,
> Stop carrying useless placards,
> Rioting, injuring,
> Causing useless trouble;
> Get going on a plan
> For a better world
> And make it yours[155]

Hedges argues that the reality of life is inescapable, which for her also means that the protesters are wasting their time because some things simply cannot be changed, like war. She advises these "kids" that "Life follows you / To every hippy joint."[156] Reality cannot be denied. The newness of this kind of protest – and the youth movement of the 1960s itself – is foreign to her. She has not yet learned the correct spelling of "hippie." She does not know how to understand the demonstrations she sees on television and in the streets. Her generation accepted the reality of two wars. But these demonstrators do not accept the wisdom of their governments. They are not ready to sacrifice themselves to what they see as a conflict that should never have involved America. This argument garners little sympathy from Hedges. For her, the hippies are "cowardly" because "It never pays / Not to face fact." She advises them to "fight for a better life" but only if "you know / What you want of it."[157]

Hedges shows herself to be aware of a changing world around her. But she did little to enter this world. She seemed to be more interested in poetry that harked back to the past. At the same time, she was fantasizing about possible future worlds. To this end, *Inside Out* opens with a poem called "Effeticus," which Hedges describes in a note as "Previously unpublished, and written in the early thirties."[158] In her last book Hedges returns to the preoccupations of a much earlier stage in her career when she was attracted to science fiction. The poem, possibly influenced by H.G. Wells's *The Time Machine* (1895), tells "the sad story of young Effeticus from a document discovered in a Simian graveyard on earth in the year A.D. 4000 by a tourist from the planet Saturn."[159]

Effeticus was born a perfect child who "was in fact a perfect little man, / As Adam was before the world began."[160] Hedges speculates about whether Effeticus is a divine being or the product of evolution. But she decides not to involve herself in an argument about creationism. Instead, she focuses on what this perfect human can bring to a crumbling universe:

> The global wars had made us without soul,
> The good and bad all melted in the whole;
> It was the strangest age that man had known,
> The single power was the State alone.[161]

Effeticus is ideally suited to repairing the war damage. He speaks thirty languages at birth and "had the keenest intellect on Earth." The biggest problem he has to solve is immortality, since the oppressive State had created a chemical "which kept a man from dying" and, as a result, people were "so indolent and bored and weak" that "They hardly ever smiled, or tried to speak!"[162] Now the state had a problem on its hands. What would it do with all these bored, immortal citizens? Effeticus was invented to solve the problem. He was "science-born and science-bred"; he was fated to be "the World-State Head" and "commander of all lands." But the State had ensured that, regardless of his immense power, Effeticus would still be subservient to its ideology. So he was programmed in such a way "That human urges would not make him sway / Or totter with the call of love or hate."[163]

Here was a superman who would be above human emotion. In this sense, he could be a ruthless saviour, the perfect person who could operate without feelings. Thus conceived, Effeticus would sit "besceptered on a lofty throne" with an "Interglobal telephone" as his crown. This way, he could "keep an eye on all the Earth / And know exactly what each man was worth."[164] The plan works well until Effeticus is twenty-one. Then, he starts to blame the State "for failing to amuse" and for neglecting the "Life-urge" within him. But the main problem for Effeticus is that he has never been taught the difference between good and evil, and so "He had confused ideas of heaven and hell." The more he learns, the more he wants to shed his role as "superman" so that he can, in his own words, "test my male virility."[165]

As he witnesses human men fighting on the planet he controls, Effeticus realizes that their battles, and the imperfection of the world, is preferable to the perfection he embodies, because at least conflict provides a route to human emotion. Effeticus has obviously read Tennyson. He understands, looking down upon the battling humans, that "it's better thus to fall / than never to have fought a fight at all."[166] So he decides to descend from his throne. Besides, his throne is only a concept, since the world has now been stripped of all the wood that might once have been used to construct it. He sits on a throne of air. He will go down to Earth and "be a lover ere I die."

Of course, the State looks upon this decision with horror: "they tried to hold him back" but to no avail. Finally, "They gave him back entire his manly glands / Preserved all these long years by doctors' hands."[167] Poor Effeticus does not know how to handle his new "manly glands." They seem to have a life of their own. He "watched aghast as he began to swell, / And swelled and swelled until at last he burst."[168] That is what happens if you cannot control your "manly glands" and refuse to serve "the State." Needless to say, Effeticus "died, poor lad, of glandular explosion," but that is preferable, Hedges reminds us, to dying by "corrosion." It turns out that Effeticus was "too effete" to handle "a draught so neat." In order to solve the problems presented by Effeticus, the State develops a new design. They will invent a new man who is more like an animal, more like "back-to-nature men in every way."[169]

By the end of the poem, Hedges has created a conundrum. Human life cannot be experienced through any kind of perfection; flawed experience is preferable to some kind of divine experience. But at the same time, it is precisely the flawed state of humankind that leads to war, useless talk, and the mindless "rule of thumb" that dominates the quotidian world. There seems to be no way out, no form of existence that remains pure and authentic. As she approached the end of her career, Hedges found herself returning to a work she had written much closer to the start of it. In some respects, she had come a long way, but in other respects, sometimes tragic, she had never moved an inch.

Inside Out includes two poems that seem appropriate to Hedges's final book. In "The Mail-Box" she meditates on what she has tried to do in her poetry:

I am a mail-box
shaking and vibrating
With the emotions
And the turbulence

Of human feelings
Put silently on paper.[170]

She writes that "When I was new" she was "proud to hold" differing emotions; she embraced both "Loves and repudiations." But now, she says, "I am old" and "my belly / Trembles with the weight / Of what I've learned." At the end of the poem, she tells us that she is "shaking and vibrating / With the world's sorrows."[171] In "Challenge" she makes a similar observation:

Some of us think it is easier to live
inside our cage of unreality
untouched by the agony of search;
but to challenge fear
is better than to snuggle
empty and bedecked
behind a cosy cloud.[172]

Perhaps the most succinct expression of Hedges's aesthetic appears in "Poet's Protest," where she struggles with the extent to which the act of writing takes things that are sacred in their ephemerality and transforms them into something debased by the permanence of words:

You say you cannot
Prison beauty in a word
Ephemeral things are sacred
So you say. You are afraid
Of moulds; yet no one else
Can say it better.
Why not make moulds
Of lovely words
And pour the moment in?[173]

Hedges was not able to resolve the tension between ephemerality and permanence. It might be more accurate to say that her poetry is about the failure of that resolution. The moments of energy that appear in a handful of her poems are prompted by her inability to unite the experience of the moment with the weight of history, her self, her past.

Geoffrey Hedges died on 26 April 1972. Doris died at home, three months later, on 14 July. A brief obituary appeared in the *Gazette*, noting that Hedges was a "well-known Montreal author" whose works had received "critical acclaim in Canada, the United States and Great Britain."[174] This was not true. Hedges's works had received little commentary over her career. She was better known as a local speaker than as a writer. What might have come as a surprise to those reading her obituary was the revelation that "she held a post in the psychological warfare division of the U.S. Office of War Information."[175] The idea that she had been involved in covert surveillance activities was something no one had heard about before. How did the *Gazette* manage to obtain this information after Hedges's death? Perhaps the paper did know about her wartime activities all along, but had decided to keep some of them secret while Hedges was still alive. There was a side to Hedges's personality that had entirely escaped public scrutiny.

The *Gazette* obituary was not accompanied by a photo. In fact, given the extent to which she was a public figure, it is remarkably difficult to find images of Doris Hedges. Only a few survive. These images were often created by the most noted photographers and painters of the day. Some of the earliest portraits were taken by the celebrated Montreal photographers William Notman and Anne Kew. Another photo, dated 1931, reproduces a painting of Hedges done by Richard Jack, Canada's pre-eminent war painter. In this picture she is looking directly at the painter.

There is challenge in her eyes, a sensuality in the partially bared shoulder, the casually draped cape. But there is also the sense that this was a woman who was comfortable in her privilege. Who designed the jewellery? The dress? How did Doris find herself in the studio of the famed Richard Jack?

There is another photo taken much later in Hedges's life, in 1954.[176] Hedges is seated under what is described as "a trompe l'oeil portrait of herself." It would be nice to be able to determine who created the painting and what kind of personality it was intended to convey. But its very presence suggests that Hedges was connected with at least one painter who was interested enough to complete the portrait. Perhaps the painting was created by her cousin, Patricia (Trudi) Nora Dawes, who built a career as an artist, as did her husband, Robert Pilot. This is the most informal picture of Hedges I have discovered. She looks happy and relaxed. She is leaning back on a couch, her hands

Figure 6.3
Doris Hedges, 1931

clasped. She seems at ease with the photographer, posing with a quizzical smile beneath the portrait of herself, as if the painting on the wall – another Doris from another time – looks down suspiciously upon the Doris who is constructing herself for the photo we are viewing.

There is no singular woman here. What gives the photo and the painting energy is the way each casts the other into doubt. For years, I have pursued her elusive story and these rare images with a passion I cannot explain. Who was this enigmatic woman? Who was Doris Hedges?

EPILOGUE

On a cold morning in April, a few years ago now, I decided to visit Doris Hedges's grave. I knew, from reading her will, that she had been cremated. Her remains are buried in the Dawes family plot, in the Sunnyside section of Mount Royal Cemetery. The cemetery covers some 165 acres on the north slope of the mountain, not far below its crucifix-topped crown. It took a while to locate the grave. When I found it, I saw immediately that, even in death, Doris had once again been erased. She lies under a large tombstone with the name DAWES in its centre, as if that's all you needed to know. The Dawes family had been so powerful, so well connected, that their surname eclipsed all others.

On the stone itself are the names of several family members who were originally buried in Lachine. Their remains had been moved to the Mount Royal site in 1928, perhaps in recognition of the fact that by that time the Dawes family had aligned itself more closely with the city than the country village where they had prospered for so many years. The bottom of the monument displays several plaques commemorating members of the family whose names could not be added to the crowded list on the upper tombstone. There, near the top, are Doris's parents, William O. Ryde and Edith Dawes, and, under them, Geoffrey P. Hedges and Doris, identified by her birth name – Doris Edith Ryde. On a smaller set of plaques, mounted on the sides of the stone lying nearest to the ground, are the names of various family servants who are also buried in the Dawes plot. Like Geoffrey Hedges, their identities have been subsumed under the family name. Even in death, they still serve the Dawes. The memorial speaks of the powerful clan that surrounded Doris her whole life. It also shows, in very concrete terms, how difficult it would have been for Doris to break free from those family ties, to assert herself as an individual who could circumvent the family's norms and expectations.

The Dawes connection provided wealth, social networks, and access to business and pleasure. At the same time, that connection made it difficult for Doris to speak out. So many of her poems are about a voice that is stifled, or about passions that end in frustration or fantasized escape. In part, Doris wrote to confess. Yet even in her confessions she had to exert control. She described what she could not speak of in her daily life: forbidden lovers, the children she never had, the solace God might offer in a modern world that had turned away from spiritual sustenance. Then there were the challenges posed by her social standing. She wanted to prove herself as an authentic member of the Dawes clan. She could be involved with charitable organizations and attend fundraising balls and banquets. But why not also start a business and make it a resounding success, in the same way her uncles had managed their railroads and banks and cricket clubs and country estates? Backed by an unlikely group of investors, Doris took the plunge.

The agency never worked. Doris lied about its successes, unable to admit defeat. Undaunted, she promoted herself relentlessly, even though she could see, over and over, that her business was going nowhere and that her writing was losing its relevance to what was modern, what had changed since the war. Part of my attraction to Doris had to do with her unmatched determination. I found myself wanting to defend her and what she tried to do, even though, in terms of her writing and business acumen, there was little to defend. I could also see how hard it was for her to express her sexuality, but express it she did, from her early poems onward. I can think of no poet in Canada who would be bold enough, in 1949, to write about "soft kisses" that went "downward into me" like "The blade of passion feeling for its mark"[1] ("The Blade") or about the ways in which "Stirred passions long asleep" tempt her to enter "Summer's lusty noon"[2] ("Reluctant Awakening"). She was curious about her era even though her style was a throwback to an earlier age. She wrote about roses, love, and redemption as if she inhabited another century. But she also wrote about robots, time travel, space aliens, computers, reincarnation, nuclear energy, abstract art, and Canada's increasing presence in the international order.

While it might sound as though Doris was a socialite by virtue of her family ties, she died childless and alone. Her will is dated 6 October 1971; she added a codicil on 21 January 1972, three months before Geoffrey died. She left her entire estate to him, but in the event that he predeceased her, she directed that $50,000 (about $325,000 in 2020 dollars)[3] be left to her nephew in England – David Paget Hedges – and that the remainder of her estate be left, in equal amounts, to the Salvation Army and the Red Cross Society of Quebec. Near the end of 1972, the Hedges's large house at 9 Redpath Place was put up for sale and an auction of her possessions was organized.

I decided to visit the Hedges residence, simply to get a sense, from the outside, of where Doris had lived. But when I walked up Redpath Avenue to Redpath Place, I saw a new building occupying the lot where the Hedges's house once stood. Her erasure was profound.

Soon after, I began to deal with that erasure by reading Doris's books and visiting the few archives that held her remaining papers. I came across a letter from Nelson Ball to Doris, written after her death. Ball was a well-known Toronto bookseller and the publisher of Weed/Flower Press in the 1960s and '70s. He was renowned for his experimental, minimalist verse. Somehow, Ball had become a fan of Hedges's poetry. He wrote to ask if she had books she wanted to sell. But he also added a fan's comment (see figure E.1).

Ball was, of course, too late. He was one of the few discerning writers in Canada who had discovered Hedges's work. Then, after his 1973 letter, the trail goes silent for decades. Hedges is not mentioned in any literary histories of Canada. Nor is the work she did in founding the first Canadian literary agency credited in those histories. When York University acquired the papers of Matie Molinaro, who started the Canadian Speakers' and Writers' Services in 1950, the archivists stated that "Canadian Speakers' and Writers' Service Ltd. was begun by Matie Molinaro in 1950 as Canada's first literary agency."[4] Since this was incorrect, I wrote to the librarians at York to explain that, in fact, it was Hedges who had started the first Canadian literary agency in 1947. However, the error in the description of the fonds remains. Doris still deserves that credit.

I thought that might be the end of the story. But then, in a routine search, I discovered that Doris had not been completely forgotten. In 2012, the editors of the best-selling *Chicken Soup for the Canadian Soul: Stories to Inspire and Uplift the Hearts of Canadians* included a line from one of Doris's poems. The line appears under the chapter heading "Kindness":

> Life is a lonely journey if we take only our bodies
> on the road and leave our hearts behind.

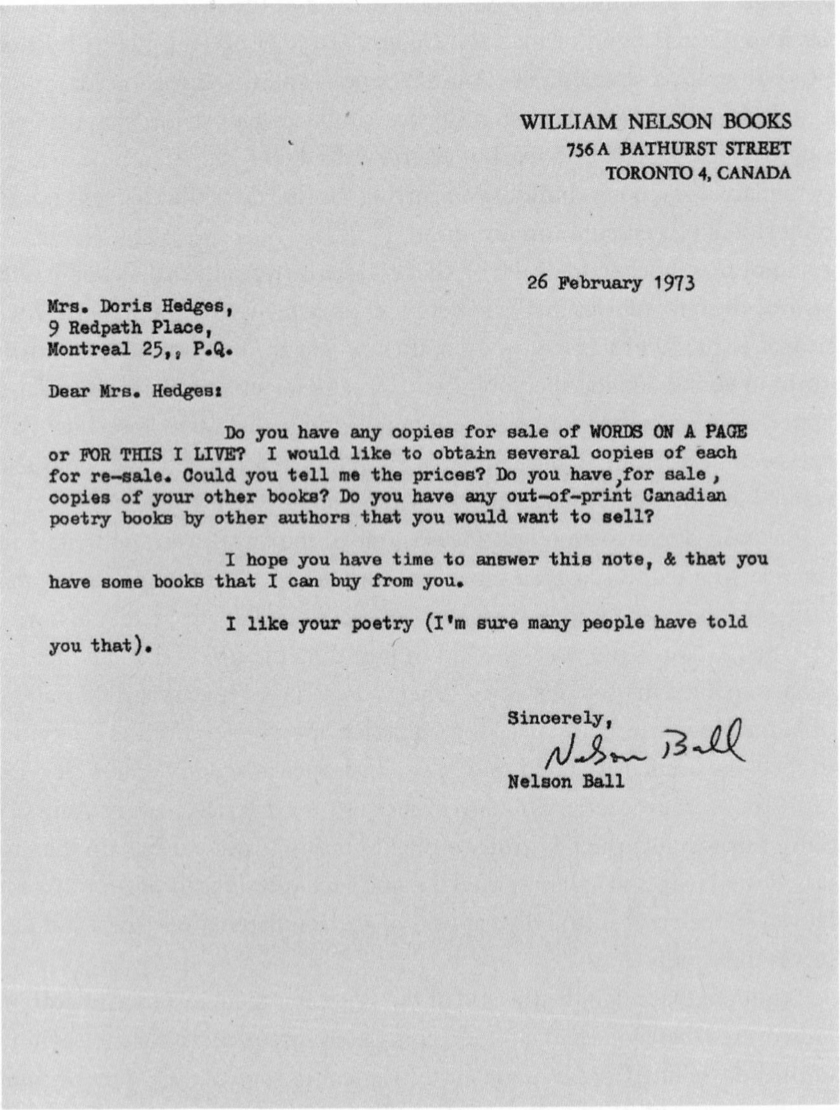

WILLIAM NELSON BOOKS
756 A BATHURST STREET
TORONTO 4, CANADA

26 February 1973

Mrs. Doris Hedges,
9 Redpath Place,
Montreal 25,, P.Q.

Dear Mrs. Hedges:

Do you have any copies for sale of WORDS ON A PAGE or FOR THIS I LIVE? I would like to obtain several copies of each for re-sale. Could you tell me the prices? Do you have, for sale, copies of your other books? Do you have any out-of-print Canadian poetry books by other authors that you would want to sell?

I hope you have time to answer this note, & that you have some books that I can buy from you.

I like your poetry (I'm sure many people have told you that).

Sincerely,
Nelson Ball
Nelson Ball

Figure E.1
Letter to Hedges from Nelson Ball, 1972

The publishers and editors of this anthology of feel-good poems and narratives about Canada knew exactly what they were looking for when they made this selection. Something inspirational. Something quotable. A memorable phrase about kindness. But there would also have been another criterion involved in making their selections: the rights to the material in the anthology would have to be inexpensive, or better, free. Although Hedges's words are used to introduce the section on "Kindness," the permissions page at the end of the book makes it clear that no rights to use those words were granted by any person or organization. This does not mean that the editors intentionally stole Hedges's material. More likely, they attempted to locate the copyright holder and hit a dead end. That is no surprise, since Doris Hedges left so few paths to follow when it came to determining the provenance of her published works. In fact, she left few paths to follow when it came to reconstructing her life. This brief excursion has followed some of those pathways. Many more remain unfound.

WORKS BY DORIS HEDGES

BOOKS

The Flower in the Dusk. Toronto: Ryerson, 1946.
Crisis. Toronto: Ryerson, 1947.
Words on a Page. Toronto: Ryerson, 1949.
Dumb Spirit: A Novel of Montreal. London: A. Barker, 1952.
Elixir: A Novel. London: A. Barker, 1954.
The Dream Is Certain. Boston: Christopher, 1954.
Robin. New York: Vantage, 1957.
For This I Live. New York: Exposition, 1963.
Inside Out. Berkshire, UK: Abbey Press, 1971.

POEMS

"Apathy." *Canadian Poetry* 1, no. 2 (1936): 26.
"Loneliness." *Queen's Quarterly* 34 (1937): 309.
"Courage." *Gazette*, 24 April 1946, 8.
"Alloy." *Canadian Poetry* 9, no. 4 (1946): 24.
"Withered Asters." *Canadian Poetry* 12, no. 1 (1948): 28.
"Convalescence of Man." *Canadian Poetry* 12, no. 4 (1949): 10.
"Onwardness." 1949, Poetry Society of America records, Manuscripts and Archives Division, New York Public Library.
"Spring." *Canadian Poetry* 21, no. 3 (1958): 9.
"Prayer." *The Golden Year: The Poetry Society of America Anthology (1910–1960)*. Freehold, NY: Books for Libraries Press, 1959–60. 130.
"Flowers Ending." *Canadian Poetry* 23, no. 1 (1959): 8.
"Falling Leaves Are Dead." *Gazette*, 27 October 1966, 6.

“Tempo.” *Canadian Poetry* 30, no. 2 (1967): 24.

“Loan of Life.” *Canadian Poetry* 31, no. 2 (1968): 33.

“Alias for Love.” *Gazette*, 6 April 1969, 6.

SHORT STORIES

“Sleds.” *Maclean’s*, 15 December 1938, 14–15, 31–2.

“The Concert.” *Cosmopolitan*, June 1940, 62–3, 109–12.

“I Put Away Childish Things.” *Good Housekeeping*, March 1943, 36–7, 156–68.

“Le Retour.” Trans. Pierre Benoit. *Le Jour*, 24 March 1943, 2.

“The Murdered Rose.” *Milwaukee Journal*, 17 June 1945, 8–9, 13.

“Flowers Have Fought.” *Montrealer*, June 1945, 17–18.

“Pipe Down, You Guys.” *Montreal Standard*, 8 March 1947, 24.

“Masquerade.” *Canadian Home Journal*, March 1957, 30–1, 74–6.

ARTICLES

(D.E.H). “The Montreal Repertory Theatre and Its Place in the Community.” *Junior League News*, October 1932, 9–10.

“Montreal Repertory Theatre News.” *Junior League News*, February 1933, 4–5.

(D.E.H). “Shakespeare’s ‘Hamlet, Prince of Denmark.’” *Junior League News*, December 1932, 6–8.

“A Time of Proving.” *Junior League News*, October 1943, 3–4.

“The Citizen and His Child.” Excerpt from broadcast, 11 March 1944. *Junior League News*, April 1944, 3–4.

“Katherine.” *Junior League News*, May 1944, 3–4.

“Montreal’s New Venture.” Excerpt from broadcast, 26 November 1944. *Junior League News*, December 1944, 4–5.

“Anomalies.” *Junior League News*, March 1945, 7.

“Error.” Correction to “Anomalies.” *Junior League News*, April 1945, 5.

“A Tango and a Feast with the Faun.” My Most Memorable Meal. *Maclean’s*, January 1957, 56.

“Commonwealth United; Canadian Woman Explains Viewpoint of Various British Nations.” *New York Times*, 2 March 1941, 103.

“Soldier-Civilian ‘Split’ Dangerous.” Speech transcript. *Gazette*, 19 June 1944, 13, 19.

LETTERS

Letter to the editor. "Conference in Moscow." *Gazette*, 20 October 1943, 8.

Letter to the editor. "Principle at Stake." *Gazette*, 24 January 1944, 8.

Letter to the editor. "Is It Weak Thinking?" *Gazette*, 17 October 1944, 8.

Letter to the editor. "Canada and the Peace." *Gazette*, 23 October 1944, 8.

Letter to the editor. "National Military Service." *Gazette*, 20 November 1944, 8.

Letter to the editor. "Is This What the People Want?" *Gazette*, 30 March 1945, 36.

Letter to the editor. "Contemporary Manners." *Gazette*, 27 December 1945, 6.

Letter to the editor. "The Controversy over Roussil's Statue." *Gazette*, 6 March 1951, 8.

Letter to the editor. "The Things at Stake in the CBC." *Gazette*, 15 June 1959, 6.

Letter to the editor. "Resents Criticism of Royal Tour." *Gazette*, 23 June 1959, 6.

Letter to Lorne Pierce. 23 January 1946. Correspondence Series, Lorne Pierce Fonds, Queen's University Archives, box 13, file 7.

Letter to Lorne Pierce. 26 January 1947. Correspondence Series, Lorne Pierce Fonds, Queen's University Archives, box 30, file 3.

Letter to W.A. Bradley. 24 January 1947. Series III, Agent Correspondence 1922–1974, William A. Bradley Literary Agency Records (1909–1982), University of Texas Archives, box 238, folder 6.

Letter to W.A. Bradley. 7 February 1947. Series III, Agent Correspondence 1922–1974, William A. Bradley Literary Agency Records (1909–1982), University of Texas Archives, box 238, folder 6.

Letter to W.A. Bradley. 18 February 1947. Series III, Agent Correspondence 1922–1974, William A. Bradley Literary Agency Records (1909–1982), University of Texas Archives, box 238, folder 6.

Letter to W.A. Bradley. 6 March 1947. Series III, Agent Correspondence 1922–1974, William A. Bradley Literary Agency Records (1909–1982), University of Texas Archives, box 238, folder 6.

Letter to W.A. Bradley. 21 March 1947. Series III, Agent Correspondence 1922–1974, William A. Bradley Literary Agency Records (1909–1982), University of Texas Archives, box 238, folder 6.

Letter to Léo-Paul Desrosiers. 30 April 1947. BAnQ Collection.

Letter to W.A. Bradley. 21 June 1947. Series III, Agent Correspondence 1922–1974, William A. Bradley Literary Agency Records (1909–1982), University of Texas Archives, box 238, folder 6.

Letter to W.A. Bradley. 24 July 1947. Series III, Agent Correspondence 1922–1974, William A. Bradley Literary Agency Records (1909–1982), University of Texas Archives, box 238, folder 6.

Letter to W.A. Bradley. 25 July 1947. Series III, Agent Correspondence 1922–1974, William A. Bradley Literary Agency Records (1909–1982), University of Texas Archives, box 238, folder 6.

Letter to W.A. Bradley. 8 Aug. 1947. Series III, Agent Correspondence 1922–1974, William A. Bradley Literary Agency Records (1909–1982), University of Texas Archives, box 238, folder 6.

Letter to W.A. Bradley. 15 October 1947. Series III, Agent Correspondence 1922–1974, William A. Bradley Literary Agency Records (1909–1982), University of Texas Archives, box 238, folder 6.

Letter to W.A. Bradley. 17 March 1948. Series III, Agent Correspondence 1922–1974, William A. Bradley Literary Agency Records (1909–1982), University of Texas Archives, box 238, folder 6.

Letter to William Arthur Deacon. 22 January 1953. MS Coll. 160, William Arthur Deacon Papers, Thomas Fisher Rare Book Library, University of Toronto.

Letter to William Arthur Deacon. 20 September 1954. MS Coll. 160, William Arthur Deacon Papers, Thomas Fisher Rare Book Library, University of Toronto.

Letter to Oakley Dalgleish. 7 October 1954. MS Coll. 160, William Arthur Deacon Papers, Thomas Fisher Rare Book Library, University of Toronto.

Letter to the editor. "Meddling in Others' Affairs." *Gazette*, 6 March 1956, 6.

THEATRE PERFORMANCES

The Perfect Alibi. By A.A. Milne, Dir. Martha Allan. Montreal Repertory Theatre, 26 March 1930. Performance.

The Constant Wife. By W. Somerset Maugham, Dir. Martha Allan. Montreal Repertory Theatre, 20 December 1930. Performance.

The Mask and the Face. By Luigi Chiarelli, Dir. Martha Allan. Montreal Repertory Theatre, 4–6 November 1931. Associate, Special Articles.

Hamlet. By William Shakespeare, Dir Martha Allan. Montreal Repertory Theatre, 26–27 December 1932. Performance.

Twelfth Night. By William Shakespeare, Dir. Cecil West. Montreal Repertory Theatre, 20–2 April 1933. Associate, Director of Publicity.

The Constant Wife (Anniversary Production). By W. Somerset Maugham, Dir. Louis Mulligan. Montreal Repertory Theatre, 23 November 1949. Performance.

RADIO SPEECHES

"Wives across the Waves." Radio Broadcast Series, 1940–1945.

"Let Us Think for Ourselves." Radio speech aired over CBO Ottawa, 19 September 1941.

"What Things Do to Us." Radio speech aired over CBO Ottawa, 24 September 1941.

"Let Us Read." Radio speech aired over CBO Ottawa, 9 February 1942.

"Enemy of Death." CBM. Speech. July 1943.

"Soldier-Civilian 'Split' Dangerous." Radio speech aired over CFCF Montreal, Saturday Night, on regular weekly program of the City Improvement League and the Municipal Service Bureau. June 1944.

"Montreal's New Venture." Radio speech aired over CFCF Montreal, 26 November 1944.

"Canadian Chronicle." CBC Radio Speech, 19 August 1945.

"British Brides." Radio speech aired over CFCF Montreal, 23 November 1945.

"The Citizen and the Atomic Bomb." Radio speech aired over CFCF Montreal, 29 June 1946.

"The Poet and the Community." Radio speech aired over CFCF Montreal, 13 May 1950.

SPEECHES

"The Place of Poetry in Modern Education." Speech given at the Canadian Authors Association Poetry Group, February 1944.

Speech given at the Professional and Business Women's Club, March 1945.

"What Do You Hope from Your New Life in Canada?" Speech given at the Acorn Club for British Wives, 5 July 1945.

"Books Are Precious." Speech given at McGill University, Spring 1949.
"Books Are Precious." Speech given at Ste-Agathe Tuberculosis Hospital, 1949.

MANUSCRIPTS

"The Poet and the Community." Draft of a radio speech aired on CFCF Montreal, 13 May 1950. Rare Books and Special Collections, McGill University.*
"The Mind of the Poet." Transcript of public speech, 1950. Rare Books and Special Collections, McGill University.
"The Poet and the Community." Transcript of a radio speech, 1950. Rare Books and Special Collections, McGill University.
"Books Are Precious." Transcript of speech given at Ste-Agathe's Tuberculosis Hospital, 1947–1948. Rare Books and Special Collections, McGill University.
"The Place of Poetry in Modern Education." Transcript of speech given at Canadian Author's Association, February 1944. Rare Books and Special Collections, McGill University.
"The Citizen and His Child." Transcript of public speech given on behalf of the Improvement League and Municipal Service Bureau to mark the start of Delinquency Prevention Week in Montreal. 11 March 1944.

*Two versions of these manuscripts exist at McGill.

REPORTS

"Report." Wartime Information Board Records. 4 August 1943. Vol. 25, dead file F-J. Library and Archives Canada, Ottawa.
Women's Canadian Club Minutes, 1933–1934. McCord Museum, P722/C,1.
Women's Canadian Club Minutes, 1934–1935. McCord Museum, P722/C,1.

UNRECOVERED MATERIAL

"The Boxing Lesson." Short story that represented Canada at 1948 London Olympics.

"Canadian Olympic Group Announced by Arts Council." *Winnipeg Tribune*, 27 March 1948, 22.

CAA Talk at the Municipal Library on 19 March 1953. "Une assemblée bilingue à La Bibliothèque Municipale." *Le Devoir*, 17 March 1953, 5.

WORKS BY DORIS HEDGES
A CHRONOLOGY

1930 *The Perfect Alibi.* By A.A. Milne. Montreal Repertory Theatre. Performance.

1930 *The Constant Wife.* By W. Somerset Maugham. Montreal Repertory Theatre. Performance.

1931 *The Mask and the Face.* By Luigi Chiarelli. Montreal Repertory Theatre. Associate, Special Articles.

1932 (D.E.H). "The Montreal Repertory Theatre and Its Place in the Community."

1932 *Hamlet.* By William Shakespeare. Little Theatre, Ottawa. Performance.

1932 (D.E.H). "Shakespeare's 'Hamlet, Prince of Denmark.'"

1933 "Montreal Repertory Theatre News."

1933 *Twelfth Night.* By William Shakespeare. Montreal Repertory Theatre. Associate, Director of Publicity.

1933–34 Women's Canadian Club Minutes.

1934–35 Women's Canadian Club Minutes.

1936 "Apathy."

1937 "Loneliness."

1938 "Sleds."

1940 "The Concert."

1940–45 "Wives across the Waves."

1941 "Commonwealth United; Canadian Woman Explains Viewpoint of Various British Nations."

1941 "Let Us Think for Ourselves."

1941 "What Things Do to Us."

1942 "Let Us Read."

1943 "I Put Away Childish Things."

1943 "What Do You Hope for Your New Life in Canada?"
1943 "Enemy of Death."
1943 "Report."
1943 "A Time of Proving."
1943 Letter to the editor. "Conference in Moscow."
1944 Letter to the editor. "Principle at Stake."
1944 "The Place of Poetry in Modern Education." Speech given at the Canadian Authors Association Poetry Group.
1944 "The Place of Poetry in Modern Education." Transcript of speech given at Canadian Authors Association.
1944 "The Citizen and His Child."
1944 "Katherine."
1944 "Soldier-Civilian 'Split' Dangerous." Radio speech.
1944 "Soldier-Civilian 'Split' Dangerous." Speech Transcript.
1944 Letter to the editor. "Is It Weak Thinking?"
1944 Letter to the editor. "National Military Service."
1944 "Montreal's New Venture." Radio speech.
1944 "Montreal's New Venture." Excerpt from broadcast.
1945 Speech given at the Professional and Business Women's Club.
1945 "Le Retour."
1945 Letter to the editor. "Is This What the People Want?"
1945 "Anomalies."
1945 "Error." Correction to "Anomalies."
1945 "The Murdered Rose."
1945 "Flowers Have Fought."
1945 "Canadian Chronicle."
1945 "British Brides."
1945 Letter to the editor. "Contemporary Manners."
1946 *The Flower in the Dusk.*
1946 Letter to Lorne Pierce.
1946 "Courage."
1946 "The Citizen and the Atomic Bomb."
1946 "Alloy."
1947 Letter to W.A. Bradley.
1947 Letter to Lorne Pierce.
1947 Letter to W.A. Bradley.
1947 Letter to W.A. Bradley.

1947 "Pipe Down, You Guys."
1947 Letter to W.A. Bradley.
1947 Letter to W.A. Bradley.
1947 Letter to Léo-Paul Desrosiers.
1947 *Crisis.*
1947–48 "Books Are Precious."
1947 Letter to W.A. Bradley.
1947 Letter to W.A. Bradley.
1947 Letter to W.A. Bradley.
1947 Letter to W.A. Bradley.
1947 Letter to W.A. Bradley.
1948 Letter to W.A. Bradley.
1948 "The Boxing Lesson."
1948 "Withered Asters."
1949 "Books Are Precious." Speech given at McGill University.
1949 "Books Are Precious." Speech given at Ste-Agathe Tuberculosis Hospital.
1949 "Convalescence of Man."
1949 *The Constant Wife* (Anniversary Production). By W. Somerset Maugham. Montreal Repertory Theatre. Performance.
1949 *Words on a Page.*
1949 "Onwardness."
1950 "The Poet and the Community."
1950 "The Mind of a Poet."
1950 "The Poet and the Community."
1951 Letter to the editor. "The Controversy over Roussil's Statue."
1952 *Dumb Spirit, A Novel of Montreal.*
1953 Letter to William Arthur Deacon.
1953 Talk. "Une assemblée bilingue à la Bibliothèque Municipale."
1954 Letter to William Arthur Deacon.
1954 Letter to Oakley Dalgleish.
1954 *Elixir, A Novel.*
1954 *The Dream Is Certain.*
1956 Letter to the editor. "Meddling in Others' Affairs."
1957 "A Tango and a Feast with the Faun."
1957 "Masquerade."
1957 *Robin.*

1958 "Spring."

1959 Letter to the editor. "The Things at Stake in the CBC."

1959 Letter to the editor. "Resents Criticism of Royal Tour."

1959 "Flowers Ending."

1959–60 Hedges, Doris. "Prayer." *The Golden Year, The Poetry Society of America Anthology (1910–1960).*

1963 *For This I Live.*

1969 "Alias for Love."

1971 *Inside Out.*

UNKNOWN DATE

"The Poet and the Community." Transcript of a radio speech, 1950. Rare Books and Special Collections, McGill University.

"The Boxing Lesson." Short story that represented Canada at 1948 London Olympics. Archives. Announcement of selection made Friday, 26 March 1948, by Canadian Arts Council, "Canadian Olympic Group Announced by Arts Council." *Winnipeg Tribune*, 27 March 1948.

NOTES

FOREWORD

1 Jordan and Patten, *Literature in the Marketplace*, 12.
2 See Lecker, "Canadian Authors and Their Literary Agents."
3 Ibid.
4 See Canadian Speakers' and Writers' Service Fonds, Clara Thomas Archives, York University.
5 *Canadian Bookman*, December 1946, 17.
6 Gerson, "The Most Canadian of All Canadian Poets," 92.
7 Hedges to Deacon, 22 January 1953, MS Coll. 160, WADP, TFRBL.
8 Hedges to Oakley Dalgleish, 7 October 1954, MS Coll. 160, WADP, TFRBL.
9 Ibid.
10 Deacon to Hedges, 20 September 1954, MS Coll. 160, Box 11, File 22, WADP, TFRBL.
11 "Rejuvenation," *Globe and Mail*, 13 February 1954, 15.
12 "Doris Hedges, Noted Author Funeral Today," *Gazette*, 17 July 1972, 37.
13 Ibid.
14 Waller, *No Ordinary Hotel*, 63.
15 Ibid., 65.
16 Murphree, "Edward Bernays's 1929 'Torches of Freedom' March."
17 "To Get a Drink You Have to Sell," Musée de Lachine, last modified 8 August 2018, http://www.villedemtl.ca/pourboireilfautvendre/en.
18 "Car 57511," *Bugatti Builder*, last modified 4 August 2008, http://www.bugatti builder.com/forum/viewtopic.php?p=3979&start=0&view=print.
19 "1937 Bugatti Type 57SC Tourer by Corscia," Sotheby's, https://rmsothebys.com/en/auctions/am19/amelia-island/lots/r0148-1937-bugatti-type-57sc-tourer-by-corsica/748541.
20 "AD. Club Speaker," *Ottawa Journal*, 18 December 1937, 9; "Fred C. Johnstone Wins High Honors," *Ottawa Journal*, 7 February 1942, 11; Broad, *Studies in Canadian Military History Series*, 63.
21 "Business Film Shown at Rotary Luncheon," *Ottawa Journal*, 14 June 1938, 21.

22 "William A. Bradley Literary Agency," HRC, University of Texas at Austin, https://norman.hrc.utexas.edu/fasearch/findingAid.cfm?eadid=00300.

23 Andresen, *Field of Vision*, 214–15.

24 Fiamengo, *Home Ground and Foreign Territory*, 4–5.

CHAPTER ONE

1 Joseph Pawley Dawes's career is summarized in Burr, "Dawes, James Pawley."

2 "The Dawes Family," Musée de Lachine, http://villedemtl.ca/pourboireilfautvendre/en/3_3/the_dawes_family.

3 Burr, "Dawes, James Pawley."

4 See "History of the Lachine Curling Club," Lachine Curling Club, http://www.lachinecurling.com/history_en.php.

5 "Writer's Club Will Be Host to D. Hedges," *McGill Daily*, 15 December 1947, https://archive.org/stream/McGillLibrary-mcgill-daily-v37-n053-december-15-1947-5336/mcgill-daily-v37-n053-december-15-1947_djvu.txt.

6 Hedges, "Books Are Precious," 3.

7 Hedges, "A Tango and a Feast," *Maclean's*, 19 January 1957, 56.

8 Ibid.

9 Ibid.

10 Ibid.

11 Ibid.

12 Hedges remembers the dinner as taking place in 1911, but the references to Nijinsky's role as the faun suggest that the year was 1912, since the ballet *L'Après-midi d'un faune* was choreographed by Nijinsky himself and first performed at the Théâtre du Châtelet in Paris on 29 May 1912. Nijinsky played the role of the faun.

13 Hedges, "A Tango and a Feast," *Maclean's*, 19 January 1957, 56.

14 Ibid.

15 "Paul Poiret," Mémoires de Guerre, last modified 14 March 2016, http://la-loupe.over-blog.net/article-poiret-paul-122369444.html.

16 Vipond, "Best Sellers in English Canada," 103.

17 The Canadian Women's Art Initiative provides this brief biography of Riter: "Mary Riter Hamilton studied in Toronto with Mary Hiester Reid, George Reid and Wyly Grier. She married at eighteen, but her husband died in 1896 and she decided to become a professional painter. She traveled to Germany and studied with Franz Skarbina in Berlin, Italy, Holland and Paris where she studied portrait painting with J. Blanche and drawing with Mereon and Gervais at the Vittie Academy. She also studied privately with Castaluchi. Two of her works were shown at the Paris Salon in 1905. She continued to travel and study in Europe, spending one year in Winnipeg, and subsequent years in Florence, Berlin, Vienna, Paris and Holland. She returned to Canada in 1911 and showed 150 paint-

ings in Toronto. At around the same time she did a number of portraits of Native Canadians which were later exhibited in Paris. She also painted scenes of the Rockies. In 1912 she painted a series of portraits of British Columbia's lieutenant governors which are still at Government House, Victoria. In 1919 she went to Europe to paint the battlefields of France and Belgium. She completed 227 canvases which were exhibited in the foyer of the Grand Opera House in Paris in 1922. She subsequently gave the paintings to the National Archives of Canada. She won the Palme Académique and was named Officier d'Académie of France in 1922. In 1925 she received a diploma and gold medal for her exhibit at the Paris Exposition Internationale. She settled in Victoria and painted many scenes and portraits until she lost her sight in 1948. There was an exhibition of her work at the Vancouver Art Gallery in 1952 and a memorial exhibition in conjunction with the work of Sophie Deane-Drummond at the Art Gallery of Greater Victoria in 1959." See "Hamilton, Mary Riter," Canadian Women Artists History Initiative, last modified 12 December 2019, http://cwahi.concordia.ca/sources/artists/displayArtist.php?ID_artist=23.

18 Vance, *A History of Canadian Culture*, 238.

19 "Canadian Passenger Lists, 1865–1935 for Doris E. Ryde," *Ancestry.ca.*

20 Dominion Bureau of Statistics, Sixth Census of Canada, 1921.

21 Harrington, *Syllables of Recorded Time*, 71.

22 Osborne, "Warscapes, Landscapes, Inscapes," 325.

23 Ibid., 327.

24 "Social and Personal," *Gazette*, 25 September 1926, 8; "Social and Personal," *Gazette*, 15 October 1926, 8.

25 Ibid.

26 183 Mansfield Street in Montreal in 1926. With the exception of one year (1929) in which they are listed as residing in London, the Hedges remained in Montreal. Lovell shows them residing at 2047 Mansfield in 1928; 1515 Chomedy in 1930; 17 Grove Park, Westmount, in 1931; 4160 Dorchester in 1932; 900 Sherbrooke Street West in 1949; and 9 Redpath Place from 1953 until their respective deaths.

27 "Social and Personal," *Gazette*, 5 October 1927, 8.

28 This career information regarding Geoffrey Hedges is derived from "G.P. Hedges, of Red Cross, dies at 75," *Gazette*, 29 April 1972, 43.

29 *Passenger Lists, 1865–1935*, Microfilm Publications T-479 to T-520, T-4689 to T-4874, T-14700 to T-14939, C-4511 to C-4542, Library and Archives Canada, n.d. RG 76-C, Department of Employment and Immigration Fonds, Library and Archives Canada, Ottawa, Ontario, Canada.

30 Linteau, *The History of Montréal*, 129.

31 "Theatre Guild in Initial Success," *Gazette*, 27 March 1930, 6.

32 "Local Amateurs Achieve Success in Second Play," *McGill Daily*, 19 December 1930, 4.

33 Booth, "The Montreal Repertory Theatre," 91.
34 *McGill Daily*, 25 November 1949, https://archive.org/stream/McGillLibrary-mcgill-daily-v39-n040-november-25-1949-9696/mcgill-daily-v39-n040-november-25-1949_djvu.txt.
35 "Lord Duncannon Scores Success in the Exacting Role of Hamlet," *Ottawa Journal*, 27 December 1932, 8.
36 "Social and Personal," *Gazette*, 4 December 1926, 18.
37 "Social and Personal," *Gazette*, 12 June 1928, 8.
38 "Social and Personal," *Gazette*, 25 June 1928, 8.
39 "Social and Personal," *Gazette*, 17 June 1929, 8.
40 "Social and Personal," *Gazette*, 2 September 1930, 8.
41 "Social and Personal," *Gazette*, 18 June 1928, 8.
42 "Social and Personal," *Gazette*, 1 September 1930, 8.
43 "Social and Personal," *Gazette*, 24 January 1931, 2.
44 Harrington, *Syllables of Recorded Time*, 164.
45 Charlesworth, "Authors and Radio," 8.
46 *The Canadian Author* 12, no. 4 (June 1935): 4.
47 Ibid.
48 Ibid., 16.
49 Ibid., 20.
50 Ibid.
51 Harrington, *Syllables of Recorded Time*, 175.
52 Leonard Brockington, "1936: CBC Radio Takes to the Air," CBC Radio Special, broadcast 4 November 1936, https://www.cbc.ca/archives/entry/1936-cbc-radio-takes-to-the-air.
53 Harrington, *Syllables of Recorded Time*, 186.
54 Hedges, "The Mind of the Poet," 3.
55 Dean Irvine notes that "*New Frontier* included a majority of women on its staff: its founder (Jean Watts), two of its four editors (Dorothy Livesay and Margaret Gould), and its business manager (Jocelyn Moore). Likely as a result of the high proportion of women involved in its production, it served as an important forum for women's writing" (see Irvine, *Editing Modernity*, 13).
56 Hedges, "Apathy," *Canadian Poetry* 1, no. 2 (1936): 26.
57 Hedges, "Loneliness," *Queen's Quarterly* 34 (1937): 309.
58 Hedges, "Sleds," *Maclean's*, 15 December 1938, 14.
59 Ibid.
60 Ibid.
61 Ibid., 15.
62 Ibid.
63 Ibid., 31.
64 Ibid.

65 Ibid., 32.
66 Ibid.
67 Ibid.
68 Ibid.
69 Ibid.
70 Ibid.
71 Ibid.
72 Rifkind, *Comrades and Critics*, 9.
73 Karr, *Authors and Audiences*, 200.
74 Irvine, *Editing Modernity*, 77.
75 Ibid., 79.
76 Ibid., 80.
77 Gerson, "The Most Canadian of All Canadian Poets," 91–2.
78 Ibid., 94.
79 Weintraub, *City Unique*, 6.

CHAPTER TWO

1 Herbert Whittaker notes that the Theatre Guild of Montreal was forced to change its name to the Montreal Repertory Theatre because a New York theatre group had copyrighted the name (see Whittaker, *Setting the Stage*, 65).
2 Weintraub, *City Unique*, 240.
3 Booth, "The Montreal Repertory Theatre," 58.
4 Ibid.
5 Ibid., 60.
6 "Doris Hedges, Noted Author Funeral Today," *Gazette*, 17 July 1972, 37.
7 Donn Mitchell, "Debutantes of the World: Unite! The Irrepressible Mary Harriman," *The Anglican Examiner*, http://www.anglicanexaminer.com/Rumsey.html.
8 "History of the Junior League," Canadian Federation of Junior Leagues, http://www.cfjl.org/about-the-alji/history-of-the-junior-league.aspx.
9 *Junior League News*, October 1939, 5.
10 Hedges, "A Time of Proving," *Junior League News*, October 1943, 3.
11 Ibid.
12 *Junior League News*, January 1944, 1.
13 Hedges, "A Time of Proving," *Junior League News*, October 1943, 3.
14 Ibid., 4.
15 *Junior League News*, October 1934, 6.
16 Hedges, "A Time of Proving," *Junior League News*, October 1943, 4.
17 Ibid.
18 Ibid.
19 Ibid.

20 McDonald, "Socialism and the English Canadian Literary Tradition," 227.
21 Ibid.
22 McKay, "For a New Kind of History," 99.
23 In its commentary on war jewellery, the Comox Air Force Museum explains that "for the military during WWI and WWII, exchanging letters and mementos kept them connected with home; this strengthened relationships while time and distance separated families. Many of the sentimental items sent home by servicemen have been referred to as sweetheart jewelry. Starting in WWI, young men began the tradition of sending the jewelry home; this custom grew even more popular during WWII. Some of it was handcrafted in the trenches but much of it was machine-made and sold to soldiers, who then sent it back home. During the Second World War, most precious metals were rationed and used to build weapons, tanks, ships, airplanes, and other machinery needed for the Allies' campaign. As a result, most of the sweetheart items from this time were made from non-precious or semi-precious materials such as Bakelite, celluloid, wood, mother-of-pearl, shell, ivory, rhinestones, enamel, and cheap, readily available wire. Though 'sweetheart' is the word used to describe the jewelry, not all of it was given to actual sweethearts; indeed it was also given to mothers, sisters, and wives." See "Along with the Letters Home – Sweetheart Jewelry," Comox Air Force Museum, last modified 14 November 2016, https://comoxairforcemuseum.ca/along-with-the-letters-home-sweetheart-jewelry/.
24 Hedges, "Books Are Precious," 7.
25 Ibid., 6.
26 Freeman, *Beyond Bylines*, 94.
27 "U-Boat Sinks Freighter in St. Lawrence," *Gazette*, 13 May 1942, 1.
28 "Let Us Think for Ourselves" (19 September 1941), "What Things Do to Us" (25 September 1941), and "Let Us Read" (9 February 1942).
29 "Montreal's New Venture" (25 November 1944) and "British Brides" (23 November 1945).
30 The interview can be accessed online. See "Audio Recording," Who was Doris Hedges?, https://dorishedges.com/audio/.
31 Keshen, *Saints, Sinners, and Soldiers*, 215.
32 "High Tribute Paid To Youth Centre," *Gazette*, 27 November 1944, 4.
33 Ibid.
34 "Sees Need for Youth Centres," *Montreal Daily Star*, 27 November 1944, 8.
35 Hedges, "The Citizen and His Child," MG 30, Series D 208, Vol. 7, LAC.
36 Ibid.
37 Ibid.
38 Ibid.
39 Ibid.
40 Ibid.

41 Myers, *Caught*, 73.
42 Ibid., 72–3.
43 Hedges, "I Put Away Childish Things," *Good Housekeeping*, March 1943, 164.
44 Ibid., 165.
45 Ibid., 156.
46 Ibid.
47 1 Corinthians 13:11.
48 Hedges, "I Put Away Childish Things," *Good Housekeeping*, March 1943, 158.
49 Ibid., 37.
50 Ibid., 167.
51 Ibid., 168.
52 Ibid.
53 Ibid.
54 Ibid., 158.
55 Ibid., 156.
56 Hedges, "The Place of Poetry in Modern Education," 1.
57 Ibid.
58 Ibid.
59 Ibid.
60 Ibid., 2.
61 Ibid., 4.
62 Ibid.
63 Ibid., 6.
64 Percy Bysshe Shelley, *A Defence of Poetry* (Portland: Thomas B. Mosher, 1910), 86.
65 William Wordsworth, "Preface to *Lyrical Ballads*," *Lyrical Ballads: 1798 and 1802* (Oxford: Oxford University Press, 2013), 112.
66 Cited in Harrington, *Syllables of Recorded Time*, 201.
67 Cited in ibid., 201.
68 Cited in ibid., 202.
69 Cited in ibid.
70 Ibid.
71 Cited in ibid., 209.
72 Ibid., 210.
73 Buitenhuis, "The CAA and Propaganda," 129.
74 Ibid., 130.
75 Young, "Academics and Social Scientists," 217.
76 Caccia, *Managing the Canadian Mosaic*, 187.
77 Balzer, *The Information Front*, 7.
78 Young, "Academics and Social Scientists," 219.
79 Ibid., 223.

80 Ibid., 224.
81 Ibid.
82 Ibid., 227.
83 Cited in ibid., 230.
84 Ibid., 233.
85 Ibid., 231.
86 Ibid., 234.
87 Ibid., 231.
88 Ibid., 235.
89 Hedges, "Report," 25 March 1943, Vol. 25, dead file F-J, WIBR, LAC, 1.
90 Ibid.
91 Ibid.
92 Saez, *Income and Wealth Inequality*.
93 Bliss, "Preface," ix.
94 Maioni, "New Century, New Risks."
95 Fahrni, *Household Politics*, 19.
96 Ibid.
97 Ibid.
98 Hedges, "Report," 25 March 1943, Vol. 25, dead file F-J, WIBR, LAC, 1.
99 Ibid., 1–2.
100 Hedges, "Report," 10 April 1943, Vol. 25, dead file F-J, WIBR, LAC, 1.
101 Ibid.
102 Ibid.
103 Ibid.
104 Hedges, "Report," 12 May 1943, Vol. 25, dead file F-J, WIBR, LAC, 1.
105 Ibid.
106 Ibid., 2.
107 Hedges, "Report," 28 May 1943, Vol. 25, dead file F-J, WIBR, LAC, 1.
108 See Claude Bélanger, "Why Did Canada Refuse to Admit Jewish Refugees in the 1930's," *The Quebec History Encyclopedia*, http://faculty.marianopolis.edu/c.belanger/quebechistory/readings/CanadaandJewishRefugeesinthe1930s.html.
109 Hedges, "Report," 28 May 1943, Vol. 25, dead file F-J, WIBR, LAC, 2.
110 Hedges, "Report," 13 June 1943, Vol. 25, dead file F-J, WIBR, LAC, 1.
111 Hedges, "Report," 30 June 1943, Vol. 25, dead file F-J, WIBR, LAC, 1.
112 Ibid., 1–2.
113 Ibid., 1.
114 Leong, "The China Mystique," xvii.
115 Hedges, "Report," 30 June 1943, Vol. 25, dead file F-J, WIBR, LAC, 1.
116 Ibid.
117 Ibid.
118 Ibid.

119 Ibid.
120 Ibid., 2.
121 Fahrni, *Household Politics*, 25.
122 Weintraub, *City Unique*, 53.
123 Hedges, "Report," 4 August 1943, Vol. 25, dead file F-J, WIBR, LAC, 1.
124 Kuffert, "Stabbing our spirits broad awake," 35.
125 Ibid.
126 Hedges, "Report," 30 June 1943, Vol. 25, dead file F-J, WIBR, LAC, 2.
127 Hedges, "Report," 4 August 1943, Vol. 25, dead file F-J, WIBR, LAC, 1.
128 Ibid.
129 Ibid.
130 Caccia, *Managing the Canadian Mosaic*, 180.
131 Ibid., 181.
132 Ibid.
133 Ibid., 182.
134 Hedges, "Report," 6 September 1943, Vol. 25, dead file F-J, WIBR, LAC, 1.
135 Doyle, *Progressive Heritage*, 104.
136 Ibid., 114.
137 Ibid.
138 Ibid.
139 Hedges, "The Murdered Rose," *Milwaukee Journal*, 17 June 1945, 8.
140 Hedges, "Flowers Have Fought," *Montrealer*, June 1945, 17.
141 Ibid.
142 Ibid.
143 Ibid.
144 Ibid.
145 Ibid.
146 Ibid.
147 Ibid., 18.
148 "Norwood Speaks to Empire Society," *Gazette*, 17 February 1945, 14.
149 "Returned Men Meet Civilians and Share News," *The Maple Leaf*, 26 October 1945, 3.
150 "Aid Empire Unity, Is Plea to Youth," *Gazette*, 9 March 1946, 17.
151 "Veteran Declared Pressing Problem," *Gazette*, 23 March 1945, 4.
152 "Lily Pons the Guest Star Tonight of Danny Kaye, Back from Tour," *Gazette*, 23 November 1945, 6.
153 Melynda Jarratt, "Pier 21," *Canadian War Brides*, http://www.canadianwarbrides.com/pier21.asp.
154 Melynda Jarratt, "Canadian Cookbook for British Wives," *Canadian War Brides*, http://www.canadianwarbrides.com/cook-book.asp.
155 Fahrni, *Household Politics*, 72.

156 "Crowds Swam through Streets as Canadians Celebrate Victory," *Gazette*, 8 May 1945, 1.

157 "Hitler's Last Days," *Security Service* MI5, https://www.mi5.gov.uk/hitlers-last-days.

158 "A-Bomb Discussed by Doris Hedges," *Gazette*, 1 July 1946, 5.

CHAPTER THREE

1 Campbell, *Both Hands*, 257.

2 Dunks, "Reading the Field of Canadian Poetry," 20.

3 Ibid., ii.

4 Ibid., 9.

5 Hutchinson, "During the Second World War Literature Reigned Supreme."

6 Dunks, "Reading the Field of Canadian Poetry," 58.

7 Brown, "Poetry," 253.

8 Carney, *Canadian Painters in a Modern World*, 140.

9 Ibid., 141.

10 Ibid., 179.

11 Laura Brandon, "Women Artists and the 1944 Canadian Army Art Exhibition," *Canadian Military History* 18, no. 1 (2009): 49, http://scholars.wlu.ca/cgi/viewcontent.cgi?article=1495&context=cmh.

12 "Second World War: Canada's War Artists' Perspective," Canadian War Museum, https://www.warmuseum.ca/cwm/exhibitions/artists/indexeng.shtml.

13 All quoted material is from the Artists' files at the Canadian War Museum. See "Second World War: Canada's War Artists' Perspective," Canadian War Museum, https://www.warmuseum.ca/cwm/exhibitions/artists/indexeng.shtml.

14 Hedges to Pierce, 23 January 1946, 2001-13-17, LPF, QUA.

15 Ibid.

16 Ibid.

17 Hedges, "The Mind of the Poet," 5.

18 Hedges to Pierce, 23 January 1946, 2001-13-17, LPF, QUA.

19 Ibid.

20 "Sleds" in *Maclean's* (1938), "The Concert" in *Cosmopolitan* (1940), "I Put Away Childish Things" in *Good Housekeeping* (1943), and "The Murdered Rose" in the *Milwaukee Journal* (1945). The story that Hedges claimed to have published in London *Graphic* cannot be located.

21 "Apathy" in *Canadian Poetry* (1936), "Loneliness" in *Queen's Quarterly* (1937), and "Alloy" in *Canadian Poetry* (1946).

22 Hedges to Pierce, 23 January 1946, 2001-13-17, LPF, QUA.

23 Hedges, *The Flower in the Dusk*, 3.

24 Ibid., 4.
25 Ibid., 5.
26 Ibid., 6.
27 Ibid., 8.
28 Ibid., 6.
29 Hedges, *Inside Out*, 25.
30 Katerberg, *Modernity and the Dilemma of North American Anglican Identities*, 137.
31 Ibid., 143.
32 Ibid., 144.
33 Marshall, *A Solitary Pillar*, 52–3.
34 Ibid., 45.
35 Hedges to Pierce, 26 January 1947, 2001-13-17, LPF, QUA.
36 Ibid.
37 Ibid.
38 Hedges, "Books Are Precious," 11.
39 Hedges to Pierce, 26 January 1947, 2001-13-17, LPF, QUA.
40 "The Flower in the Dusk by Doris Hedges," *Gazette*, 28 December 1946, 9.
41 Hedges to Pierce, 26 January 1947, 2001-13-17, LPF, QUA.
42 Ibid.
43 Ibid.
44 Contract between Hedges and Ryerson Press, 21 July 1947, Ryerson Press Collection, Ryerson University, 4.
45 Ibid.
46 Birney, *Spreading Time*, 69.
47 Ibid.
48 Ibid., 70.
49 Ibid.
50 Ibid., 71.
51 "The Long November," *Véhicule Press*, http://www.vehiculepress.com/q.php?EAN=9781550653779.
52 "Poetry by Montreal Authors," *Gazette*, 1 November 1947, 24.
53 Bailey, "New Books," 420.
54 Ibid.
55 Ibid.
56 Brown, "Poetry," 263.
57 Hedges, *Crisis*, 1.
58 Ibid., 2.
59 Ibid., 3.
60 Ibid.

61 Ibid., 4.
62 Ibid., 5.
63 Ibid., 6.
64 Ibid., 8.
65 Ibid., 9.
66 Ibid., 10.
67 Ibid.
68 Ibid., 16.
69 "Writers Are Held Frustrated, Slack," *Gazette*, 3 November 1947, 3.
70 "Group Is Praised on Rehabilitation," *Gazette*, 1 December 1945, 20.
71 MacSkimming, *The Perilous Trade*, 30.
72 Ibid., 31.
73 For a detailed discussion of the arts in Canada in the war years, see Litt, *The Muses, the Masses, and the Massey Commission.*
74 Birney, *Spreading Time*, 70.
75 Vance, *A History of Canadian Culture*, 315.
76 "Doris Hedges, Noted Author Funeral Today," *Gazette*, 17 July 1972, 37.
77 *Dalhousie Review* 27, no. 1 (1947): 2; *Canadian Bookman* (1947): 17; *Evening Citizen*, 14 December 1946, 8.
78 "AD. Club Speaker," *Ottawa Journal*, 18 December 1937, 9.
79 *Globe and Mail*, 23 March 1946, 18; *The Times* (London), 16 November 1987, 18.
80 Hoare to Bradley, 6 May 1946, Series III. Agent Correspondence, 1922–1974, Subseries C. Foreign Agents, 1924–1968, Box 238, WABLAR, HRHRC.
81 Ibid.
82 George L. Parker, "The Publishing Industry in Canada 1918 to the Twenty-First Century," McMaster University Library, http://pw20c.mcmaster.ca/hpcanpub/case-study/publishing-industry-canada-1918-twenty-first-century.
83 Hoare to Bradley, 6 May 1946, Series III. Agent Correspondence, 1922–1974, Subseries C. Foreign Agents, 1924-1968, Box 238, WABLAR, HRHRC.
84 Bradley to Hoare, 11 July 1946, Series III. Agent Correspondence, 1922–1974, Subseries C. Foreign Agents, 1924–1968, Box 238, WABLAR, HRHRC.
85 Ibid.
86 Hoare to Bradley, 26 August 1946, Series III. Agent Correspondence, 1922–1974, Subseries C. Foreign Agents, 1924–1968, Box 238, WABLAR, HRHRC.
87 Ibid.
88 Hoare to Bradley, 11 October 1946, Series III. Agent Correspondence, 1922–1974, Subseries C. Foreign Agents, 1924–1968, Box 238, WABLAR, HRHRC.
89 Hoare to Bradley, 30 October 1946, Series III. Agent Correspondence, 1922–1974, Subseries C. Foreign Agents, 1924–1968, Box 238, WABLAR, HRHRC.
90 Ibid.

91 Hoare to Bradley, 30 December 1946, Series III. Agent Correspondence, 1922–1974, Subseries C. Foreign Agents, 1924–1968, Box 238, WABLAR, HRHRC.

92 "Gladdis Joy Lowe (1902–1972) published variously as Joy Tranter, Gladdis Tranter, G.J. Tranter or under her full married name, Gladdis Joy Tranter. A versatile professional author, she wrote poetry, fiction, non-fiction, and plays." See "Tranter, Gladdis Joy," Canada's Early Women Writers, Simon Fraser University, https://digital.lib.sfu.ca/ceww-815/tranter-gladdis-joy.

93 Tranter to Clay, 23 November 1946, MS Coll. 160, Box 24, File 30, WADP, TFRBL. Clay was Secretary of the Canadian Authors Association and editor of the periodical *Canadian Author*, from 1942 to 1946. See Charles Clay Fonds, Library and Archives Canada, https://www.collectionscanada.gc.ca/literaryarchives/027011-200.030-e.html.

94 Clay to Tranter, 25 November 1946, MS Coll. 160, Box 24, File 30, WADP, TFRBL.

95 Hedges to Bradley, 24 January 1947, Series III. Agent Correspondence, 1922–1974, Subseries C. Foreign Agents, 1924–1968, Box 238, Folder 6, WABLAR, HRHRC.

96 Ibid.

97 Hedges to Bradley, 7 February 1947, Series III. Agent Correspondence, 1922–1974, Subseries C. Foreign Agents, 1924–1968, Box 238, Folder 6, WABLAR, HRHRC.

98 Klaus-Peter Friedrich, "An Eventful Life," The American Association for Jewish Studies, http://www.aapjstudies.org/index.php?id=120.

99 Hedges to Bradley, 6 March 1947, Series III. Agent Correspondence, 1922–1974, Subseries C. Foreign Agents, 1924–1968, Box 238, Folder 6, WABLAR, HRHRC.

100 Bradley to Hedges, 14 March 1947, Series III. Agent Correspondence, 1922–1974, Subseries C. Foreign Agents, 1924–1968, Box 238, WABLAR, HRHRC.

101 Hedges to Bradley, 21 March 1947, Series III. Agent Correspondence, 1922–1974, Subseries C. Foreign Agents, 1924–1968, Box 238, Folder 6, WABLAR, HRHRC.

102 Ibid.

103 Bradley to Hedges, 25 June 1947, Series III. Agent Correspondence, 1922–1974, Subseries C. Foreign Agents, 1924–1968, WABLAR, HRHRC.

104 Friskney and Gerson, "The Author and the Market," 135.

105 Ibid., 134.

106 Hedges to Bradley, 8 August 1947, Series III. Agent Correspondence, 1922–1974, Subseries C. Foreign Agents, 1924–1968, Box 238, Folder 6, WABLAR, HRHRC.

107 Hedges to Bradley, Series III. Agent Correspondence, 1922–1974, Subseries C. Foreign Agents, 1924–1968, Box 238, Folder 6, WABLAR, HRHRC.

108 Ibid.

109 Hedges to Bradley, 17 March 1948, Series III. Agent Correspondence, 1922–1974, Subseries C. Foreign Agents, 1924–1968, Box 238, Folder 6, WABLAR, HRHRC.

110 Xenia Seriabine to Hedges, 22 March 1948, Series III. Agent Correspondence, 1922–1974, Subseries C. Foreign Agents, 1924–1968, Box 238, WABLAR, HRHRC.

111 Kendrick Lee, "Newspaper Supply," Editorial Research Reports 1947, CQ Researcher, published 5 September 1947, library.cqpress.com/cqresearcher/cqresrre1947090500.

112 Thomson to Bradley, July 1947, Series III. Agent Correspondence, 1922–1974, Subseries C. Foreign Agents, 1924–1968, Box 238, WABLAR, HRHRC.

113 "1946 Interest Rates, Inflation, and War," *Economic Populist*, last modified 2 March 2008, http://www.economicpopulist.org/content/1946-interest-rates-inflation-and-war.

114 "Writers Are Held Frustrated, Slack," *Gazette*, 3 November 1947, 3.

115 Ibid.

116 Ibid.

117 Ibid.

118 "Writer's Club Will Be Host to Mrs. Hedges," *McGill Daily*, 15 December 1947.

119 "Doris Hedges Meets McGill Writer's Club," *McGill Daily*, 17 December 1947.

120 Ibid.

121 Colin Hill, "*Canadian Bookman* and the Origins of Modern Realism in English-Canadian Fiction," *Canadian Literature* 195 (2007): 100.

122 The twists and turns of *Cabbagetown*'s editorial history are recounted in Stuewe, *The Storms Below*.

123 Eustace to Garner, 7 November 1947, Folder 2065, Series 1, Box 1, File 1, HGF, QUA.

124 Eustace to Hedges, November 1947, Folder 2065, Series 1, Box 1, File 1, HGF, QUA.

125 Garner to Taylor, 5 February 1948, Folder 2065, Series 1, Box 1, File 1, HGF, QUA.

126 Ibid.

127 Garner to Taylor, Folder 2065, Series 1, Box 1, File 1, HGF, QUA.

128 Ibid.

129 Fortin, "Hugh Garner."

130 Fortin, "Letter to the author."

131 Seriabine to Hedges, 22 March 1948, Series III. Agent Correspondence, 1922–1974, Subseries C. Foreign Agents, 1924–1968, Box 238, WABLAR, HRHRC.

132 Ibid.

133 "Canadian Olympic Group Announced by Arts Council," *Winnipeg Tribune*, 27 March 1948, 22. (Note: "The Boxing Lesson" has not been recovered.)

134 Cited in Stanton, *The Forgotten Olympic Art Competitions*, 11.

135 Stanton, *The Forgotten Olympic Art Competitions*, 2.

136 Ibid.

137 "Social and Personal," *Gazette*, 23 August 1947, 15.

138 "Craftsmanship in Art of Writing Is Placed Ahead of Inspiration," *Gazette*, 3 April 1948, 7.

139 Ibid.

140 Ibid.

141 "What Are the Odds of Getting a Book Deal?," *Jericho Writers,* https://jerichowriters.com/getting-a-publishing-deal/.

CHAPTER FOUR

1 Ince, "The Vocabulary of Freedom in 1948," 48–9.

2 François-Marc Gagnon, "Borduas, Paul-Émile," *Dictionary of Canadian Biography*, http://www.biographi.ca/en/bio/ borduas_paul_emile_18E.html.

3 Gagnon notes that "in 1946 and 1947 Borduas and the Groupe Automatiste held exhibitions in a series of makeshift galleries: at 1257 Rue Amherst in Montreal (20–29 April 1946); at the house of Mme Julienne Gauvreau, the mother of Pierre and Claude, 75 Rue Sherbrooke Ouest in Montreal (15 Feb.–1 March 1947)." At this time, Hedges and her husband were living at the Ritz-Carlton Hotel, a few blocks away from the Gauvreau house on Sherbrooke. See ibid.

4 "Art Gallery Owner Receives Summons in Statue Dispute," *Gazette*, 7 March 1951, 10.

5 Ibid.

6 "Scandal! Vice, Crime, and Morality in Montreal, 1940–1960," Centre d'histoire de Montréal, http://ville.montreal.qc.ca/portal/page?_pageid=9077,118275570&_dad=portal&_schema=PORTAL.

7 Ibid.

8 Hedges, "The Controversy over Roussil's Statue," *Gazette*, 6 March 1951, 8.

9 Ibid.

10 Ibid.

11 Ibid.

12 Ibid.

13 Jean Ampleman, "Notre Temps," photocopy in MRT papers in National Theatre School. See Booth, *The Montreal Repertory Theatre*, 87.

14 Léger, "Alfred Pellan, scénographe."

15 Ibid.

16 The poem was selected for inclusion in the Poetry Society of America's anthology of compelling poetry published in 1949.

17 Hedges, *Words on a Page*, 1–2.

18 Ibid., 15.

19 Ibid., 40.

20 Quoted on dust jacket to *Words on a Page.*

21 Hedges, *Words on a Page*, 11.

22 Ibid., 14.

23 Ibid.

24 Trudeau, *The Asbestos Strike*, 344.
25 Trudeau, *Memoirs*, 62–3.
26 Hedges, *Words on a Page*, 18.
27 Ibid., 7.
28 Ibid., 18.
29 Ibid., 24.
30 Ibid., 25.
31 Ibid.
32 Ibid., 26.
33 Ibid., 28.
34 Ibid., 32.
35 Ibid., 36.
36 Ibid.
37 A similar version was given two other times – see Hedges's bibliography.
38 Hedges, "Books Are Precious," transcript of speech given at Ste-Agathe's Tuberculosis Hospital, 1947–1948, RBSC.
39 Ibid.
40 Ibid.
41 Ibid.
42 Ibid.
43 Ibid.
44 Ibid.
45 Ibid.
46 Ibid.
47 Ibid.
48 Ibid.
49 Ibid.
50 Ibid.
51 Two versions of this talk are held in Rare Books and Special Collections at McGill University. One is titled "The Poet and the Community" and the other "The Mind of the Poet," but both essays cover much of the same ground. Because the second manuscript cannot be dated, the discussion here melds the commentary made by Hedges in both addresses.
52 Hedges, "The Poet and the Community," 1.
53 Ibid., 2.
54 Ibid., 4.
55 Ibid., 3.
56 Ibid., 4.
57 Ibid., 1.
58 Ibid.
59 Ibid., 3.

60 Ibid., 2.
61 Ibid., 3.
62 Ibid., 1–2.
63 Ibid., 4.
64 Hedges, "The Mind of the Poet," 2.
65 Ibid.
66 Ibid., 1.
67 "Books," YM-YWHA *Beacon*, 15 January 1953, 2.
68 Litt, *The Muses, the Masses, and the Massey Commission*, 22.
69 Ibid.
70 Ibid., 23.
71 Ibid.
72 Ibid., 36.
73 *Royal Commission on National Development*, 228.
74 Ibid., 229.
75 *Dumb Spirit*, back cover.
76 Hedges, *Dumb Spirit*, 62.
77 *The Encyclopedic Theosophical Glossary* notes that in theosophy, "spirit" is a term that "means incorporeal intelligences of a high degree, such as dhyanis or planetary spirits, those hosts of arupa (bodiless) monads or egos which spring more or less directly from the universal consciousness or cosmic spirit. Thus the spiritual monad in man is, strictly speaking, a spirit as derivative directly from the cosmic intelligence, mahat or mahabuddhi manifesting through mahat. Spirits exist in almost limitless ranges of hierarchical classes, highest, intermediate, and lower."
78 For a commentary on the history of Canadian theosophy and its evolution in the postwar years, see McCann, *Vanguard of the New Age*. McCann observes that "the experiments that situate the Theosophists on the most radical edge of Protestantism have a genealogical link with the efflorescence of interest in Eastern religion in the 1960s and early 1970s and with the more recent explosion of interest in the practices of yoga. The worldview and religious ideas of Theosophists like Albert Smythe offer a window onto a process of transformation that has culminated in what Steven Sutcliffe calls 'the discourse of "New Age"' Spirituality. This approach to religion has a great deal to tell us about contemporary forms of religiosity, which are so often noninstitutional, deritualized, and individualistic in approach. It is also highly abstracted and radically disembedded from cultural community" (144). For an introduction to the development of the theosophical movement in Canada, see Lacombe, "Theosophy and the Canadian Idealist Tradition."
79 Hedges, "The Mind of the Poet," 2.
80 Ibid.

81 Hedges, *Dumb Spirit*, 11.
82 Ibid., 218.
83 Ibid., 11.
84 Ibid., 85.
85 Ibid., 103.
86 Ibid., 124.
87 Ibid., 140.
88 Ibid., 8.
89 Ibid., 39.
90 Ibid., 137.
91 Ibid., 84–5.
92 Ibid., 85.
93 Ibid., 121.
94 Ibid., 120.
95 Ibid., 6.
96 Ibid.
97 Ibid., 7.
98 Ibid., 12.
99 Ibid., 46.
100 Ibid.
101 Ibid., 47.
102 Ibid.
103 Ibid., 48.
104 Sibley, "The Duality in Messages about Female Sexuality," 73.
105 Hedges, *Dumb Spirit*, 141.
106 Ibid., 36.
107 Ibid., 37.
108 Ibid.
109 Ibid., 146.
110 Ibid., 147.
111 Ibid., 185.
112 Ibid., 186.
113 Ibid.
114 Harriet Hill, "Facts and Fancies," *Gazette*, 8 May 1952, 16.

CHAPTER FIVE

1 "Social and Personal," *Gazette*, 29 October 1952, 17.
2 "To Let Heated House," *Gazette*, 5 November 1926, 14.
3 Harriet Hill, "Facts and Fancies," *Gazette*, 31 December 1952, 13.
4 Ibid.

5 Harriet Hill, "A Dog's Eye View of Humanity," *Gazette*, 29 March 1952, 21.
6 Ibid.
7 *Junior League News*, March 1945, 7.
8 Ibid.
9 *Winnipeg Free Press*, 6 February 1954, 10.
10 Hedges, *Elixir*, 5.
11 Ibid., 10.
12 Ibid., 18.
13 *Winnipeg Free Press*, 6 February 1954, 10.
14 Bissell, "Letters in Canada," 268.
15 Hedges, *Elixir*, 94.
16 Ibid., 49.
17 Ibid., 38.
18 Ibid., 36.
19 Ibid., 25.
20 Ibid.
21 Ibid., 45.
22 Ibid., 29.
23 Ibid., 24–5.
24 Ibid., 44.
25 Ibid., 18.
26 Ibid., 26.
27 Ibid., 79–80.
28 Ibid., 80.
29 Ibid.
30 Ibid.
31 Ibid., 81.
32 Ibid.
33 Ibid.
34 Ibid.
35 Ibid.
36 Ibid.
37 Ibid., 61.
38 Ibid., 63.
39 Ibid., 64.
40 Ibid.
41 Ibid., 94.
42 Ibid., 99.
43 Ibid.
44 Ibid., 98.
45 Ibid.

46 Ibid., 115.
47 Ibid., 98.
48 Ibid., 117.
49 Ibid., 92.
50 Ibid., 111.
51 Ibid., 113.
52 Ibid., 114.
53 Ibid., 92.
54 Ibid.
55 Ibid., 93.
56 Ibid.
57 Ibid., 139.
58 Ibid., 93.
59 Ibid., 99.
60 Ibid.
61 Ibid., 98.
62 Ibid., 115.
63 Ibid., 116.
64 Toops, "The Lavender Scare," 91.
65 Ibid., 95.
66 Ibid., 99.
67 Belshaw and Light, "Queer and Other Histories."
68 Hedges, *Elixir*, 9.
69 Ibid., 58.
70 Ibid., 75.
71 Ibid., 161.
72 Ibid., 146.
73 Ibid., 46.
74 Ibid., 27.
75 Ibid.
76 Ibid., 190.
77 Ibid., 191.
78 Frost, "The Lesbian Pulp Fiction That Saved Lives."
79 "Lack of Professional Attitude Noted in Canadian Writers," *Gazette*, 27 February 1954, 4.
80 Ibid.
81 Ibid.
82 Ibid.
83 Harriet Hill, "Facts and Fancies," *Gazette*, 27 October 1954, 11.
84 "The Christopher Publishing House," *Bibliopolis*, https://books.bibliopolis.com/main/find/publisher/The%20Christopher%20Publishing%20House.html.

85 Sean B. Murphy, "Portraits of Ophthamology at McGill University 1876–1998," McGill Ophthalmology, https://www.mcgill.ca/ophthalmology/files/ophthalmology/history_of_ophthalmology.pdf.
86 Daniel 2:45.
87 Hedges, *The Dream Is Certain*, 7.
88 Ibid., 8.
89 Ibid., 9.
90 Ibid., 10.
91 Ibid.
92 Ibid.
93 Ibid., 13.
94 Ibid.
95 Ibid., 14.
96 Ibid.
97 Ibid., 15.
98 Ibid., 19.
99 Ibid., 20.
100 Ibid., 21.
101 Ibid.
102 Ibid.
103 Ibid., 22.
104 Ibid., 23.
105 Ibid.
106 Ibid.
107 Ibid., 24.
108 Ibid.
109 Ibid., 25.
110 Ibid.
111 Ibid., 26.
112 Ibid., 27.
113 Ibid., 28.
114 Ibid.
115 Ibid.
116 Ibid., 29.
117 Ibid., 30.
118 Ibid.
119 Ibid.
120 Ibid.
121 Ibid., 31.
122 Ibid.
123 Ibid.

124 Ibid.
125 Hedges to Deacon, 22 January 1953, MS Coll. 160, WADP, TFRBL.
126 Ibid.
127 Ibid.
128 Hedges to Deacon, 20 September 1954, MS Coll. 160, WADP, TFRBL.
129 Hedges to Dalgleish, 7 October 1954, MS Coll. 160, WADP, TFRBL.
130 Ibid.
131 I have been unable to locate the second of these two letters to Dalgleish.
132 Deacon to Hedges, 25 October 1954, WADP, TFRBL.
133 Ibid.
134 Ibid.
135 Ibid.
136 Ibid.
137 Scott's article was later reprinted as part of the introduction to Whalley, *Writing in Canada.*
138 Scott, "The Canadian Writers' Conference," 96.
139 Ibid., 97.
140 Ibid., 98.
141 Hedges, "Meddling in Others' Affairs," *Gazette*, 6 March 1956, 6.
142 *McGill Daily*, 23 February 1956, 1.
143 Hedges, "Meddling in Others' Affairs," *Gazette*, 6 March 1956, 6.
144 Ibid.
145 Ibid.
146 "Human Rights Law," *Canada's Human Rights History*, https://historyofrights.ca/history/human-rights-law/2/.
147 Kihika, "Ghosts and Shadows," 42.
148 "Person to Person," *Gazette*, 23 March 1956, 11.
149 "Conversation Piece," *Gazette*, 7 January 1957, 9.
150 "Person to Person," *Gazette*, 23 March 1956, 11.
151 "Conversation Piece," *Gazette*, 7 January 1957, 9.

CHAPTER SIX

1 As Mariana Gosnell notes, by 1955 "Boeing Stratocruisers, Lockheed Constellations, and Douglas DC-6s had sleeping accommodations for transatlantic passengers. But unlike the beds on today's airplanes, which are do-it-yourself flip-down 'lie flat' seats with blanket and pillow, the earlier ones were meant to evoke long-distance train travel, which still had an allure suggestive of luxury and comfort: upper and lower berths with mattresses and sheets, Pullman-style curtains for privacy, windows, reading lights, and sometimes breakfast in bed." First-class accommodation was "about as spacious as a modern hotel room."

See Suzy Strutner, "This Is What Your Flight Used to Look Like (and It's Actually Crazy)," *Huffpost*, last modified 6 December 2017, https://www.huffingtonpost.ca/entry/air-travel-1950s_n_5461411.

2 Hedges, "Masquerade," *Canadian Home Journal*, March 1957, 31.

3 Ibid.

4 Ibid., 76.

5 Ibid., 31.

6 Ibid., 74.

7 Hedges, *Robin*, 79.

8 Ibid., 13.

9 Ibid., 176.

10 Ibid., 99.

11 Ibid., 154.

12 "Robin," *Gazette*, 7 December 1957, 33.

13 Ibid.

14 Hedges, *Elixir*, 53.

15 Ibid., 88.

16 Donald Cranstone, "Mineral Resources," *Canadian Encyclopedia*, last modified 4 March 2015, https://www.thecanadianencyclopedia.ca/en/article/mineral-resources.

17 Howard Sullivan notes that "the most active of the subsidy houses are Exposition, Vantage, and Pageant. During 1956 they issued 135, 223, and 112 new titles respectively, and shared with Macmillan, Doubleday, Oxford, McGraw-Hill, and other major publishers a place on the list of the thirty-one houses producing one hundred or more new books" (see Sullivan, "Vanity Press Publishing," 111). In 1957, the year that *Robin* was published, Vantage "advertised itself as the sixth largest publisher in the United States" (see ibid., 12).

18 Ibid., 105.

19 Laquintano, "The Legacy of the Vanity Press and Digital Transitions."

20 Ibid.

21 Ibid.

22 Hedges, *Robin*, 9.

23 Ibid., 11.

24 Ibid., 12.

25 Ibid., 26.

26 Ibid.

27 Ibid.

28 Ibid., 32.

29 Ibid., 173.

30 Ibid., 23.

31 Ibid., 61.

32 Ibid.
33 Ibid.
34 Ibid., 124.
35 Ibid., 125.
36 Ibid., 140.
37 Ibid., 34.
38 Ibid., 35.
39 Ibid., 38.
40 Ibid., 52.
41 Ibid., 96.
42 Ibid., 97.
43 Ibid., 95.
44 Ibid., 141.
45 Ibid., 96.
46 Ibid., 99.
47 Ibid., 101.
48 Hanson, "Sixties Scoop."
49 Sinclair and Dainard, "Sixties Scoop." Sinclair and Dainard also write: "With no additional financial resources, provincial agencies in 1951 inherited a litany of issues surrounding children and child welfare in Indigenous communities. With many communities under-serviced, under-resourced and under the control of the *Indian Act*, provincial child welfare agencies chose to remove children from their homes rather than provide community resources and supports."
50 Hedges, *Robin*, 90.
51 Kyle Mizokami, "The Tests That Showed the World the Horrifying Power of Nuclear Weapons," *Popular Mechanics*, 5 July 2016, https://www.popularmechanics.com/military/weapons/a21667/bikini-nuclear-tests-legacy/.
52 While Operation Crossroads was the subject of considerable criticism, it also inspired fashion design. "Paris Swimwear designer Louis Réard adopted 'Bikini' for his new line of swimwear during Operation Crossroads. Réard's bikini was not the first two-piece swimsuit, but he explained that "'like the bomb, the bikini is small and devastating.'" See "Operation Crossroads," Atomic Heritage Foundation, https://www.atomicheritage.org/history/operation-crossroads.
53 "A-Bomb Discussed by Doris Hedges," *Gazette*, 1 July 1946, 5.
54 "Atomic Timeline," Atomic Heritage Foundation, https://www.atomicheritage.org/history/timeline.
55 Gordon Edwards, "Reactor Accidents at Chalk River," Canadian Coalition for Nuclear Responsibility, http://www.ccnr.org/paulson_legacy.html.
56 Jeremy Whitlock, "Entering the Nuclear Age," *Legion*, 1 September 2003, https://legionmagazine.com/en/2003/09/entering-the-nuclear-age/.
57 Hedges, *Robin*, 142.

58 Ibid., 143.
59 Ibid., 90.
60 Ibid., 142–3.
61 Ibid., 91.
62 Ibid.
63 Ibid.
64 Ibid., 105.
65 Ibid.
66 Ibid.
67 Ibid.
68 Ibid.
69 Ibid., 106.
70 Ibid.
71 "My Fur Lady," UPI, 24 September 1982, https://www.upi.com/Archives/1982/09/24/The-cast-of-My-Fur-Lady-Canadas-most-successful/4245401688000/; "My Fur Lady," McGill Library, https://www.mcgill.ca/library/branches/mua/virtual-exhibits/campus-life/my-fur-lady.
72 Hedges, "Spring," 9.
73 Hedges, "Resents Criticism of Royal Tour," *Gazette*, 23 June 1959, 6.
74 Ibid.
75 Ibid.
76 Ibid.
77 Mills, *The Empire Within*, 18.
78 Ibid.
79 Ibid.
80 Ibid.
81 Ibid., 20.
82 Cited in Mills, *The Empire Within*, 20.
83 "Facts and Fancies," *Gazette*, 4 November 1959, 13.
84 Hedges, *Words on a Page*, 130.
85 "Facts and Fancies," *Gazette*, 4 November 1959, 13.
86 "Social and Personal," *Gazette*, 22 January 1960, 21.
87 "Social and Personal," *Gazette*, 8 March 1960, 21.
88 "Social and Personal," *Gazette*, 16 May 1960, 31.
89 "Social and Personal," *Gazette*, 15 July 1960, 19.
90 "Social and Personal," *Gazette*, 27 February 1961, 29.
91 "Social and Personal," *Gazette*, 5 September 1961, 22.
92 "Social and Personal," *Gazette*, 5 March 1962, 27.
93 "Social and Personal," *Gazette*, 7 June 1962, 19.
94 "Social and Personal," *Gazette*, 12 September 1962, 35.
95 "Social and Personal," *Gazette*, 14 March 1963, 21.

96 "Social and Personal," *Gazette*, 19 July 1963, 9.
97 Laquintano, "The Legacy of the Vanity Press and Digital Transitions."
98 Ibid.
99 Ibid.
100 Uhlan, *The Rogue of Publishers' Row*, 43. Uhlan's memoir proved to be incredibly popular. The first edition was published in 1956. By 1980 it was in its sixtieth edition.
101 "Calculate the value of $960 in 1963," *Dollar Times*, https://www.dollartimes.com/inflation/inflation.php?amount=960&year=1963.
102 Hedges, *For This I Live*, 11.
103 Ibid., 12.
104 Ibid., 13.
105 Ibid., 15.
106 Ibid., 17.
107 Ibid., 18.
108 Ibid.
109 Ibid., 21.
110 Ibid.
111 Ibid., 23.
112 Ibid., 24.
113 Ibid., 25–6.
114 Ibid., 29.
115 Ibid., 30.
116 Ibid., 33.
117 Ibid.
118 Ibid., 34.
119 Ibid., 38.
120 Ibid., 39.
121 Ibid., 35.
122 Ibid., 36.
123 Ibid., 37.
124 Ibid., 40.
125 Ibid., 43.
126 Ibid., 45.
127 Ibid., 47.
128 Ibid., 51.
129 Ibid., 57.
130 Ibid., 58.
131 Ibid., 62.
132 Ibid.
133 Ibid., 64.

134 Ibid., 72.
135 Ibid., 75.
136 Ibid., 79.
137 Marcus Van Steen, "For This I Live," Ottawa *Citizen*, 8 August 1964, 14.
138 Hedges, "Tempo," 24.
139 Hedges, "Loan of Life," 33.
140 Hedges, "Alias for Love," 6.
141 Apparently, Hedges did find a way of placing *Inside Out* in at least one Canadian bookstore, since it was advertised for sale in Montreal's Ogilvy's department store in December of 1971.
142 Hedges, *Inside Out*, 13.
143 Ibid.
144 Ibid., 15.
145 Ibid.
146 Ibid., 20.
147 "Pocket Computer May Replace Shopping List," *New York Times*, 3 November 1962, 23.
148 Hedges, *Inside Out*, 14.
149 Ibid., 15.
150 Ibid., 16.
151 Ibid., 25.
152 Ibid., 17.
153 Ibid., 16.
154 Ibid.
155 Ibid., 14.
156 Ibid.
157 Ibid.
158 Ibid., 9.
159 Ibid.
160 Ibid.
161 Ibid.
162 Ibid.
163 Ibid., 10.
164 Ibid.
165 Ibid., 11.
166 Ibid.
167 Ibid., 12.
168 Ibid.
169 Ibid.
170 Ibid., 18.
171 Ibid.

172 Ibid., 22.

173 Ibid., 23.

174 "Doris Hedges, Noted Author Funeral Today," *Gazette*, 17 July 1972, 37.

175 Ibid.

176 "Lack of Professional Attitude Noted in Canadian Writers," *Gazette*, 27 February 1954, 4.

EPILOGUE

1 Hedges, *Crisis*, 8.

2 Hedges, *Words on a Page*, 28.

3 "Value of 1972 Canadian Dollar Today," *Inflation Tool*, https://www.inflationtool.com/canadian-dollar/1972-to-present-value.

4 "Fonds F0280 – Canadian Speakers' and Writers' Service Fonds," York University Library, https://atom.library.yorku.ca/index.php/canadian-speakers-and-writers-service-ltd-fonds.

BIBLIOGRAPHY

ARCHIVES

Canadian Speakers' and Writers' Service Fonds (CSWSF), Clara Thomas Archives (CTA), York University.
Queen's University Archives (QUA), Queen's University.
Hugh Garner Fonds (HGF)
Lorne Pierce Fonds (LPF)
Rare Books and Special Collections (RBSC), McGill University.
Wartime Information Board Records (WIBR), Library and Archives Canada (LAC), Ottawa.
William A. Bradley Literary Agency Records (1909–1982) (WABLAR), Harry Ransom Humanities Research Center (HRHRC), University of Texas at Austin.
William Arthur Deacon Papers (WADP), Thomas Fisher Rare Book Library (TFRBL), University of Toronto.

SOURCES

Andresen, Mark. *Field of Vision: The Broadcast Life of Kenneth Allsop*. Victoria: Trafford, 2004.
Bailey, Alfred G. "New Books." *Dalhousie Review* 28, no. 4 (1947): 419–20.
Balzer, Timothy. *The Information Front: The Canadian Army and News Management during the Second World War*. Vancouver: University of British Columbia Press, 2011.
Bélanger, Claude. "Why Did Canada Refuse to Admit Jewish Refugees in the 1930's?" *L'Encyclopédie de l'histoire du Québec / The Quebec History Encyclopedia*. http://faculty.marianopolis.edu/c.belanger/quebechistory/readings/CanadaandJewishRefugeesinthe1930s.html.
Belshaw, John, and Tracy Penny Light. "Queer and Other Histories." *Canadian History, Post Confederation*. BC Open Textbook Project. https://opentextbc.ca/postconfederation/chapter/hidden-histories/.
Benson, Susan Porter. "Living on the Margin: Working-Class Marriages and Family Survival Strategies in the United States, 1919–1941." *The Sex of Things: Gender and*

Consumption in Historical Perspective, ed. Victoria De Grazia and Ellen Furlough. Berkeley: University of California Press, 1996.

Birney, Earle. *Spreading Time: Remarks on Canadian Writing and Writers 1904–1949*. Montreal: Véhicule, 1980.

Bissell, Claude T. "Letters in Canada." *University of Toronto Quarterly* 23, no. 3 (1954): 268.

Bliss, Michael. "Preface." *Report on Social Security for Canada 1943*. Toronto: University of Toronto Press, 1975.

Booth, Philip. "The Montreal Repertory Theatre 1930–1961: A History and Handlist of Productions." MA thesis, McGill University, 1989.

Broad, Graham. *Studies in Canadian Military History Series, A Small Price To Pay: Consumer Culture on the Canadian Homefront, 1939–45*. Vancouver: University of British Columbia Press, 2013.

Brown, E.K. "Poetry." Letters in Canada. *University of Toronto Quarterly* 16, no. 3 (1947): 246–55.

– "Poetry." Letters in Canada. *University of Toronto Quarterly* 17, no. 3 (1948): 257–65.

Buitenhuis, Peter. "The CAA and Propaganda during the Second World War." In *History of the Book in Canada*, vol. 3: *1918–1980*, ed. Carole Gerson and Jacques Michon, 129–30. Toronto: University of Toronto Press, 2007.

Burr, Gordon. "Dawes, James Pawley." *Dictionary of Canadian Biography* 13 (1901–1910). http://www.biographi.ca/en/bio/dawes_james_pawley_13E.html.

Caccia, Ivana. *Managing the Canadian Mosaic in Wartime: Shaping Citizenship Policy, 1939–1945*. Montreal: McGill-Queen's University Press, 2010.

Campbell, Sandra. *Both Hands: A Life of Lorne Pierce of Ryerson Press*. Montreal: McGill-Queen's University Press, 2013.

Canadian Cook Book for British Brides. Women's Voluntary Services Canada. 1945.

Carney, Lora Senechal. *Canadian Painters in a Modern World: Writings and Reconsiderations*. Montreal: McGill-Queen's University Press, 2017.

Charlesworth, Hector. "Authors and Radio." *Canadian Author* 12, no. 4 (1935): 8–9.

Doyle, James. *Progressive Heritage: The Evolution of a Politically Radical Literary Tradition in Canada*. Waterloo, ON: Wilfrid Laurier University Press, 2002.

Dunks, Gillian. "Reading the Field of Canadian Poetry in the Era of Modernity: The Ryerson Poetry Chapbook Series, 1925–1962." MA thesis, University of British Columbia, 2013.

Fahrni, Magda. *Household Politics: Montreal Families and Postwar Reconstruction*. Toronto: University of Toronto Press, 2005.

Fiamengo, Janice, ed. *Home Ground and Foreign Territory: Essays on Early Canadian Literature*. Ottawa: University of Ottawa Press, 2014.

Fortin, Marc. "Hugh Garner, The 'One Man Trade Union' of Publishing." McMaster University Library. http://hpcanpub.mcmaster.ca/hpcanpub/case-study/hugh-garner-one-man-trade-union-publishing-audio-recording.

– Letter to the author. 18 May 2018.

Freeman, Barbara M. *Beyond Bylines: Media Workers and Women's Rights in Canada.* Waterloo, ON: Wilfrid Laurier University Press, 2011.

Friskney, Janet B., and Carole Gerson. "The Author and the Market: Writers and the Market for Fiction and Literature." In *History of the Book in Canada*, vol. 3: *1918–1980*, ed. Carole Gerson and Jacques Michon, 131–8. Toronto: University of Toronto Press, 2007.

Frost, Natasha. "The Lesbian Pulp Fiction That Saved Lives." *Atlas Obscura*. 22 May 2018. https://www.atlasobscura.com/articles/lesbian-pulp-fiction-ann-bannon.

Gerson, Carole. "'The Most Canadian of All Canadian Poets,' Pauline Johnson and the Construction of National Literature." *Canadian Literature* 158 (1998): 90–107.

Gosnell, Mariana. "When Airplanes Had Beds." *Smithsonian Air and Space*. January 2013. https://www.airspacemag.com/history-of-flight/when-airplanes-had-beds-125048102/.

Hanson, Erin. "Sixties Scoop." Indigenous Foundations. UBC First Nations and Indigenous Studies. http://indigenousfoundations.arts.ubc.ca/sixties_scoop/.

Harrington, Lyn. *Syllables of Recorded Time: The Story of the Canadian Authors Association 1921–1981*. Toronto: Simon and Pierre, 1981.

Hill, Colin. "*Canadian Bookman* and the Origins of Modern Realism in English-Canadian Fiction." *Canadian Literature* 195 (2007): 100.

Hill, Harriett. "A Dog's Eye View of Humanity." *Gazette*, 29 March 1952, 21.

Hutchinson, George. "During the Second World War Literature Reigned Supreme: How Displacement and Migration Created an Unexpected Literary Boom." *Literary Hub*. 26 January 2018. https://lithub.com/during-world-war-ii-literature-reigned-supreme/.

Ince, Judith." The Vocabulary of Freedom in 1948: The Politics of the Montreal Avant-Garde." *Journal of Canadian Art History/Annales d'histoire de l'art canadien* 7 (1982): 36–45.

Irvine, Dean. *Editing Modernity: Women and Little-Magazine Culture in Canada, 1916–1956*. Toronto: University of Toronto Press, 2008.

Jordan, J.O., and Robert L. Patten, eds. *Literature in the Marketplace*. Cambridge, Cambridge University Press, 1995.

Karr, Clarence. *Authors and Audiences: Popular Canadian Fiction in the Early Twentieth Century*. Montreal: McGill-Queen's University Press, 2000.

Katerberg, William H. *Modernity and the Dilemma of North American Anglican Identities, 1880–1950*. Montreal: McGill-Queen's University Press, 2001.

Keshen, Jeffrey A. *Saints, Sinners, and Soldiers: Canada's Second World War*. Vancouver: University of British Columbia Press, 2004.

Kihika, Maureen. "Ghosts and Shadows: A History of Racism in Canada." *Canadian Graduate Journal of Sociology and Criminology* 2, no. 1 (2013): 35–44.

Kuffert, Leonard. "'Stabbing our spirits broad awake': Reconstructing Canadian

Culture, 1940–1948." In *Cultures of Citizenship in Postwar Canada, 1940–1955*, ed. Nancy Christie and Michael Gauvreau, 27–62. Montreal: McGill-Queen's University Press, 2003.

Lacombe, Michelle. "Theosophy and the Canadian Idealist Tradition, A Preliminary Exploration." *Journal of Canadian Studies* 17, no. 2 (1982): 100–18.

Laquintano, Timothy. "The Legacy of the Vanity Press and Digital Transitions." *Journal of Electronic Publishing* 16, no. 1 (2013). https://quod.lib.umich.edu/j/jep/3336451.0016.104?view=text;rgn=main.

Lecker, Robert. "Canadian Authors and Their Literary Agents." *Papers of the Bibliographical Society of Canada* 54, no. 1–2 (2016): 93–102.

Léger, Danielle. "Alfred Pellan, scénographe." BAnQ. http://www.banq.qc.ca/a_propos_banq/publications/a_rayons_ouverts/aro_89/aro_89_dossier2.html#pellan.

Leong, Janis Karen. "The China Mystique: Mayling Soong Chiang, Pearl S. Buck and Anna May Wong in the American Imagination." PhD dissertation, University of California Berkeley, 1999.

Linteau, Paul-André. *The History of Montréal*. Trans. Peter McCambridge. Montreal: Baraka, 2013.

Litt, Paul. *The Muses, the Masses, and the Massey Commission*. Toronto: University of Toronto Press, 1992.

Livingstone, Richard. *The Future in Education*. Cambridge: Cambridge University Press, 1941.

MacSkimming, Roy. *The Perilous Trade: Publishing Canada's Writers*. Toronto: McClelland and Stewart, 2003.

Maioni, Antonia. "New Century, New Risks: The Marsh Report and the Postwar Welfare State in Canada." Institute for Research and Public Policy. 1 August 2004. http://policyoptions.irpp.org/magazines/social-policy-in-the-21st-century/new-century-new-risks-the-marsh-report-and-the-postwar-welfare-state-in-canada/.

Marshall, Joan. *A Solitary Pillar: Montreal's Anglican Church and the Quiet Revolution*. Montreal: McGill-Queen's University Press, 1995.

McCann, Gillian. *Vanguard of the New Age: The Toronto Theosophical Society, 1891–1945*. Montreal: McGill-Queen's University Press, 2012.

McDonald, Larry. "Socialism and the English Canadian Literary Tradition." *Essays on Canadian Writing* 68 (1999): 213–41.

McKay, Ian. "For a New Kind of History: A Reconnaissance of 100 Years of Canadian Socialism." *Labour/Le Travail* 46 (2000): 69–125.

Mills, Sean. *The Empire Within: Postcolonial Thought and Political Activism in Sixties Montreal*. Montreal: McGill-Queen's University Press, 2010.

Mount, Nick. *Arrival: The Story of CanLit*. Toronto: Anansi, 2017.

Murphree, Vanessa. "Edward Bernays's 1929 'Torches of Freedom' March, Myths and Historical Significance." *American Journalism* 32, no. 3 (2015): 258–81.

Myers, Tamara. *Caught: Montreal's Modern Girls and the Law, 1869–1945*. Toronto: University of Toronto Press, 2006.

Osborne, Brian S. "Warscapes, Landscapes, Inscapes, France, War, and Canadian National Identity." In *Place, Culture and Identity: Essays in Historical Geography in Honour of Alan R.H. Baker*, ed. Iain S. Black and Robin A. Butlin, 311–33. Quebec: Les Presses de l'Université Laval, 2001.

Owram, Doug. *The Government Generation: Canadian Intellectuals and the State 1900–1945*. Toronto: University of Toronto Press, 1986.

Reisner, M.E. *The Measure of Faith: Annals of the Diocese of Montreal, 1760–2000, John Irwin Cooper's The Blessed Communion: The Origins and History of the Diocese of Montreal, 1760–1960*. Toronto: Anglican Book Centre, 1995.

Rifkind, Candida. *Comrades and Critics: Women, Literature, and the Left in 1930s Canada*. Toronto: University of Toronto Press, 2008.

Royal Commission on National Development in the Arts, Letters and Sciences. Ottawa: Queen's Printer, 1951.

Saez, Emmanuel. *Income and Wealth Inequality: Evidence and Policy Implications.* October 2014. https://www.policyalternatives.ca/sites/default/files/uploads/publications/lecture_saez_UBC14.pdf.

Scott, F.R. "The Canadian Writers' Conference." *University of Toronto Quarterly* 25, no. 1 (1955): 96–103.

Sibley, Michelle. "The Duality in Messages about Female Sexuality, 1950–1960." *Lehigh Review* 19 (2011): 71–6.

Sinclair, Niigaanwewidam James, and Sharon Dainard. "Sixties Scoop." *Canadian Encyclopedia*. Last modified 22 October 2019. https://www.thecanadianencyclopedia.ca/en/article/sixties-scoop.

Stanton, Richard. *The Forgotten Olympic Art Competitions*. Victoria: Trafford, 2000.

Stuewe, Paul. *The Storms Below: The Turbulent Life and Times of Hugh Garner.* Toronto: James Lorimer, 1988.

Sullivan, Howard A. "Vanity Press Publishing." *Library Trends* 7, no. 1 (1958): 105–15.

Talbot, Emile. "Literature and Ideology in the Thirties: Fictional Representations of Communism in Quebec." *International Journal of Canadian Studies* 20 (1999): 67–80.

Toops, Jessica. "The Lavender Scare: Persecution of Lesbianism during the Cold War." *Western Illinois Historical Review* 5 (2013): 91–107.

Trudeau, Pierre Elliott. *The Asbestos Strike.* Toronto: James Lewis and Samuel, 1974.

– *Memoirs.* Toronto: McClelland and Stewart, 1993.

Uhlan, Edward. *The Rogue of Publishers' Row*. New York, Exposition, 1956.

Vance, Jonathan F. *A History of Canadian Culture*. Don Mills, ON: Oxford University Press, 2009.

Vipond, Mary. "Best Sellers in English Canada, 1899–1918: An Overview." *Journal of Canadian Fiction* 24 (1979): 96–119.

Waller, Adrian. *No Ordinary Hotel: The Ritz-Carlton's First Seventy-Five Years.* Montreal: Véhicule, 1989.

Weintraub, William. *City Unique: Montreal Days and Nights in the 1940s and '50s.* Toronto: Robin Brass Studio, 1996.

Whalley, George, ed. *Writing in Canada, Proceedings of the Canadian Writers' Conference Held at Queen's University July 1955*. Toronto: Macmillan, 1956.

Whitlock, Jeremy. "Entering the Nuclear Age." *Legion: Canada's Literary History Magazine*, 1 September 2003. https://legionmagazine.com/en/2003/09/entering-the-nuclear-age/.

Whittaker, Herbert. *Setting the Stage: Montreal Theatre 1920–49*. Montreal: McGill-Queen's University Press, 1999.

Young, William R. "Academics and Social Scientists versus the Press: The Policies of the Bureau of Public Information and the Wartime Information Board, 1939 to 1945." *Historical Papers. Canadian Historical Association* 13, no. 1 (1978): 217–40.

INDEX